Powers of the Mind

Powers
of the Mind

The Reinvention of Liberal Learning in America

Donald N. Levine

THE UNIVERSITY OF CHICAGO PRESS   *Chicago and London*

DONALD N. LEVINE is the Peter B. Ritzma Professor of Sociology at
the University of Chicago, where he served as dean of the College from
1982 to 1987. He is the author of several books, including *Visions of
the Sociological Tradition, The Flight from Ambiguity,* and *Wax and
Gold: Tradition and Innovation in Ethiopian Culture.*

The University of Chicago Press, Chicago 60637
The University of Chicago Press, Ltd., London
© 2006 by The University of Chicago
All rights reserved. Published 2006
Printed in the United States of America

15 14 13 12 11 10 09 08 07 06   1 2 3 4 5

ISBN 10: 0-226-47553-0 (cloth)
ISBN 13: 978-0-226-47553-0 (cloth)

Library of Congress Cataloging-in-Publication Data

Levine, Donald Nathan, 1931–
    Powers of the mind : the reinvention of liberal learning in America /
Donald N. Levine.
        p.   cm.
    Includes bibliographical references and index.
    ISBN-13: 978-0-226-47553-0 (cloth : alk. paper)
    ISBN-10: 0-226-47553-0 (cloth : alk. paper)
    1. Education, Higher—United States—Curricula. 2. Curriculum
change—United States. 3. Education, Higher—Philosophy. I. Title.
    LB2361.5.L48 2006
    378′.012—dc22

                                                            2006011264

♾ The paper used in this publication meets the minimum requirements
of the American National Standard for Information Sciences—
Permanence of Paper for Printed Library Materials, ANSI Z39.48-1992.

The failure to decide what students should be required to learn keeps the teacher from functioning as, and perhaps from becoming, a responsible adult. There is no one to teach young people but older people, and so the older people must do it. *That they do not know enough to do it, that they have never been smart enough or experienced enough or good enough to do it, does not matter.* They must do it because there is no one else to do it. This is simply the elemental trial—some would say the elemental tragedy—of human life: the necessity to proceed on the basis merely of the knowledge that is available, the necessity to postpone until too late the question of the sufficiency and the truth of that knowledge.   WENDELL BERRY

Contents

Preface

Whatever else happened that year, 1987 witnessed a strange turn in the reading habits of the American public. For forty-five weeks, a tortuous sermon about higher education stood on the *New York Times* list of best-selling hardcover nonfiction, selling more than one million copies. Written by University of Chicago professor Allan Bloom and packaged with a foreword by Saul Bellow, *The Closing of the American Mind: How Higher Education Has Failed Democracy and Impoverished the Souls of Today's Students* delivered a full-bodied attack against the deterioration of university curricula. Bloom called the mid-1960s, when this decline accelerated, a time of "unmitigated disaster. . . . The old core curriculum—according to which every student in the college had to take a smattering of courses in the major divisions of knowledge—was abandoned."

Responses to this publication startled me. Shaped, like Bloom, by the common core of the "Hutchins College" of the University of Chicago, I yearned to restore the values that it had embodied. As dean of the university's undergraduate college—called simply "the College"—in the 1980s, I searched widely to find hints of interest in the liberal arts curriculum. This surprise best seller suggested that the public was hungering for universities to reaffirm a clarified educational mission. It seemed to signify a certain resonance with Bloom's point that the crisis of liberal education in our time reflected not so much the incoherence among principles of understanding the world as our incapacity even to discuss this incoherence.

Nevertheless, in certain respects both the book itself and the public's response distressed me. Although I sympathized with Bloom's critique of universities for changing requirements in accord with political demands rather than educational principles, his call to restore an old-time curriculum seemed misguided. To my mind, the need was not to restore some old set of requirements but to reinvent a curriculum that pursued high educational goals with methods and materials suited to the times. In fact, it was upsetting to see that Bloom's book paid almost no direct attention to educational principles and curricular structures, and it was dismaying to read his definition of "the old core curriculum" as a "smattering of courses in the major divisions of knowledge."

This vagueness elicited an array of impassioned responses to *The Closing of the American Mind,* positive and negative, most of which went wide of the mark insofar as they meant to target the curriculum of Chicago's College. For indeed, Bloom's tract was widely viewed as championing a curriculum, exemplified at Chicago, that required all students to absorb a canon of Great Books of the Western World. However understandable this interpretation, due to Chicago's association with the Great Books movement spearheaded by Robert Maynard Hutchins and Mortimer Adler, it grossly misrepresented what the Chicago curriculum had achieved. For that reason, I resolved to write a book of my own, to be titled *The Chicago Tradition of Liberal Learning,* in order to present a firmly documented account of what really happened at Chicago.

It was little comfort to come upon Martha Nussbaum's diatribe against Bloom in the *New York Review of Books.* While applauding her critique of how Bloom depicted American college students and his simplistic accounts of intellectual history, I found myself concerned that in the enthusiasm of her attacks against old-style elitism, she was losing sight of the importance of producing intellectually and morally qualified leaders. What is more, I found myself offended by her assertion that "required lists of Great Books encourage passivity and reverence, rather than active critical reflection." This jab distorted what goes on in any educational program I know of that relies on so-called Great Books. It also could be taken as implying some comment about the widely acclaimed curriculum at Chicago, even though Nussbaum herself did not at the time make that connection explicitly.

A dozen years later, she made the implication explicit. Entering the fray during a widely publicized dispute about the curriculum at the University of Chicago, Nussbaum demeaned that curriculum in the *Chicago Tribune* by caricaturing it as rigid and unchanging, deadening the minds of students, and useful mainly "for students who are ill-prepared, lacking in confidence or bent on narrowly defined pre-professional studies." Such an attitude was what I feared might evolve from those hostile respondents to Bloom's book who associated his position with the College. The skirmishes surrounding the Chicago Core curriculum in 1999 only fortified my resolve to set things right about the Chicago experience.

Over the course of working on my manuscript since the early 1990s, the project came to be driven by additional concerns. I experienced growing frustration over the difficulties of sustaining any reasoned discussion about the liberal curriculum. The flurry of interest in Bloom's book had little constructive impact on educational discourse. It figured only as an opening shot in the culture wars between those who upheld the notion of a traditional canon and those who attacked a presumptively uniform tradition of readings by white Western males in favor of a much more inclusive "smattering" of texts. This warfare produced much heat and little light. Even those who tried to "teach the conflicts," giving the ideologies of the combatants equal time, attended to questions regarding the proper representation of authors read but let the question of what it means to be liberally educated fall by the wayside.

That complex of degradations was soon overwhelmed by a more ominous threat: a tendency to deal with questions of educational content in terms of the increasingly fashionable business notion of a bottom line. Students came to be classified as output or tuition-generating units, faculty as teaching and grant-generating units, and laws of supply and demand superseded the norms of authentic learning. Departments of education began to close out positions that taught the history and philosophy of education. As I worked on this book over the years, the latter complex of problems came to distress me far more than the common misrepresentation of the Chicago tradition. My project thus had to be reinvented. It became an effort to provoke fresh thought about the liberal curriculum by setting forth concrete ideas about how to direct that discourse in ways that respond to current circumstances. Of course, to no one's surprise, I found that Chicago's past may have a good deal to teach us about facing the future.

This project has changed in another respect since I began to work on it. I have come to believe in a need to integrate awareness of the mind as itself embodied—working in and through the nervous system—into a program of liberal learning appropriate for the twenty-first century. I propose to incorporate some of the wisdom of bodymind learning espoused for millennia in Asian cultures and for more than a century in the West. My appreciation for such learning comes through more than a quarter century of regular practice of a variety of bodymind disciplines—tai chi, yoga,

Zen, Alexander work, Feldenkrais work, and, above all, aikido, in which I have held the rank of *sandan* (third-degree black belt) since 1999. It reflects as well a delayed response to a point that Joseph Schwab was fond of making, that " the effect of a curriculum whose end was training of the intellect pure and simple would be a crippled intellect" ([1954] 1978, 125). This appreciation has led me to some of the innovative ideas I set forth in part 3 and also to conceive the whole education process in terms of a master metaphor of inhaling (chapter 9) and exhaling (chapter 10).

Finally, my perspective has changed in the direction of foregrounding the theme of dialogue in my discourse about liberal education. My involvement with this theme developed in the course of producing *Visions of the Sociological Tradition* (1995), in which I advocated a "dialogical narrative" in place of the sequence of narratives about the discipline that had appeared earlier. This aspect of my thought was reinforced by the Festschrift in my honor generously produced by Charles Camic and Hans Joas, titled *The Dialogical Turn* (2004). I also came to emphasize the powers pertinent to experiencing dialogue as a framework for organizing my teaching activity (as will become clear in chapter 12). At the risk of getting ahead of my story, I might suggest that these last two interests converge: inhaling and exhaling is the physical equivalent of engaging in dialogue.

In broaching a critical discussion of problematic issues of undergraduate education, I have left to the side a number of issues that tend to monopolize public discourse on our educational system. Several issues in contemporary debates about liberal education—such as diversity, education for citizenship, connections with the professions, and assessment of learning outcomes—will not be engaged directly. The goal of drawing those debates toward serious engagement with curricular matters offers a mammoth challenge by itself. And introducing the potential contributions of the University of Chicago's experience necessitates a nontrivial encounter with the distinctive Chicago tradition.

Consider, for example, the peculiar ceremony that transpires every autumn, when students on the verge of entering the College assemble in stately Rockefeller Chapel. While college matriculants elsewhere get oriented through little more than tugs-of-war and ice-cream socials, the hapless Chicago first-years, in addition, must listen to an oration—one of the few they will ever hear at their prospective alma mater.

One strange thing about this ceremony is that, year after year, the oration has the same title, "The Aims of Education." The other strange thing is that, year after year, the content of that address is radically different, amounting, in the words of the dean who introduces them, to "a combination of academic laissez-faire and sheer faculty ingenuity." Listen to historian Karl Joachim Weintraub, who speaks of striving "for the self-disciplined life in which alone the spirit, the mind, taste, judgment, and ultimately wisdom can grow and flourish." Or to classicist Danielle S. Allen, who praises friendship as "crucial to encountering what is novel, alien, and unsettling, and such is the business of learning." Or to Provost Geoffrey Stone, who challenges matriculants to "exercise the responsibility of freedom — to test what you are taught at every turn; to challenge your teachers, your classmates, and yourselves; to choose your own values and your own beliefs."

My own take on that assignment is that it is preposterous because, strictly speaking, there are *no* universally valid "Aims." So why do I keep going to that ceremony and discussing with small groups of students afterward what the orator has said? It is because that discussion, that discourse, figures among the noblest things that humans can do — and I remain proud to belong to a university community that keeps that discourse alive.[1]

1. The Bloom 1987 quotation is from page 320. For my earlier attempts to disabuse people of the notion of the Hutchins College as a Great Books curriculum, see Levine 1985a and 1992. For a critique of the response to the culture wars by "teaching the conflicts," see Goldfarb 2004. Andrew Abbott's essay "Academic Intellectuals" (2004) offers a succinct analysis of many trends — such as massification and commodification — that threaten good academic work. A parallel inquiry, concerning the idea of the university, has also figured notably in the Chicago tradition, as in *The Idea of the University of Chicago* (Murphy and Bruckner 1976) and the 2000–2001 symposium "The Idea of the University" (iotu.uchicago.edu). Martha Nussbaum's review of Bloom's book, entitled "Undemocratic Vistas," appeared in the *New York Review of Books* (see Nussbaum 1987). The quotation from her piece in the *Chicago Tribune* appeared on March 11, 1999. Quotations from the "Aims" addresses are from Boyer 1997, 5, 287, and 254, and from Allen 2001, 2.

Acknowledgments

Of the hundreds of good people who helped this project along over so many years, I must limit my express appreciation to a select number:

—to Douglas Mitchell of the University Press, whose manifold virtues have been sung by so many Press authors for so long, there is no rhetoric left with which to praise him;
—to Adam Kissel, without whom this book could not have been completed, and whose steadfast collaboration, language skills, editorial brilliance, wise counsel, and substantive contributions, especially on rhetoric, proved invaluable;
—to Benjamin Cornwell, who stepped in at a crucial juncture as the project was nearing completion and caught on to the challenge with amazing quickness;
—to a parade of intelligent and industrious assistants between 1990 and 2005, including Craig Cunningham, Daniel Braithwaite, Nilesh Patel, and Dan Kimmel;
—to my fastidious manuscript editor, Lori Meek Schuldt;
—to Charles Camic and Hans Joas, who took more seriously than I could have dreamed my thoughts on the theoretical significance of dialogue;
—to many colleagues who read one or another chapter, among whom the late, unfailingly wise reader Wayne Booth must be noted in particular;
—to Paul Sanders, who helped me work out a number of issues related to the pursuit of the project;
—to devoted, inspiring aikido educators, most particularly Shihans Mitsugi Saotome, Hiroshi Ikeda, Frank Doran, and the late Fumio Toyoda;
—to Dean of the College John Boyer, whose ongoing support of this project was essential to its completion;

— to Provost Geoffrey Stone, who provided special support at a critical juncture;

— to my wife Ruth, for hanging in there and trying to ensure I didn't take myself too seriously;

— to Natanyel Bohm-Levine and Zoe Jadelyn Levine Melnick, for smiling at the future; and of course

— to the University of Chicago: fostering mother, responsive subject, stimulating matrix, collegial milieu, arrogant place, architectural inspiration, ethical beacon, and sine qua non of this inquiry.

Prologue: Missing Resources in Higher Education

What's *wrong* with this picture?

The American system of higher education may be the finest in the world. The numbers at least count in its favor. The proportion of our populace who pursue higher learning is the highest in the world. The Bureau of Labor Statistics projects that teaching at the postsecondary level is expected to constitute the second-largest-growing occupation for the decade after 2002.[1] Conceived as an industry, higher education appears healthier than any other part of the American economy.

It has also been emulated the world over. Whatever the vicissitudes of political attitudes toward the United States, its universities have presented an object of constant admiration — in Europe, all over Asia, and throughout the Southern Hemisphere. Since the 1950s, students from other countries have regarded American universities as the site of choice for college and especially graduate training. Reforms of established educational institutions in Europe and their erstwhile colonies have tended to imitate American innovations.

For all this robustness, knowledgeable observers nevertheless have warned for some time that our educational sector may be in serious trouble — and not just at precollegiate levels. Sober educators have talked about "social hurricanes" to describe the scene they face, a scene marked by a massive influx of new student populations, a decline in academic standards, diminished respect for teaching, weakened salience of written texts, overly programmed competitiveness, and organizational inertia in the face

1. See Horrigan 2004, table 4.

of critical challenges. Once-sanguine presidents of universities such as Harvard, Dartmouth, Berkeley, and Stanford have become Cassandras.[2]

Much of the alarm focuses on funding. Government support for higher education has diminished steadily, rising operational costs have outstripped revenues, and students and their families have come to shoulder crushing debt burdens. For some time, talented and accomplished PhD's have found few job openings. Increasing numbers of liberal arts colleges have been forced to close their doors.

Perhaps the slack commitment to resources reflects a waning of attitudes that might support adequate funding. It does appear that academic sentiment has lost touch with a pervasive and persuasive sense of broader purpose. Narrow vocationalism, mindless consumerism, grade inflation, and curricular fragmentation have led to demoralized campus milieus. In milieus where the communal good has long figured as an important goal, particularisms of ethnicity and gender tend to dominate, and self-interest rules. Cheating and plagiarism among college students have increased exponentially. Faculty have come increasingly to put personal self-interest above commitment to institutional interests by giving themselves diminished teaching loads and diverting university resources to outside business ventures and consultations. Instead of the old environment of communal purpose and moral inspiration, cynicism has come to flourish like ragweed.[3]

Under these conditions, and with alternate learning resources provided by new educational technologies and work training programs, many have questioned the extent to which college education remains meaningful. In some families these questions simply get suppressed as they grudgingly accommodate the greater expense of education, like that of costlier gasoline, as a brute fact of contemporary life. Those who persist in demanding

2. Derek Bok writes that "universities share one characteristic with compulsive gamblers and exiled royalty. . . . There is never enough money to satisfy their desires . . . the prospect of new revenue is a powerful temptation that can easily lead decent people into unwise compromises, especially when they are under pressure to accomplish more than they can readily achieve by conventional means" (2003, 9). The dean of onetime optimistic spokesmen for the modern American university, Clark Kerr, has come to voice apprehension about whether the university's inherited commitment to rational inquiry can be sustained, albeit long after he had already conceded that general education in the nation's universities is an "absolute disaster" (Kerr 2001). For a collection of sober appraisals of the contemporary university, see *The Future of the City of Intellect: The Changing American University* (Brint 2002).

3. On the diffusion of cynicism as a more general societal pathology, see Gore 1994 and Goldfarb 2004.

a rationale for the tab, and look to colleges to make the case for such expensive learning, may be disappointed. Mostly what they find is the blithe promise that academic degrees offer credentials to well-paying jobs. If they look more closely, they find curricula structured to recruit students into the conventional academic disciplines.[4]

The decline of the vision of liberal learning as a training ground for mature human beings and informed citizens has consequences: graduates are less equipped, while personal, public, and environmental decisions have become more demanding than ever. At a time of exponentially growing environmental degradation, the public has tolerated statements denying such threats and undermining the scientific institutions that investigate them. Our elected leaders supported a costly and self-destructive war virtually unanimously, when the most informed professionals produced analyses projecting serious negative international and domestic fallouts. Even if our educational system cannot produce a citizenry capable of informed deliberation about complex matters, it is essential that modern societies have the benefit of an intellectual elite educated well beyond their occupational specialties.[5]

Modern society has come to rely on occupations requiring a range of specialized skills, and the modern university has come increasingly to serve as a training ground for such skills. Beyond that function, universities continue to be haunted by a dimly recalled sense of mission to provide an educational experience that transcends these mundane concerns. It does so by addressing a realm of freedom against that of practical necessity and by connecting persons to a realm of ultimate concerns. All of these senses have been involved historically in the concept of liberal learning, and it is in the evolution of that notion that we find the philosophical grounds for articulating a rationale for our learning in our time.

The scandal of higher education in our time is that so little attention gets paid, in institutions that claim to provide an education, to what it is that

4. However, as Andrew Abbott (2002) has argued contrary to common belief, getting a college education really does not count for very much in enabling people to get jobs that pay better than they would have gotten some other way. And former dean of the Chicago College Jonathan Z. Smith (1983, 1993) has argued contrary to common belief that there is little value in forcing students to select a major; the primary benefit of the major system goes to the professionals whose interests are served by recruiting students into their fields.

5. The grim alternative is portrayed by an astute historian: "America's unofficial mandarinate, the Northeastern establishment, crumbled in the last quarter of the twentieth century. The result is a social experiment in the contemporary United States as audacious, in its own way, as that of Soviet collectivism, an attempt to have a government without a governing elite" (Lind 2006).

college educators claim to be providing. Factories, hospitals, armies, software corporations—all support departments of research and development; all require training to produce their goods and services; they all position agents of quality control to screen the output. Ironically, universities typically lack structures designed to investigate matters of both undergraduate and graduate education. Yet liberal education concerns what is arguably the most important of all human goods—the wherewithal for leading good lives as human beings and citizens—and questions of education figure among the most complex of all human problems.

Absent such structures, the default locus for authoritative decisions about curriculum and teaching lodges in academic departments and business offices. The latter demand programs that, at best, do little more than prepare students for lucrative occupations and, at worst, mirror the fads of a fickle consumerist culture. They also ensure the growing role of athletic providers in the university marketplace. The former yield instructional offerings derived from the personal preferences of intellectual specialists. Members of a faculty appointed and paid by departments understandably give pride of place to departmental interests and expectations, and they tend to think, like General Motors, that what is good for the faculty is good for the students.

The hegemony of departmental authority in American colleges and universities puts a growing premium on faculty research and publication at the expense of teaching that is oriented to the growth of students. On many campuses there is more communication among researchers about what they are doing than among teachers, even though research is thought to be a lonely pursuit while teaching purports to be a form of communication. Instead of minding the imperative to optimize the growth of students, most universities offer little or nothing to counter the interests of scholarly specialists or fractious consumers.

This is not to say that those interests should be submerged. What is crucial is to balance them with a critical mass of talents and efforts devoted to the task of liberal learning. The repertoire of experiments in liberal learning undertaken in the first part of the twentieth century has been all but forgotten. Apart from a few notable institutional exceptions and valiant efforts by some associations concerned with higher education, the undergraduate curriculum is attended by pluralistic ignorance and hasty afterthoughts.[6]

---

6. The Association of American Colleges and Universities has played a constant, heroic role in working to recover and revitalize traditions of liberal learning in the United States. Reports of a number of such efforts in small undergraduate programs, albeit restricted to the humanities, are assembled in Nelson and Associates 2000.

At the University of Chicago, from time to time, a combination of special institutional structures (faculty charged with undergraduate teaching, college deans with their own budgets, the mechanism of the staff-taught course), exceptional presidential leadership and rhetoric (Burton, Hutchins, Levy), and traditions of intense faculty concern with education (Wilkins, McKeon, Faust, Coulter, Schwab, Redfield, Axelrod, McNeill, Riesman, Sally, Cochrane) have imbued the institution with a supply of brains and energy sufficient to generate excellent educational thought and practice. Before it disappears, this work needs to be recorded and reconsidered. Whatever its local difficulties of circumstance—and they have been recurrent and often severe—the University of Chicago has long been distinguished by a relatively clear sense of its academic mission. This helps account for its long-standing reputation as "a teacher of teachers." In the current shortage of moral and intellectual resources for energizing higher education, Chicago's experience may be seen as exemplary in two senses—as a source of inspirational educational ideas and, no less important, as a model of ways in which local institutional traditions can be drawn on to inspire educational practice.

In describing the Chicago experience, this book aims not primarily to correct errors or even to plead a special case. I seek to set forth, in as much complexity as space permits, the ideals and practices of an extraordinary educational venture animated by an ethos expressed by Robert Maynard Hutchins's dictum, "It is probably fair to say that American universities . . . ought to do anything and everything to reduce their income from student fees. This is because most of the things that degrade them are done to maintain or increase this income" (1936, 5).

Not that universities do not need money, Hutchins added, or that they should not try to get it; "I mean only that they should have an educational policy and then try to finance it, instead of letting financial accidents determine their educational policy" (1936, 5). In words that ring true a half century later, he decried "the peculiar mixture of shallowness and volatility which marks the discussion and practice of education in America" and complained that "in mid-century, conformity is still preferred to agreement; tasks are undertaken before they are defined; ideas are forgotten before they are tested; problems are replaced before they are solved; and battles are lost which never were joined."

The Chicago approach to liberal education has from the outset been a tradition of developing educational policy and then trying to finance it, rather than the reverse. The great question before American higher education is whether that commitment can survive, at Chicago or anywhere else, into the twenty-first century.

I

Crises of Liberal Learning in the Modern World

1

The Place of Liberal Learning

"Liberal learning" is a commonplace. Locating that place requires four rough distinctions.

One rough distinction concerns the timing of what is learned. To begin with, individuals learn what they must know to become human beings in their particular society. This learning happens early and involves widely shared patterns. A second phase occurs during adolescence and after; it involves learning special, often specialized, matters humans must know to function as adults.

A second distinction concerns the content of what is learned—whether it concerns ways to engage in social relations and play social roles or the complex of ideas whereby people impart meanings to their environment.[1] The term *socialization* refers to the former, that is, experiences whereby persons learn their positions in networks of social relations and how to behave toward others in those networks. On the other hand, the process of assimilating the meanings in one's culture we designate as *enculturation*.

Both distinctions reflect features unique to humans. The exceptionally long maturation period of humans accounts for the distinction between primary and secondary phases of learning. The distinction between learning social roles and absorbing cultural symbols indicates that while other

1. This distinction is especially rough, since cultural symbols are also required for social interaction.

animal species exhibit well-defined patterns of social interaction, humans alone rely essentially on symbols.[2]

These two distinctions combine to identify four sites of learning experience:

1. *Primary socialization* teaches general ways of relating to people — for example, to be loyal to those to whom they are bonded or to show respect to people according to their social status.
2. *Secondary socialization* teaches how to play special adult roles: how to be a carpenter or a healer, organization man or entrepreneur, political leader or church follower.
3. In *primary enculturation,* individuals internalize the common features of their society's culture — its language and music, heroes and holidays, beliefs about the world and basic values — whether piety, industry, military courage, beauty, or the like.
4. In *secondary enculturation,* individuals acquire ideas reserved for adults and, often, only for selected adults.

Liberal learning figures as a particular form of secondary enculturation. It evolves when special teachings are adduced to create what is considered a "higher" kind of human being. It instantiates a third distinction, between the acquisition of adult *popular* culture, common to all adults, and some form of *elite* culture. Elite secondary enculturation (distinct from elite secondary socialization, which prepares persons for high-status governance or technical occupational roles) has taken two main forms. Associated with the ethics of two world-historical cultural transformations, this pair of forms embodies a fourth distinction, between what I shall call *civilized* learning and *liberal* learning.

Sites of Secondary Enculturation

COMMON ADULT CULTURE   In speaking of the popular, common-sense form of secondary enculturation, I refer initially to small, undifferentiated societies where a homogeneous culture is shared by virtually the whole adult community. Although such societies may possess lore known

2. Herring gulls, for example, feed, migrate, and sleep in flocks. Three-spined sticklebacks live in schools and have complex interactions. Other species — ants, honeybees, roosters — practice division of labor and social stratification. While all such species have ways of communicating, they do not rely on symbols, nor can those few outlier species that appear to learn a few symbols organize them into systems with distinctive properties.

only to specialists such as shamans or chieftains, their basic religious notions, magic, science, and artistic forms are common property. Secondary
enculturation takes the form of initiating young people into this adult lore.
Such initiations may involve dramatic transitional rites—through such
ordeals as scarification, prolonged fasting, or circumcision—when the
young person is taught the sacred myths and traditions of the community
as well as the names of their gods and stories of their works; or it may occur casually, with youngsters educated informally by relatives and village
elders.

Comments of Australian Aborigines exemplify this sort of learning,
which prevailed over most of human history. "I tell my kids stories when
they come hunting with me. I show them how to hunt, fish, get bush
tucker—these are good things to eat." "In my life when I was young he was
teaching us how to hunt and telling us stories every day. I always remember
the things he was teaching me—language, places, skins, clans, *djang*
(dreaming) sites, sacred places. He is still teaching me." Such teaching was
unwritten; it was *unstructured;* it occurred *anywhere* and everywhere; it involved *no specialized lore.* And it was essential for a group's survival. When
such teachings were lost, individuals might find new subsistence skills, but
their culture could not survive and their lives were drained of meaning. Another Aborigine said, "When I look at a lot of aboriginal people who don't
have their culture I feel sad for them. You don't really feel that you have a
place of belonging."

And so, for example, young people of the Kuku Yalanji clan would learn
to use juice of green ants to heal sore throats and chest colds; to make and
use fire sticks; to climb trees to collect honey, possums, bird eggs, and fruits;
to build traps to snare scrub turkeys. They learned what to do with water
lilies (eat their roots and stems, make cakes by wrapping their ground seeds
in the lily's leaves and cooking them in sand under hot coals); who among
them could eat stingrays or eels (elders only); who could eat food a child
brings from hunting (only the godparents); what to say when someone dies
(not mention their name); how to identify "sacred" or "dangerous" places
created by the First People (marked by cairns, stone arrangements); and
what rules to follow and obligations to assume with respect to people, animals, and places. Before outsiders with superior weapons forcibly in-
truded, these people lived smart, alert, often happy lives, in tune with the
surround of nature, their community of people, and their encompassing
world of spirits. What they learned was common to all, at least to members
of the same age and gender groups, and all of their learning related to ways
to survive and live together effectively. For them, a higher level of human

being amounted simply to anyone who conformed particularly well to customary expectations.[3]

"CIVILIZED" ELITE CULTURE   Ancient forms of liberal learning emerged from a long process of differentiation from the customary thoughtways of commonsense culture. The germs of these systems appeared in speculations about life and the world that took shape in what Paul Radin described in *Primitive Man as Philosopher* (1927). Over time such notions developed into traditions of philosophy, theology, and fine arts transmitted through formal schools of instruction. These traditions formed the cultural core of what we refer to as *historic civilizations*.

The historic civilizations evolved separate tracks for secondary enculturation. We sometimes speak of their cultures as divided into a high culture and a low culture, what Redfield called a "Great Tradition" and a "Little Tradition."[4] For illiterate members of such societies, secondary enculturation would follow the commonsense pattern. But for those who, by special position or by talent and ambition, learned how to read, secondary enculturation could also take the form of acquainting them with the great texts of their high culture. In Imperial China this enculturation involved study of the analects of Confucius and the historical writings of Confucian scholars; in Hindu civilization, the Vedas and Upanishads; in Jewish civilization, the Bible, Talmud, and Midrash; in the Christian tradition, the Old and New Testaments and other sacred literature, with variants such as Ethiopian Orthodox Christian texts and an esoteric type of poetry; and in Islamic civilization, the Qur'an and the Hadith.

Notable in all these traditions is a shift from using cultural forms solely for purposes of adjustment to natural and social worlds to ways of honoring them as guides to transcending worldly habits and thereby producing a higher, "civilized" type of humanity. Most of their prophetic works appeared around the sixth century BCE—a crucially formative period in world history, which Karl Jaspers ([1949] 1953) has described as an "Axial Age"—when a number of powerful cultural developments took place independently in China, India, Iran, Palestine, and Greece. An era of simultaneous destruction and creation, the Axial Age redirected cultural

3. This material draws on conversations with survivors of the Kuku Yalanji clan, Queensland, from a compilation of their oral traditions (Fisher and Ross-Kelly 1996), and on interviews with Australian Aborigines exhibited at the Warradjan Culture Centre, Northern Territory, Australia.

4. Among many valuable accounts of the process by which great traditions are formed, see Redfield 1956 and Shils 1981.

symbols from a basically utilitarian, adaptive function toward a self-conscious striving for transcendence and self-determination. Jaspers represented this historic transformation as a process of spiritualization (*Vergeistigung*), whereby humans came to reorient their lives through adherence to transcendent spiritual directives.[5] The elevated character of these texts meant that the primary outcome of studying them was to reinforce their sacral authority.

"LIBERAL" ELITE CULTURE   In contrast with those types of elite enculturation that focused on mastery of the texts and doctrines of an Axial civilization, another type stressed the production of an especially cultivated type of person. In ancient China, this type became the preeminent ideal of the gentleman-scholar. During the latter sixth century BCE,, Confucius described this ideal as one who possesses wisdom, courage, and magnanimity, and who is accomplished in courtesy, ceremony, and music. He stressed the virtue of sincerity and held that education was a means to gain an enlightened mind, enlightened in the sense of coming to grasp the remarkable harmonies of nature. Classical Chinese education attempted to produce a broadly cultivated man through a program that included both literary and martial training. The curriculum codified during the Chou period consisted of six subjects, sometimes called the liberal arts of classical Chinese education: rituals, music, archery, charioting, writing, and mathematics.

A Japanese variant of this conception employed the idiom of "polishing" the person. In medieval Japan, this idiom became crystallized in the ideal of *bu-bun,* the cultured warrior, who received training in the various arts of combat and in such other arts as calligraphy, poetry, and tea ceremony—arts closely associated with traditions of Zen Buddhism.

In the West, the form of liberal education designed to produce elite persons is usually traced to ancient Greece around the sixth century BCE, reaching generative depth in the "educational century" of Athens, from about 450 to 350 BCE. The educational ideal formulated there, *paideia,* denoted an aspiration to use culture as a means to creating a higher type of human being. The Greeks believed, we are told, that education in this

5. This notion of reversal of orientation through *Vergeistigung* was prominent among many social thinkers of his time, including Weber, Simmel, and Scheler. They all "visualized, beyond a level of self-consciousness emerging out of natural experience, an almost physical turning against natural process in order to subordinate it to some sort of transcendent ideal" (Levine 2003).

sense "embodied the purpose of all human effort. It was, they held, the ultimate justification for the existence of both the individual and the community" (Jaeger 1939, xvii).

This type of elite learning celebrated not the authority of sacred texts but the formation of adults with special qualities. Aristotle's *Politics* (1255b, 1258b, 1337a) remains a locus classicus of this formulation. Aristotle distinguished between education that is liberal, meaning appropriate to a free man (*eleutheron*), and education suited for slaves and servile classes. The distinction was made on the basis not of subject matter but of the spirit in which a subject is pursued. One may pursue a subject out of necessity, as learning a trade may be necessary to earn a living. One may study something for its utility, as reading is useful because it enables one to decipher signs. Or one may pursue a subject because of peer pressure, as the fashionable "thing to do." But by definition, to act from necessity is not the mark of being free; to seek utility everywhere is not suited for those who are great-souled and free; and to follow some pursuit because of the opinion of other people, says Aristotle, would appear to be acting in a menial and servile manner.

In contrast to motives of this sort, Aristotle describes motives to learn that befit a free person: learning that is undertaken for its own sake and appropriate for promoting a good life. Although Aristotle certainly does not deny the need to study useful arts, he insists that they should not constitute the whole point of learning. Free people should study drawing, he urges, not merely to avoid being cheated in buying and selling furniture, but for the liberal reason that this study makes one observant of bodily beauty.

Aristotle's notion of what this education should consist of rested on the teachings of Socrates and Plato and featured the philosophical pursuit of truth. This view of liberal education was by no means shared by all prominent educators of the time. Indeed, the "education century" was marked by acrimonious competition among educators. Isocrates, who commanded a larger following than Aristotle, emphasized civic activities and therewith promoted arts of discourse as the most suitable education for free men.[6]

Proponents of both views directed their teachings to those who were of high status—free, not slaves or servile, and wealthy enough to have the leisure time to spend on educational pursuits. They believed that the ennobling education proper to free persons should include a physical as well as intellectual component. In later centuries, cultivation of the body

6. Kimball (1986) argues that these two traditions, philosophical and rhetorical, between them organized the whole universe of discourse about liberal education over the past twenty-five centuries.

disappeared as a component of liberal training, so that intellectual arts alone emerged as suitable subjects for liberal learning.[7] The Greeks named these intellectual arts arithmetic, geometry, astronomy, music, grammar, rhetoric, and dialectic. During the Roman Republic, the prominence of legal and political issues disposed educators to feature the cultivation of rhetorical skills as the prime component of liberal teaching. Looking to Isocrates as a model, these proponents of oratory, most notably Quintilian and Cicero, identified a set of arts proper for free citizens, which they designated as *artes liberales.*

Although early Christian fathers were wary of such "pagan" subjects, by the fourth century CE, figures such as St. Augustine were able to embrace major parts of the classical liberal curriculum. When invasions swept aside traditional Roman schools, the church, needing a literary culture for its clergy, sustained educational traditions that Rome had adapted from the Greeks. By the sixth century, Christian educators including Cassiodorus and Isidore of Seville codified the liberal arts into an encyclopedic education. Their curriculum organized human knowledge into seven fundamental disciplines, divided into two groups: the *trivium,* consisting of the disciplines of grammar, logic (sometimes dialectic), and rhetoric; and the *quadrivium,* comprising arithmetic, geometry, astronomy, and music (the ancient Pythagorean program of mathematics). Transmitted by monastics for centuries, this curriculum entered secular universities during the Renaissance.

The liberal arts tradition came to the United States with the Puritan divines in Massachusetts. It was instituted in American colleges in a framework that combined Protestant piety and *mental discipline,* a term that came to embrace the approach to disciplines found in the Renaissance curriculum. The core of this curriculum consisted of Greek and Latin languages and literatures, biblical studies, and moral philosophy. Well into the nineteenth century, the political and cultural elites of Western Europe and the Americas were groomed on curricula of this sort, programs of liberal cultivation inspired by Renaissance culture.

The Modernity Revolutions

From the eighteenth century onward, Western philosophers of education came to evolve new rationales and directions for liberal learning. They and the educational administrators who followed in their wake were

7. In East Asia, the martial arts continued to be taught as a form of personal cultivation, largely in Taoist monasteries (Levine 1984).

responding to momentous changes in their societal and cultural environments. For thinking about those changes, the notion of modernity, however ambiguous its sense and contested its meanings, offers a point of reference. It symbolizes the sense of a radical discontinuity between earlier forms of social order and the sense, perhaps for the first time in Western history, that the "modern" or novel did not have pejorative overtones.

None of the ingredients of modernity was unprecedented. What happened was that their momentum picked up enormously; that change as such, or "progress," came to be accepted as a good thing; and that those changes came to be supported by active striving. Acceleration of long-brewing changes, celebration of the new, and intimations of intentionality have led many to refer to the transformations that ushered in the modern order with the trope of revolution. We hear of the industrial and the democratic revolutions, the scientific revolution, the managerial revolution, the education revolution, the communications revolution, the social revolution, and the like. What may be called a complex of modernity revolutions conveniently represents the diverse transformations of recent centuries and offers a framework for looking at the educational challenges they have posed.

MODERNITY AS DIFFERENTIATION   In most accounts of modernity, changes associated with the improvement of production and the enhancement of commerce have figured prominently. They form the centerpiece of what Adam Smith ([1776] 1976) viewed as a new type of society, which he described as "commercial" in contrast to the previous "agricultural" type of society. For Smith, the central features of modern society included major improvements in the productivity of labor resulting from an unprecedented extension of occupational differentiation. In Smith's thought, differentiation connoted the division of labor in production and exchange, a process of *functional specialization*. Others extended this notion to signify specialization in all spheres of life including science, politics, administration, military and ecclesiastical structures, as well as the economy, and later to signify the separation of different institutional sectors or spheres of action from one another.

Differentiation also designates processes whereby individuals become increasingly distinct and unlike one another. Georg Simmel represented this transformation in terms of two contrasting processes. One, the *emancipation* of individuals from social constraints, included the transposition of jural responsibility from collectivities to individuals and the shift from a pattern of compulsory group affiliations based on birth and propinquity to a pattern of voluntary associations. A contrasting process, *individuation*, features the authentic development of every distinctive personality.

This kind of individuation Simmel found in the enlargement of groups that creates more space for the expression of individuality; the transition from a condition where mental activity is circumscribed by shared beliefs to one that permits individualized intellectual achievement; and the individuated constellation of affiliations based on membership in multiple voluntary groups. Both of these patterns of personal differentiation were accentuated by two central features of modern societies: widespread use of money as an abstract generalized medium of exchange and concentration of people in large cities.[8]

MODERNITY AS DEMOCRATIZATION   A second complex of modernization processes was famously treated by that consummate analyst of what he called "a world . . . quite new," Alexis de Tocqueville ([1840] 1988, 12). Tocqueville's observant eye focused on a number of transformative processes, including political centralization, popular sovereignty, and popular mobilization. This array of processes have in common the extension of connections between a political center and peripheries, such that the center becomes more effective in influencing the peripheries and at the same time more accessible to and affected by them. Using somewhat different terms and emphases, these processes have been analyzed further through Comte's notion of the steady expansion of modern society toward a global humanity, G. H. Mead's linkage of national-mindedness to an emerging international community, and accounts of modern state formation by such scholars as Norbert Elias, Reinhard Bendix, Karl Deutsch, and Clifford Geertz.

8. For Simmel's writings on individualism, see Simmel 1971, esp. chaps. 15–18 and 20; see also Simmel [1890] 1989 and Levine 1981 and 1991c. Other analysts of modernity have interpreted individualization in different ways. Durkheim's cult of the individual and W. I. Thomas's description of "individualization of behavior" as a process of "evolution" also emphasized individuation. Thomas connected this process with "mechanical inventions, facilitated communication, the diffusion of print, the growth of cities, business organization, the capitalistic system, specialized occupations, scientific research, doctrines of freedom, the evolutionary view of life, etc., [whereby] the family and community influences have been weakened and the world in general has been profoundly changed in content, ideals, and organization" (1923, 70). Robert Redfield adduced twelve types of evidence for processes of individuation in the modernization of four Yucatecan communities (1941, 355–57). Eisenstadt views the importance of conscious moral choice among members of fundamentalist movements as an indicator of the modern emphasis on the autonomy of human will (1999, 91).

Tocqueville considered the secular trend of equalization of social status to be the dominant phenomenon of modern society. Although he found this phenomenon most pronounced in the United States, he interpreted it as a master trend for all societal orders.[9] For Hegel, too, the extension of rights guaranteed by formalized law figured as a master trend over the ages. Weber likewise depicted the extension of rational-legal bureaucracy as a core process of modern society, which had the inexorable leveling effect of status difference from the pressure to treat all persons equally before rational-legal norms. This theme has been emphasized by writers as diverse as Adam Smith and Ortega y Gasset. T. H. Marshall synthesized much thought on the subject by enumerating the array of rights—civil, political, and social—that were progressively enacted and extended throughout modern populations.

MODERNITY AS RATIONALIZATION   Some theorists have eyed the progressive accumulation of knowledge as key to the modern epoch. In the wake of a century of idealization of physical science by French philosophes, Comte advanced this view decisively. He took the maturation of biology and the arrival of sociology ("social physics" at first) as positive sciences to be markers of the new era (Levine 1995, chap. 7). The hallmark of the new age would be the guidance of societal development on the basis of positively grounded social knowledge. Hegel's idealist view of world history offered an alternative version of this conceit by identifying modernity with the triumph of reason through history. Hegel also drew a clear distinction between objective and subjective rationality, the former consisting of the progressive embodiment of a struggle to attain perfected systems of morality in the state and its laws and the latter consisting of the growth of self-consciousness and the articulation of that self-consciousness through art, religion, and philosophy.

Simmel likewise distinguished between such objectified forms as science, ethics, art, and philosophy, on the one hand, and subjective culture, or cultivation, on the other. Unlike Hegel, he saw the creation of objective culture in the modern world far outstripping subjective culture. Weber investigated the development of objectified forms of modern Western rationality in virtually all institutional and cultural spheres. Christopher Jencks and David Riesman (1968) linked the phenomenal growth of knowledge with the ascendance of research priorities as a modernizing process that had revolutionized the academic world. Daniel Bell (1966) took the

---

9. The prospect of its inexorability, he said, filled him with *une sorte de terreur religieuse.*

centrality of objectified knowledge as the key identifying feature of late capitalism, which he called "postindustrial society."

Modernization has also been viewed in terms of transformations in personal conduct. Smith applauded the virtuous character traits that engagement in the modern economy tends to foster. Commercial society inclines people to be industrious rather than idle and to manifest a frugality that eventuates in savings and capital investment. Weber famously put his finger on this change as an essential part of the conversion to modern Western capitalism, by identifying subjective rationalization—the ascetic, methodical organization of daily activities in this world—as essential to the operation of this new economic system. Inverting Weber's notion, Karl Mannheim tied the functional rationalization of worldly activities to a heightened level of self-regulation. Bendix investigated how industrial managers deliberately sought to extend this new kind of discipline to factory workers in Russia and the United States.

On a different tack, Freud analyzed the discontents of modern civilization tied to a heightened level of control of natural impulses. In *The Civilizing Process* ([1936] 2000), Norbert Elias documented the slow and steady control of psychic drives over the past millennium. Michel Foucault spoke of the modern "disciplinary society" in which civil and state apparatuses utilize a variety of correctional techniques (Foucault 1979, 215–16). More generally, this phenomenon has been so notable that it has been described as a "disciplinary revolution" (Gorski 1993). The major agent of this transformation in recent centuries has been the institution of primary education, where pupils are taught punctuality, orderliness, and other forms of self-control along with basic academic skills.

Liberal Education Encounters Modernity

The curriculum for liberal learning in the West was never entirely frozen nor invulnerable to dismissive attacks. As Richard McKeon observed, the liberal arts have been the target both of reformist energies and of complaints about their plight throughout Western history—from the controversies of Alexandria and Rome to the present: "Even before the technical learning and rhetorical pedantry of the Hellenistic Age, the Greeks of the classical period . . . lamented the inauspiciousness of their times for the use or development of the liberal arts" (1964a, 36).

In the decades before and after the American Civil War, however, plaints about the liberal curriculum increased in volume and tone, inspiring educational reforms that were responsive to the evolving needs and discontents of modern life. These reforms involved sharp reconsiderations of what had long been defined as "liberal" learning. The road to these reforms was paved by philosophers who had taken a fresh look at what it meant to become a superior human being.

PHILOSOPHICAL FOUNDATIONS OF NEW FREEDOMS   Classical Western notions of learning, however different in content, pitched liberal education as superior to popular culture by virtue of its transmission of some common set of intellectual disciplines worthy of free persons. By contrast, early modern philosophies of education extolled experiences that enabled students to shape themselves in accord with their unique inner identities. This new emphasis involved a shift from the ideal of the properly cultivated adult to that of the suitably individuated adult.

The mode of liberal education that strives for individuated learning reflects ideals of independence and individuality crystallized through the Enlightenment and the Romantic movement. In the Enlightenment, appeals to individual reason became prominent, both causing and reflecting changes in patterns of enculturation. Thus, Charles Camic (1983) suggests in his study of eighteenth-century Scotland, it was through overcoming long-ingrained patterns of dependence and particularism that changes in both domestic and scholastic institutions propelled students into kinds of learning experiences that fostered universalism and intellectual independence.

For the Romantics, the core educational notion was to attend to each student's distinctive features as points for cultivation rather than to adhere to a canon of texts or encyclopedias of knowledge. Rousseau's *Émile*, an advocate of drawing out the student's genuine natural responses, is generally considered the archetype of this type of learning. It was exemplified by Goethe, with his focus on personal development (*Bildung*), and codified by the great educator Wilhelm von Humboldt, who put man's goal as "the highest and most harmonious development of his powers"—a goal that required variety, not uniformity, of stimulation, and secure guarantees of personal freedom (1993, 10).

In the course of the nineteenth century, this notion of individuated learning became endowed with the same transcendent significance as the previous forms, civilized learning and common liberal learning. It thereby embodied what may be called a second axial transformation, one in which individuality as such came to be sacralized. "Nothing is at last sacred but the integrity of your own mind," proclaimed Ralph Waldo Emerson, whose influential essays celebrated the notions of Self-Reliance and Man Thinking ([1841] 1940, 352). Centering on what Durkheim described as the modern "cult of the individual," this ideal was illuminated by Simmel's analyses of self-formation, modern love, and student-centered peda-gogy.[10] Indeed, Simmel purported to be elucidating the common linguis-tic usage of the concept of culture (*Kultur*) by defining it in terms of the cultivation (*Bildung*) of individuals through the selective incorporation of objective cultural productions. Individuated learning was emphasized no less in Dewey's appeal for teachers to attend to the immediate experience of pupils and the enhancement of their powers of understanding and in the idealization of the creative, autonomous individual by thinkers such as Freud and Weber.[11]

RECONSTRUCTING LIBERAL LEARNING IN NEW ENGLAND
The classical view of a liberal curriculum came under attack on three grounds. By virtue of its association with an elite, the classical curriculum seemed *ill suited for all free men*. For adhering to a curriculum of classical languages and literatures, it was faulted for *failing to accommodate new kinds of knowledge*. By imposing uniform requirements on a population with diverse proclivities, it appeared to *neglect the distinctive talents of students and the capacities for choice essential to free citizens*.

In line with those objections, proponents of individuation sought to re-lax fully common requirements for higher learning. Early initiatives to do so — such as those propounded in the 1820s by professor George Ticknor at Harvard and by the state legislature of Connecticut — could not sur-mount harsh opposition. The University of Vermont provided a more fa-vorable ambience. Around 1830, university president James Marsh insti-tuted a number of reforms, including such individualized options as part-time study, flexible time requirements, informal assessments, and the country's first elective system. From then on, the elective system slowly gained ground intermittently in several places, notably Harvard, which had a fairly extensive system of electives in place when its most renowned spokesman, Charles William Eliot, became Harvard's president in 1869. In Eliot's words:

> How to transform a college with one uniform curriculum into a university without any prescribed course of study at all is a problem, which more and more claims the attention of all thoughtful friends of American learning and education. . . . A university of liberal arts and sciences must give its students three things: (1) Freedom in choice of studies, (2) Opportunity to win academic

10. See Simmel 1971, chaps. 16–17; Levine 1991c.
11. In sociology, this ideal was prominent in the writings of W. I. Thomas (1966) and David Riesman (1950). On Freud and Weber, see Levine 1985b, chap. 8.

FIGURE 1 The place of modern liberal learning, circa 1900

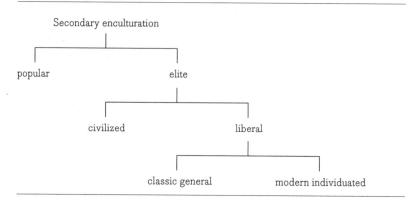

distinction in single subjects or special lines of study, (3) A Discipline which distinctly imposes on each individual the responsibility of forming his own habits and guiding his own conduct. (Eliot [1885] 1898, 12)

Invoking the Emersonian principle of letting young people follow their own stars, Eliot argued that a well-instructed youth of eighteen can select for himself a better course of study than any college faculty could possibly select for him and that the formula of a common learning ignored the individual traits of different minds. He encouraged Harvard to enlarge the number of free electives and to enrich the curriculum with numerous new courses. Thanks largely to Eliot's forcefulness and Harvard's prestige, many American institutions moved rapidly to transform the liberal curriculum into a field for electives.

Harvard's innovations in fact reconfigured the modern university in line with such central imperatives of modernization as specialization and cultural rationalization. By valorizing a growing number of disciplines, universities expanded the range of research activities. The elective system freed faculty from obligations to teach a common curriculum and gave them more time and teaching outlets for their specialized investigations. It also provided employment for a larger number of faculty. These changes moved Harvard closer to the model of the German university, whose advocates insisted that the sole mission of the American university should be to further the frontiers of knowledge. They also helped cement the foundations for curricular electivity.

Half a century after the Connecticut legislature's hapless appeal for a curriculum "adopted to the spirits and wants of the age," the elective system and the idea of specialized majors had become popular. As a result of these changes, the classical liberal ideal effectively dissolved. It was replaced by an "image of liberal education so various in its parts that all free men could find and choose freely whatever suited their personal interests" (R. Thomas 1962, 62). This image changed the construction of liberal elite culture to incorporate historically unprecedented levels of personal freedom. This shift produced radical changes in what was signified by the notion of liberal learning and of educating for freedom.[12] By the middle of the twentieth century, this notion had so thoroughly eroded the traditional liberal curriculum that one educator concluded that it did not matter what contents were included in the liberal arts curriculum, "so long as their pursuit frees the individual to develop as his inclinations and his capacities may direct" (Sack 1962, 222).

The evolving types of educational programs described in this chapter can be represented schematically as in figure 1.

12. For a more differentiated analysis of the meanings of freedom, see Levine 1985b and the references cited therein.

2

The Movement for General Education

Riding high on waves of the modernity revolutions, the elective system bore affinities with their major processes. Specialized production for expanding markets brought dramatic improvements in the standard of living—allowing frugal peasants to live better than savage kings—and achievements that surpassed pyramids, aqueducts, and cathedrals. Before long, the norm of occupational specialization became hegemonic in Western society. Loosening the constraints of custom brought the gifts of personal freedom to inhabitants of the modern urban world.

The elective system advanced specialization and individuation directly; indirectly, it advanced the rationalization of culture. By enabling faculty to teach their specialties, the elective system freed faculty time for specialized research and supported the growth of research universities, and so it gave a boost to original scholarship and the increase of autonomous disciplines. By submitting students to the rigors of specialized work, it enhanced the rationalization of personal discipline, a consequence also celebrated by Eliot.

Nevertheless, these trends did not yield unmitigated benefits, let alone exhaust the critical ingredients of modernity, and the curriculum that supported them soon came under attack. Undergraduates were jumping into elective courses without any thought of where their academic specialties and personal predilections fit into broader schemes of things. The lopsided effects of privileging electives and early specialization seemed to threaten the human and civic values associated with liberal learning as traditionally understood; these ill effects set in motion fresh waves of reform. Public intellectuals and educators decried the extent to which universities were yielding to what they regarded as the crass philistinism of the vocational colleges and the sterile specialization of the research universities, thereby abandoning their responsibility for the proper development of young people. In the pithy words of Archibald MacLeish,

> The latter part of the last century was made forever famous in the history of higher education in America by the introduction of the so-called elective system, a system under which each individual student was to supply his own definition of education and set out to save his soul under the uncritical eye of a faculty which was to offer only what was demanded of it. (MacLeish 1920, 366)

Calls to reform collegiate education in the decades around 1900 thus issued in distinctive efforts to reshape liberal elite culture. Hoping to restore a program of common learning, these reformers nevertheless turned their backs on the classical curriculum of the previous century. What they sought were fresh ways to recover an essential and irreducible humanity made possible solely by breadth of learning. The initiatives to reinvent liberal learning which they pursued converged under what came to be called the *general education movement.* This phenomenon was unique to the United States and may well constitute one of the country's major contributions to the history of higher education.

Fallout from the Modernity Revolutions

From afar, the general education movement might appear to be unific. It was in fact powered by a variety of impulses and ideas, and it manifested an array of curricular principles and forms. These developments turned on different issues linked with the modernity revolutions. Some bids to restore general education aligned with certain master trends of modernization — chiefly, the push toward national integration. But most took a countercyclical form. Directed to counteract the more noxious consequences of modernity, educational critics augmented critiques of modernity that had formed an integral part of its history.

Table 1 presents a paradigm of benefits and harmful consequences of the modernity revolutions to help us analyze this complex of issues. From that wide-ranging and rich discourse, I mention only features that bear on questions of liberal learning.

TABLE 1 Modernity revolutions and their effects

Process	Differentiation		Democratization		Rationalization	
	Specialization	Individuation	Unification	Equalization	Cultural	Personal
Revolution	Industrial	Urban-commercial	Integrative	Social	Academic	Disciplinary
Benefits	Commerce, goods	Freedom	Efficacy	Justice	Knowledge	Civility
Disadvantages	Personal atrophy; social deficits	Hyperspecialization; alienation; consumerism	Repressive centralization; Violence	Mediocrity	"Tragedy of culture"; Jacobinic barbarities	Psychic repression

Although the needs for occupational specialization, urban commerce, and rationalization were well served by the elective system, the modernizing needs of democratic nation building were not so well served. Political unifications brought pacification of larger territories, extended rights for citizens, mobilized citizenries to combat disasters, expanded access to primary education, and promoted equal rights under the law. A culture of pure specialization and individuation could not ignite the political energy needed to secure these benefits. Even the most enthusiastic supporters of the division of labor and the commercial order could not but condemn such pernicious effects as their erosion of public spirit and civic virtues and the extremes of privatization.[1] Individuating processes were also indicted for producing social deficits, due to the withdrawal of personal energies from communal activities.[2] Such deficits have engendered recurrent calls for educational programs to create an engaged and informed public and a sophisticated leadership.

Specialization also led to the truncated development of human personalities. It produced deformations of the sort that Comte depicted as "minds that are very able in some one respect and monstrously incapable in all others" (1975, 274). Specialized rationalization cultivated increasingly diverse, mutually unintelligible languages, which undermined the ability of educated citizens to live in a common symbolic universe and eroded the grounds for a coherent, meaningful worldview. Concerns about such deficits motivated recurrent calls for curricula that would provide a broad context of knowledge and represent the interconnectedness if not the unity of knowledge.

Other concerns stemmed from the leveling entailed by social democratization. Tocqueville noted the lesser quality of those who became political leaders under egalitarian conditions as well as the debasement of cultural standards. Others faulted the equalizing trends of modernity for

1. Repetition of simple operations rendered workers "as stupid and ignorant as it is possible for a human creature to become," and the dexterity thus acquired came "at the expense of [a person's] intellectual, social, and martial virtues" (A. Smith [1776] 1976, II, 303). Smith thereby indicted the division of labor for rendering people unfit for rational conversation and unsuited for making sensible judgments regarding private and public interests. Tocqueville quipped that as the division of labor advances, "art makes progress but the artisan regresses" (Tocqueville 1840, bk. 2, ch. 20). Marx famously analyzed ways in which divided labor led to the alienation of producers from their products, their creative powers, and their fellow men.

2. More recently, such processes have been linked to a diminishing pool of persons ready to assume public responsibilities and constitute other forms of social capital (Sennett 1977, Putnam 2000).

reducing the pool of people willing to assume the burdens of public leadership and equipped to maintain standards for cultural productions. Enfranchisement of the masses was associated with less well-informed policy decisions, promoting vulnerability to demagogues and despots, and entailing the tyranny of the majority, with attendant suppression of minority views. For such problems, the push behind general education reflected desires to uphold standards of excellence.

Simmel's notion of the "tragedy of culture" depicted another discontent of what we have called the rationalization of culture. For Simmel, modernity was marked by the accelerated production of "objective culture": all those created forms of symbolic work such as science, art, music, philosophy, and the like. This enormous output has taken place at the expense of subjective culture, that is, of the capacity of human subjects to engage and digest those objective forms for the sake of their personal growth. As a result, he said, modern man feels himself in a typically problematic situation—"his sense of being surrounded by an innumerable number of cultural elements which are neither meaningless to him nor, in the final analysis, meaningful. In their mass they depress him, since he is not capable of assimilating them all, nor can he simply reject them, since after all they do belong *potentially* within the sphere of his cultural development" (Simmel 1968, 44).

Finally, the very pace of change in the modernity revolutions produced reactions that observers found troubling, if not alarming. Tocqueville ([1840] 1988) observed that under conditions of rapid cultural change in which grounding religious beliefs were eroded, people were likely to look for strong political authorities as a surrogate for authoritative directives, and Durkheim ([1897] 1951) identified waves of disorientation that swelled the rates of suicide. Simmel found that the tempo of modern life addicts the populace to fevered consumerism and to "the superficiality, the sensual frenzy and the hollow splendour of modern amusements." Due to the lability of modern conditions, the "lack of something definite at the center of the soul impels us to search for momentary satisfaction in ever-new stimulations, sensations and external activities [which become manifest] as the tumult of the metropolis, as the mania for traveling, as the wild pursuit of competition and as the typically modern disloyalty with regard to taste, style, opinions and personal relationships" (Simmel [1896] 1997, 260; [1907] 1978, 484).

More recent analysts have pointed to the traumatic strains that attend the loss of any existing social patterns. Emancipation from traditional, hierarchical authority had its psychological downside. Scrutinizing a variety of common psychological reactions to such changes, Weinstein and Platt argue that since for most of human history autonomous initiative was not prized and personal and social autonomy were rarely demanded, the uniquely modern wish to be free has generated a good deal of guilt and anxiety. These feelings have led to regressive solutions that take violent forms, including both the revolutionary imposition of new values in excessive and polarized fashion and the radical enforcement of a return to traditional values (Weinstein and Platt 1973, 1969; Parsons 1942; Lechner 1985).

Quest for a New Common Learning

Keeping such issues in mind, we can better distinguish the diverse voices behind the calls for new kinds of general education. Their early statements attended to five major challenges:

1. the need to cultivate public spirit and civic intelligence;
2. the need to overcome one-sided intellectual specializations;
3. the need to overcome intellectual anarchy;
4. the need to uphold standards in face of leveling;
5. the need to help persons become more centered and reflective, in order to the cope with the acceleration of change and of cultural productivity.

One early appeal for general education resonated with those critics who decried a growing *privatization of outlook* in the modern era. Among prominent early figures of this sort, Paul Chadbourne of Wisconsin, who became president of Williams College in 1872, stressed the need to ground the training students received to become artisans, farmers, lawyers, merchants, ministers, and the like on a general education: "The very theory of our government demands a broad culture for all our young people. The time comes when they must choose their special pursuits, but all that is needful to fit them for the duties of citizenship they should enjoy in common" (Chadbourne 1869, 335).

President A. Lawrence Lowell of Harvard similarly defended a broad experience of general education because "democracies have the greater need of widely diffused general education," since "all men partake of the character of rulers . . . [and] ought to be trained in some measure for that duty" (Lowell 1934, 104–5). John Dewey and George Herbert Mead worried that their contemporary society had not developed the kinds of public consciousness needed for pluralistic urban communities and advocated new educational programs to cultivate habits of social cooperation and to elevate discourse about public problems.

Another impulse sprang from a concern about the democratization of culture and the intensified need for cohorts qualified to meet demanding academic criteria and to upgrade American standards.[3] Tocqueville had warned of the *debasement of taste* attendant upon the unchecked egalitarianism and utilitarianism of Americans, and the expansion of educational opportunities after the Civil War did little to check those tendencies. By the 1870s, leaders of all the major American colleges affirmed that standards of admission must be raised and that secondary schools must share the responsibility for elevating standards of general education. William Rainey Harper of Chicago sent shocks throughout the secondary school system of his day in 1892 by refusing to admit matriculants on the basis of high school certificates and instead requiring them to pass entrance examinations in a broad range of subjects. A quarter century later, John Erskine created his influential Great Books course at Columbia in order to force students to engage demanding classics directly as well as to polish unwashed Americans through immersion in a great tradition.

A third impulse stemmed from a reaction to the *specialization of perspectives* in urban-industrial society. Educators who decried the excessive narrowness generated by academic specialization expressed an impulse to restore an educational program whose goal it was to create a well-rounded human adult. They included Henry Tappan of the University of Michigan, an early advocate of general education on grounds that the "true idea of education is the development of the soul in all its faculties." Tappan appealed for an educational program to provide "that large and generous culture which brings out the whole man, and which commits him to active life with the capacity of estimating from the highest points of view all . . . knowledges and agencies" (Tappan 1851, 15–16).

Finding such an ideal mocked by unchecked specialization and the excesses of the elective system, educators such as Woodrow Wilson were aroused to attack programs of specialized training that did not rest on a solid general education. Wilson claimed that the drift toward specialization was producing "a new ignorance" produced by "separate baronies of knowledge, where a few strong men rule and many ignorant men are held

3. On this point, Eliot was theoretically at one with critics of the elective system. However, he had assumed that students coming to college would already have received sufficient general education in public high schools and that even if they hadn't, it mattered little, because college would force them to catch up.

vassals"; he defended the "generalizing habit" based on a broad survey of the field of knowledge, without which "it is hard to see how a man is to discern *the relations of things,* upon the perception of which all just thought must rest" (Wilson 1925, 224).

Perhaps the most ambitious impulse of all reflected a wish to do counteract what was coming to be perceived as a condition of *intellectual anarchy* in modern times. Echoing Auguste Comte, who had insisted that the fragmenting outlooks of industrial civilization needed to be balanced by a coherent philosophy that connected the fields of special knowledge produced by the positive sciences, Archibald MacLeish declared that the failure of colleges to formulate a common and acceptable definition of liberal education reflected the "intellectual anarchy" that marked contemporary culture as a whole (MacLeish 1920, 363).

Among American educators, Alexander Meiklejohn of Amherst made history by declaring that one could not talk about a unified curriculum without discussing the unity of knowledge and that the hesitation to speak about the unity of knowledge was all too conspicuous in educational deliberations. If faculty agreed that it was all right for students to secure a degree simply by putting together a smattering of disconnected fragments of knowledge, they would never sustain the will to search for a unified understanding of knowledge that could ground a coherent general education (Meiklejohn 1922).

Finally, there were those who focused on the moral and mental challenges of living in an increasingly complex and labile society. Writing in Germany of the time, Max Weber railed against dilettantes and held high the ideal of specialized training for responsible professional work, but he also warned that processes of rationalization threatened to turn human actors into robots, living in steel-hard shells of bureaucracy and capitalist enterprise. To counter this, Weber advocated a strenuous process of education for judgment, a process which prodded people to think critically for themselves and to escape the unreflective determination of social decisions by value habits and emotions built into public language and conventional practice. His contemporary Georg Simmel pursued kindred lines of thought, holding that students should be directed to reflect on all of their formative experiences: the moral decisions they make, the curricula they are asked to follow, the directives they receive, the ways in which all subjects they study connect to their individual lives (Levine 1991c).

Perhaps none of the educational thinkers analyzed the linkage between social change and educational reform so profoundly as did John Dewey. For students at all levels, Dewey considered it a prime desideratum to equip

TABLE 2 Motives for the reform of liberal education

Modernizing Process	Direction of Reforms	Educational Directives		Representative Educators
		Individuated Education	General Education	
Specialization	Create specialized curricula	Invent specialized courses, majors		Eliot
Individuation	Create distinctive personalities	Provide electives		Eliot Dewey
Cultural rationalization	Organize knowledge	Develop academic disciplines		Eliot Weber
Discipline	Create a disciplined self	Promote self-discipline		Eliot Weber
Political unification	Prepare for national citizenship, reflective patriotism		Educate for civic participation	Chadbourne Lowell Dewey
Social equalization	Counter mediocrity due to leveling		Educate for depth, elevate standards	Harper Erskine Scholz
Hyperspecialization	Counter one-sided personal growth		Promote well-rounded personal growth	Tappan Wilson
Hyperindividuation	Counter privatization, intellectual anarchy		Surmount intellectual anarchy	MacLeish Meiklejohn
Hypertrophy of rationalized culture	Counter rigidity, alienation of subjects		Promote reflection, creativity, subjective culture	Simmel Dewey
Accelerated change	Promote adaptive, centered person		Promote centered, critical thinking	Simmel Dewey

students with the ability to think for themselves in the midst of changing circumstances, avoiding the opposed perils of rigid attachment to old thoughtways and responding to change by collapsing into impulsivity.

Richard Scholz, second president of Reed College and moving figure behind Reed's drive for general educational reforms in the 1920s, stands out as an educator who articulated each one of these concerns. His inaugural address, "Fitness for Freedom," highlighted the need for educational goals that promote civic-mindedness, breadth of learning, intellectual coherence, heightened cultural standards, and virtuous self-realization. He did so in words that merit revisiting eight decades later: "Never before was the relation of scholarship to patriotism, of learning to life, so obvious *and* so fundamentally necessary. . . . We need today a unified reinterpretation of the whole of existence. . . . The content of a liberal education will integrate in a larger synthesis the results of the humane and the natural sciences, of the history and creative achievements of man's past and present" (1922, 3, 6, 8).

My general thesis thus far has been that the revolutionizing processes of modernity demanded a number of novel educational adaptations, including those affecting the traditional site of liberal learning. Certain reforms were undertaken in support of the modernizing changes in question. Others were advocated as ways to overcome the discontents associated with them. And some of them have been propounded as ways to elevate the agents of and responses to these changes to a higher level of human functioning.

Table 2 summarizes motives for the reform of liberal education as characterized by various modernizing processes. The modernizing process of *specialization* required training programs to produce specialists. For such purposes, Weber and Durkheim alike declared, the era of the generally educated scholar-gentleman was over. Yet many critics challenged their position and sought to counter the ill effects of hyperspecialization with educational programs to broaden the horizon of the rising specialist.

The modernizing process of *individuation* required that individuals be liberated from constricting social conventions. For that purpose, uniform modes of socializing adults had to be reduced or ended. Yet extremes of individuation hampered the promotion and transmission of common cultural understandings and communally appreciated objects.

The modernizing process of *political unification* required that individuals learn to overcome parochialisms and to support new forms of national participation. For such purposes, curricula celebrating the histories, languages, and cultures of nations would be important as means to overcome the tendencies toward privatization and parochialism. Yet uncritical acceptance of national dogmas and authoritative pronouncements entailed new forms of enslavement and required special educational experiences to create an informed citizenry.[4]

The modernizing process of *social equalization* required that individuals be exposed to lessons about the rights to which all members of the community are entitled. For such purposes, attitudes regarding exclusiveness needed to be overcome. Yet the tendency toward leveling implied a trend toward mediocrity, which could be countered only by educational programs that sought to elevate standards.

The modernizing process of *cultural rationalization* required institutions to promote the advancement of knowledge. Advances in objectified knowledge required new resources and disciplinary organizations for higher levels of academic work. For this purpose, methods to control bias and personal inclinations had to be devised. But the commitment to objectification threatened the development of cultivated subjects, which could be countered only be educational programs aimed at personal culture.

The modernizing process of *discipline* required that institutions craft lessons about ways to control oneself for achievement and communal participation. New habits needed for modern society — civility, literacy, punctuality, integrity — required a diffusion of various forms of personal discipline. For such purposes, impulsivity and anarchy need to be overcome. Yet the repression of spontaneity implied a trend toward rigidity and uniformity, which could be countered only by educational programs that sought to enhance spontaneity.

These and other concerns raised questions about curriculum design that were more complex and challenging than proponents of liberal elite culture have ever had to face. Those questions cannot be answered quickly or definitively. To begin to deal with them adequately requires institutional arrangements dedicated to them. Numerous colleges have devoted attention to them and enacted innovative curricula on the basis of

4. Senator Robert Byrd (2003) has expressed this point eloquently: "There is a power which can serve as a check against abuses by a government or by government officials and that power is the power of the informed citizen — one who has read enough, who understands enough, who has developed a base of knowledge against which to judge truth or falsehood. Participation in the great debates of our time must not be relegated to the power elites in Washington. An informed citizenry has to participate, ask questions, and demand answers and accountability to make a country like ours work."

deepgoing investigation and reflection. We shall note a number of these curricula in chapter 8.

One place even tried to build ongoing conversations about the aims and methods of general education in the fabric of its institutional life. That was something else.

II

Enter Chicago

3

The Making of a Curricular Tradition

In the history of liberal learning in the West, the University of Chicago maintained a tradition of engagement unique in range and depth. Chicago's story throws light on how such a tradition works.

Enter Chicago

It started with an idea. Never mind that the project was driven by the sectarian ambitions of Baptist philanthropists or financed by their sometimes ill-gotten gains. What counted, for the world, was an establishment devoted to uninhibited forays in the quest for truth. From the outset, the University headed forth with a notion and strove to make it real, not just let things happen. Chicago took shape as an intentional community designed to promote scholarly excellence.[1]

Deliberateness was no less marked in what became the undergraduate division. The University grew, intones its first major chronicler, Thomas Goodspeed, "in accordance with a fully elaborated educational plan" (1916, 130). Indeed, the undergraduate program began with a raft of radical innovations, often called "educational experiments," which were

1. To be sure, its intentions could not always transcend the inhibitions of a surrounding philistine culture. Intellectual titans such as Thorstein Veblen or W. I. Thomas and the distinguished president Max Mason would be driven out by what today seem like trivial sexual escapades. Its freedom of inquiry could be threatened, though not shaken, by hysterical reactions against perceptions of radical teachings.

periodically reviewed. A quarter century into its history, Goodspeed interviewed faculty to see which features of Chicago's plan had been dismissed, which modified, and which retained for their educational value (1916, 148 ff.). Later, a committee report observed that "education at the University of Chicago has always been experimental, namely in demanding constant self-criticism on the part of the faculty, open-mindedness for the future as in the past to proposed changes, and a keen sense of responsibility to our students" (College Curriculum Committee 1934, 2). Half a century later, former college dean F. Champion Ward happily found the University "once again . . . prepared to re-examine the collegiate function and then try to realize in practice the implications of that enquiry" (Levine 1985a, 51). *Reflect, experiment, reflect, revise*—that seems to have been the driving spirit.

Despite all that, the undergraduate teaching function was never unproblematic at Chicago. Founder William Rainey Harper became the first American university president to make research the primary concern of an academic institution.[2] Soon after the University opened, he observed, "From the beginning the College work of the University has been recognized as something subordinate to Graduate School work. . . . If the income of the University is used in providing suitable instruction for the great army of undergraduates, it will be impossible . . . to make provision for the smaller, but . . . more important body of graduate students" (Harper 1892, sec. 8).[3] Harper's zeal for research was matched by the faculty he recruited, scholars eager to make Chicago the premier research university in the world. In short order, they achieved just that.[4] Brimming self-consciousness about this mission led them to reflect with special

2. Well before entering office, he signaled his intention to make the University "from the very beginning an institution of the highest rank and character"—a research university that "might be born full-fledged" (William Rainey Harper to John D. Rockefeller, 9 August 1890, John D. Rockefeller [Founder] Correspondence, 1886–1892, Box 1, Folder 11, Special Collections, Joseph Regenstein Library, University of Chicago, Chicago). Goodspeed reminisced that Harper "wanted from the outset a great graduate university, with an undergraduate department as a temporary concession to the weakness of the founder and the Chicago brethren" (1916, 297).

3. William Rainey Harper to the Trustees of the University of Chicago for the Year Ending June 30, 1892, sec. 8, Special Collections, Joseph Regenstein Library, University of Chicago, Chicago.

4. This mission was dramatized by issuing scholarly publications through a university press, the first in the country. Its centrality to the institution located it inside the central administration building for more than three decades—just as earlier, for more than three decades, the central administration itself was located inside the main research library.

intensity about the goals, concepts, and methods of disciplined inquiry. Not by accident did many disciplines take their modern form at Chicago, nor by chance did there arise so many "Chicago schools."

Uncorrected, this emphasis on research, pursued by independent professors investigating whatever they wished, gave short shrift to undergraduate teaching. Harper tried repeatedly (without success) to farm out the first two years of college work to nearby academies so that the faculty could "devote its energies mainly to . . . strictly University work" (University of Chicago 1891, 3).[5] Many faculty shared the aversion to undergraduate teaching flaunted by Charles Whitman in zoology.[6] Some departments wooed scholars by relieving them from undergraduate teaching. The young chemist whose plaintive response to his dean's appeal for faculty to teach in the College—"I'd like to help you, but my faculty pays off for research" (Ward 1962, 125)—enacted a scene that must have occurred thousands of times.

Under Harry Pratt Judson, a dean under Harper and the University's president from 1906 to 1923, the prioritizing of graduate instruction and research reached its zenith. After World War I, Judson complained publicly about siphoning funds from graduate teaching and research into undergraduate instruction. Soon after, the University Senate affirmed: "[Since] State Universities are able and obliged to provide for the great mass of college students, the time has come to base our policy more definitely upon the obvious truth that this University can perform its most distinctive service to education through its graduate and professional schools. The limitation of undergraduate instruction appears to be complementary to this."[7] The respected graduate dean and university press director, Gordon J. Laing, lamented that the burden of undergraduate teaching at Chicago "probably cuts the productivity of many departments in two" (PR 1926–27, 7). Laing dreamed of what might be possible "if the

5. Harper's main initiative in that direction was to try to locate a junior college at Morgan Park Academy, a campus the University took over following the move of the Baptist Union Theological Seminary to Hyde Park as the University's Divinity School.

6. For expressions of Whitman's famous aversion to teaching, see Newman 1948, 220–21; Maienschein 1988, 165–67. However, before coming to Chicago, Whitman defended vigorously the teaching vocation, which he defined in a distinctive way as enhancing the student's ability to do research. So defined, "to exclude teaching [from the laboratory] would shut out the possibilities of the highest development" (quoted in Blake 1966, 127).

7. University Senate Minutes, 18 September 1922, Special Collections, Joseph Regenstein Library, University of Chicago, Chicago. In Chauncey Boucher's memorable description, under Judson "the College came to be regarded by some members of the family as an unwanted, ill-begotten brat that should be disinherited" (Boucher 1935, 1).

institution were entirely free from undergraduate entanglements" and imputed to those who thought the contrary "a delectable simplicity and charming naiveté" (Laing 1927, 201). In his inaugural address of November 1929, young President Robert Maynard Hutchins noted that many faculty members wanted the university to "withdraw from undergraduate work, or at least from the first two years of it" (Hutchins 1930, 12–13); a few years later, he tried in vain to relocate the bulk of the undergraduate body to the Northwestern campus in Evanston.[8] Indeed, as late as 1969, following a protracted student sit-in, then President Edward Levi talked about reducing College enrollment to about five hundred, and a prominent colleague commented, "If this sort of thing keeps up, maybe we'll just have to abolish the College."[9]

The notion that, unlike all other American universities, the College at the University of Chicago could be thought of as expendable lent a certain intensity, poignancy even, to efforts to make it flourish. Those efforts, paradoxically, also originated with Harper, who wanted to link the university research enterprise with an undergraduate program that suited its intellectual caliber. This goal accorded with the wish of his prime benefactor, John D. Rockefeller, and other founding donors, whose grants to the university in 1889–90 were designated for an undergraduate college. If Harper failed to farm out the undergraduate function, then he wanted the university to create an exemplary undergraduate program right at home. He thereby used the University's authority to elevate academic standards in the Chicago metropolitan area and throughout the Midwest.[10] When it appeared that Harper's University was not developing the exemplary college he envisioned, the faculty decided not to abandon it but instead "to develop it to a position of strength in its field comparable to that of our graduate schools in their fields" (Boucher 1935, 1).

Over the years, efforts to mount such a program produced tumult and tribulation and left a legacy of great moment to all who care about liberal

8. Soon afterward, former history professor William E. Dodd wrote Hutchins, "I think it unwise for a large endowed institution to continue to offer undergraduate work, especially in a region where there are four State universities not far away.... The one thing which modern civilization needs is absolutely free university work on a research level" (Boyer 1999, 46).

9. Edward Levi, personal communication with author.

10. These initiatives included an innovative program of extension courses and a College for Teachers. The University has maintained an active outreach program ever since. In the past generation, it has been manifest chiefly in the downtown programs of continuing education and in numerous conferences and seminars for faculty of the Associated Colleges of the Midwest.

learning. This chapter explores that legacy by looking at its innovative curricular and pedagogical ideas and at institutional factors that engendered all that innovation.

Forming and Nurturing a Tradition

Contrary to some perceptions, cultural traditions do not constrain action rigidly. Like language, their elements are continuously reproduced, recreated, and revised. Like language, they provide tools with which to define changing situations, tools that become sharpened or transfigured in their use. As illumined by Chicago social thinkers Richard McKeon (1967) and Edward Shils (1981), traditions reveal themselves as resources for empowerment and creativity.

Since Chicago's tradition mandated the application of experimental thought to curricular matters, its College faculty continuously revised their curriculum. Commenting on the innovations of the early 1930s, President Hutchins observed, "The attitude of the University is experimental because it is willing to try some things when success is not guaranteed. It is willing to change if change seems, on reflection, to be desirable. But it is not striking out blindly in the effort to do something new merely because it is new" (Hutchins 1936, 188).

This inclination grew so enmeshed in the lifeway of the university that it came to be taken for granted.[11] Hutchins celebrated the revised curriculum of 1942 by noting that it completed a process begun fifty years before under Harper. Efforts to rethink the curriculum in 1984 began with a tribute to the curricular landmarks of 1892, 1905, 1920, 1931, 1942, 1958, and 1965. The past continuously prods those responsible for Chicago's educational tradition to experiment and supplies ideas to be drawn on in novel ways.[12]

11. During my tenure as dean, it seemed self-evident that the faculty should be asked to undertake a searching review of our curricular structure. It took relatively little effort to encourage nearly a hundred members of our faculty to spend a year reviewing a dozen dimensions of our undergraduate program. This review took place through an institutional exercise of self-examination we called Project 1984: Design Issues and culminated in a four-day retreat at Starved Rock State Park that produced its own set of deliberations. See University of Chicago College Center for Curricular Thought 1984a and 1984b.

12. As dean of the College, I once brought to the attention of the heads of our undergraduate programs in biology and physical science some curricular ideas from our natural science programs from the 1920s. Their response was, "You mean we had something like this once? Why did we ever give it up?" They proceeded to create a pair of two-year sequences in the natural sciences that have served as models of the University of Chicago faculty's creativity. One course, The Evolution of the Natural World, offers an integrated six-quarter sequence that first examines the evolution of the physical universe and then the

Themes of the Chicago Tradition

From the manifold outcroppings of the University of Chicago's curricular history, a number of generative themes stand out. Viewed together, they suggest a profile of the Chicago approach to liberal education. These themes did not appear all at once, nor were they continuously evident even after they did appear. However attenuated, each of them remains to this day a constitutive element of the Chicago approach. Those themes include:

- a commitment to *demanding academic standards;*
- the ideal of a *coherent program of general education;*
- the appointment, in a research university, of *faculty dedicated to the function of undergraduate teaching;*
- creation of *interdisciplinary curricular structures;*
- a distinctive focus on the *cultivation of human powers* suited for all members of a democratic society;
- respect for differences in students' abilities and motivations by offering *flexible pacing* of their journeys through the baccalaureate curriculum;
- inventing ways to *enhance independent inquiry;*
- conducting *research on curricular questions and teaching practices;*
- promoting *pluralism about and within the curriculum;* and
- an ethos of *enfolding undergraduates within a community of scholars.*

DEMANDING ACADEMIC STANDARDS   The generative idea behind Harper's design for collegiate education was the notion of preparing a body of students to be able to perform at the highest level of graduate study. Notes scribbled in one of his famous red notebooks begin "1. A high standard" and end "14. No conditions allowed."[13] Given this point of departure, the organization of the University had to be seamless, all components pointing to the execution of advanced graduate work and research.

Harper signaled his seriousness about academic excellence with an

---

evolution of life on earth and explores the interconnections between the two. The other, Form and Function in the Natural World, describes the architecture of atoms and molecules, the forms and functions of cells and multicellular animals, and the interactional structures of animate communities. Both sequences contrast dramatically with The Nature of the World and Man, which initially inspired them.

13. William Rainey Harper, Red Book III, 1089, Special Collections, Joseph Regenstein Library, University of Chicago, Chicago.

innovation that sent ripples through the secondary school system. Instead of accepting undergraduates on the basis of their high school certificates, the University adopted a policy of requiring entrance examinations in all required subjects—English, history, and mathematics in all cases, along with varying combinations of foreign languages and science. "This policy has been adopted," Harper wrote, "because no greater service to the cause of education in the great country west of the Alleghanies [*sic*] could be rendered than a determined and persistent effort to raise the standard of admission to college. . . . If we are to have graduate students able to do the highest work, they must come to us . . . with a preliminary education of an accurate and thorough character."[14] This new admissions policy so diverged from the prevailing American system that four years later it was modified—not the last time an attractive Chicago educational innovation encountered tough resistance from conventions clung to elsewhere.

Even so, the idea of holding University of Chicago undergraduates to an exacting standard was durably implanted and never died. Awarding financial aid on the sole basis of merit reinforced this expectation. Once admitted, matriculants to the Harper-designed College followed a rigorous course of study to ready them for proper university work. Harper promoted this rigor with two innovations. First, in order to enable students to concentrate on academic work, he divided courses into *majors* and *minors*. In Harper's plan those terms meant that the student concentrated upon one major class for ten to twelve hours of classroom work or lectures per week and one minor class for four to six hours. "Concentration on a single subject is impossible," Harper noted, "if at the same time the student is held responsible for work in five or more additional subjects."[15] Although this scheme soon gave way to a requirement of three courses per quarter, the intention to promote concentrated study remained (Goodspeed 1916, 152). Moreover, the idea of compressing substantial work on a single subject into a short period was retained in the summer quarter, where it has remained ever since. Concentrated intensity became a hallmark of education in the College.

Harper's other innovation was to transform the conventional four-year baccalaureate program into two sets of sequential colleges. For promoting what Harper and his colleagues referred to as the "University Spirit," he thought it essential to distinguish between the first two years of general academic schooling and the last two years devoted to independent

14. Harper to Trustees.
15. Ibid.

investigation. At first these two colleges were named the Academic and University Colleges, later the Junior and Senior Colleges.[16]

Harper's two-college system deviated from the accustomed division of undergraduates into freshmen, sophomores, juniors, and seniors. Combined with provisions enabling students to complete their work at varying paces, this departure alarmed those who feared that his plan might destroy any sense of class spirit. To this objection, Harper responded,

> There is a certain kind of class spirit which ought to be destroyed. A class spirit which rises superior to the College spirit and to the spirit of scholarship deserves no existence. This plan will develop a spirit of scholarship and will in no way interfere with the companionship. By other means that most valuable of all student acquisitions—strong friendships—will be cultivated.[17]

The plan, then, was to use the University College courses to prepare students for graduate university work and to use the Academic College courses to ready students for the demanding work of the University College. This plan involved an unprecedented effort: *to design a two-year program of general education that had a specific purpose and a coherent curriculum,* a frame that became foundational for Chicago curricular thought for the ensuing century.

COHERENT GENERAL EDUCATION   How should one design a coherent program of education when it is to be devised as preparation for specialized academic work? Harper saw the Junior College as a continuation of the students' secondary school work, designed to prepare them for serious university study. The Junior College offered students the general culture and intellectual discipline essential for such study, failing which they could not enter the portion of undergraduate study that was oriented toward university work. The Junior College was thus described as a "clearing-house" between the secondary school and the "higher work of the Senior College and Graduate Schools" (PR 1892–1902, 109). In so viewing the Junior College, Harper and his colleagues consistently *considered the Junior College curriculum as the final part of a six-year period*

16. These sets initially included junior and senior Colleges of Arts, Literature, and Science. Later, a Junior College of Philosophy, a Senior College of Commerce and Administration, and a College for Teachers were added. For a while after 1902, the Colleges were further subdivided by gender, despite strenuous protests from feminists on and off the faculty.

17. Harper to Trustees.

of preparation for university work rather than part of a four-year collegiate program, a concept that Hutchins would steadfastly defend and finally implement.

Once again, President Harper initiated the dialogue. He assigned Junior Colleges the task of transmitting sufficient "general culture" to enable students to proceed to the more demanding work of the Senior Colleges. For Harper, that meant "a study of the great heritage we have received from the past" (PR 1898–99, xxiv). The idea that the aim of general education was to provide students with a general orientation to their cultural universe resonated at the University for many years. It became the generative principle for the curricular structure promoted by President Ernest Burton in the early 1920s. Burton conceived general education as aiming "to help each student to acquire such a knowledge of the physical universe, of the history of the race, of the structure of society, and of the nature of the individual, that . . . he may have a sense of where he is" (PR 1924–25, 21–22). With that in mind, he encouraged his talented dean of the College, Ernest Hatch Wilkins, to design survey courses to orient students in the major fields of human knowledge.

The idea of devoting the first two undergraduate years to general education inscribed itself indelibly into the tradition of curricular thought at Chicago and constrained generations of faculty to deliberate about the nature of general education. The broader notion—that precollegiate work should comprise fourteen years of study—converged with the thinking of educators who envisioned an ideal educational program consisting of six years of elementary school, then four years each of middle school and college preparatory school. Known as the 6-4-4 plan, this schema, whose seeds were planted in the 1890s, sprouted three decades later as a full-dress recommendation in the 1924 report of Dean Ernest Hatch Wilkins. The Wilkins report recommended a 6-8 plan culminating in a Junior College separated from the Senior College, and it urged a sharp distinction between general education and professional training. The plan eventually became operational in the College curriculum of 1942: a full-blown four-year undergraduate program of general education set to commence after the tenth year of precollegiate schooling.[18]

The less-radical version of this notion was more enduring. The idea of constructing a self-contained *junior* college curriculum was pursued in a

18. The four-year curriculum in general education, based on completion of requirements for fourteen yearlong course sequences, is described in Ward [1950] 1992. A mere schematic representation offers no insight into the extraordinary intellectual coherence this curriculum embodied, but it may be suggestive:

1928 report of a Senate Committee on the Undergraduate Colleges and implemented with the New Plan of 1931, which mandated a two-year program of general education. It was restored in 1958 when a coherent two-year general education curriculum became the first half of a four-year baccalaureate program, and it was reconfigured in the 1966 curriculum, which mandated one year of collegewide general education plus one year of general education prescribed by each collegiate division. One outcome of the yearlong curricular review known as Project 1984 was the restoration in 1986 of a two-year collegewide program of general education. The decanal call that initiated that review began with a paean to curricular coherence. It defined the hallmarks of a coherent curriculum as "one whose parts have an orderly and logical relation to one another, and whose organization expresses those values and beliefs about an educated person that are shared by the faculty who teach it," and listed the advantages of a coherent curriculum as securing "for our students, a rationale to make sense of a large number of requirements, so those requirements can be viewed as meaningful elements of their intellectual development rather than as arbitrary impositions; for our faculty, a context to facilitate more intelligent participation in a common enterprise; for the public, a means of presenting what our College has to offer in a more visible, more intelligible, and more persuasive manner"[19] (Levine 1983, 4–5).

Those responsible for the University of Chicago's curriculum perforce have agonized more than most faculties elsewhere about the extent to which their general education program manifests coherence—and they also sustain a century-old debate about the proper content of that program. Although the founding faculty agreed with Harper that Junior Colleges should prepare students for serious university work, throughout the University's first decade they "disagreed vehemently over the ingredients

First Year	*Second Year*
Social Sciences 1	Social Sciences 2
Humanities 1	Humanities 2
Natural Sciences 1	Natural Sciences 2
English	Mathematics

Third Year	*Fourth Year*
Social Sciences 3	History of Western Civilization
Humanities 3	Observation, Interpretation, and Integration
Natural Sciences 3	
Foreign Language	

19. Donald N. Levine, "Back to Business as Usual?" Minutes of the College Faculty, 12 May 1983, 4–5, Special Collections, Joseph Regenstein Library, University of Chicago, Chicago.

of the culture upon which true university study should rest" (Storr 1966, 311). Broadly speaking, their conception of the junior college curriculum has taken four forms. In the Harper era, it involved a common curriculum of mathematics, Latin, English, history, natural science, and German and/or French designed to prepare students for programs that would lead to focused academic research or professional training. Following the Boucher report of 1928 and the New Plan of 1931, it involved general survey courses designed to help students understand the world they would live in. In the Four-Year Program conceived experimentally in 1937 and mandated in 1942, it was held to foster a set of powers — to understand key ideas and methods of the natural and social sciences, to appreciate literature and the arts, and to express oneself clearly and effectively — deemed important for all members of a democratic society. And in the curriculum of the Levi years in the late 1960s, under Dean Wayne Booth, some defined it as learning languages of the different disciplines in order to gain access to the various academic specialties.

FOR A DEDICATED UNDERGRADUATE FACULTY   It became clear early on that to maintain an undergraduate program of high quality would require the services of some faculty who were devoted to and specially qualified for undergraduate teaching assignments. Harper thought an independent faculty was needed to guide students through the Junior College. At his instigation, a special faculty group was formed to manage the Junior College and, after a trial decade, this plan for a distinct Junior College faculty with independent powers was officially approved (PR 1892–1902, xcvi).[20]

During the Judson years, due to declining interest in undergraduate programs and swelling enrollments after World War I, the use of regular faculty to teach Junior College classes diminished. Large classes taught by ill-prepared graduate students became the norm. In reaction, some senior faculty pushed for educational programs up to the University's high standards. Inspired by Dean Wilkins, the 1924 Commission Report proclaimed:

> The success or failure of The College as an educational institution will depend primarily upon the teaching ability . . . of the men and women employed as teachers. . . . The primary duty of the administrative officers of The College is the selection of a staff of high teaching ability and personality, and the

20. By one account, "those who taught in the Junior Colleges were viewed as advanced secondary teachers, like the masters of the sixth form in English public schools" (Orlinsky 1992, 32).

maintenance of this high quality through elimination of the unfit and constant alertness in discovering teachers of promise. . . . The College is not an institution for research, and the teachers though they may well be potential scholars, should be free from any constraint to accomplish anything but success in teaching.[21]

The Commission then made the revolutionary recommendation of a *college faculty independent of departments,* appointed on recommendation of the dean of the College, organized in interdisciplinary groups formed for curricular purposes.

These efforts culminated with the appointment of Hutchins, who moved quickly to provide budgetary support to the Junior College.[22] This funding enabled Dean Chauncey Boucher to substitute regular instructors for what he called a "Coxey's army of graduate students" and to hire a number of distinguished faculty, including no less a figure than Thornton Wilder, "in an endeavor to provide for our undergraduate students the most inspiring, and hence the best, instructors to be had" (PR 1929–30, 47). Only through making the undergraduate teaching program a serious part of the University's mission could faculty be induced to devote the energy needed to make it excellent. Hutchins established a firm institutional basis for doing so. In 1932 he gained Faculty Senate approval to empower the College dean to recommend appointments to the College faculty without departmental status, a move accompanied by a clause about expecting a "large proportion" of the College faculty to be members of departmental faculties also.[23] *From that time until the present, the dean of the College at the University of Chicago has been authorized to make faculty appointments exclusively in the College.* For decades, this exceptional power enabled the College to appoint outstanding persons more active in teaching and course development than in research; active scholars who did not comport with the predilections prevailing in their departments; and practitioners of the fine arts (Ward 1992, 92).

Two other Chicago firsts reinforced the movement to strengthen the commitment of high-powered faculty to teaching undergraduates. In the

21. CFC Report 1924, 8–9, Special Collections, Joseph Regenstein Library, University of Chicago, Chicago.

22. Following the divisional reorganization of 1930, the College was given its own budget, to "consist of that portion of the salaries of the members of the faculty that represented the share of their time and attention that was devoted to College work." Minutes of the University Senate, 22 October 1930, University Archives, Special Collections, Joseph Regenstein Library, University of Chicago, Chicago.

23. Ibid., 19 November 1932.

late 1930s, an anonymous donor provided funds for three $1,000 awards
to be bestowed annually for outstanding college teaching. Later named
after the donor's parents, the Llewellyn John and Harriet Manchester
Quantrell Awards have been presented every year since 1938. Selected
by an anonymous committee which evaluates nominations submitted by
students, awardees have been celebrated at the June College Convocation and, more recently, announced at the annual meeting of the College
faculty.

Another development affected the very fabric of the university's organization—the emergence of joint appointments as the modal status for
members of the arts and sciences faculties. Throughout the Hutchins years,
undergraduate courses were taught largely by staffs appointed on a College-only basis. At times the proportion of College-only faculty grew as
high as 60 percent. Eventually, this pattern dug unhealthy divisions between the graduate and undergraduate faculties and deprived undergraduates of instruction by some of the University's scholar-teachers. Under
the leadership of provost, acting College dean, and then university president Edward Levi in the 1960s, the separation was largely overcome, even
though Levi himself insisted upon the crucial importance of having the
College retain the right to make its own appointments. The bold Levi
plan, proposed to the faculty in a notable memorandum of August 25,
1964, led to the differentiation of the faculty along horizontal rather than
vertical lines. It did so by establishing five collegiate divisions whose
members, heads (the "masters"), and governing committees enjoyed enhanced authority by virtue of holding appointments jointly in the College
and a graduate department. The collegiate divisional structure manifested the Chicago policy of having a separate College faculty not only
teach undergraduates but also assume full responsibility as a corporate
body for the curriculum and its prosecution. It also enabled faculty who
might vote one way when considering departmental priorities to vote
differently when acting as members of a collegiate division. It is largely
through this cumbersome but intermittently effective internal role differentiation, rather than through a College faculty consisting of separate persons, that Chicago now directs special faculty resources to the undergraduate teaching function.[24] The University of Chicago's persistent

24. As a close observer describes this situation, "The regime of joint appointments
between the College and the graduate departments has meant that faculty looking out for
departmental interests and those protecting the College's interests are, generally speaking,
the same persons. This means that the tensions generated by conflicts among multiple faculty responsibilities are expressed less between groups of faculty, but are rather internal-
ized within each faculty member's position" (Orlinsky 1992, 71).

commitment to institutional arrangements that channel faculty energies of quality into the undergraduate curriculum contradicts, as Ward has put it, "the common assumption in academe that rigorous general higher education of interest to critical and demanding students can be achieved without altering the institutional setting within which it is carried on or the career lines of those who are expected to provide it" (Ward 1992, 95).

INTERDISCIPLINARY CURRICULAR STRUCTURES In and of themselves, interdisciplinary structures are not particularly valuable. It is what they make possible that commends them. Regarding research, escape from disciplinary boundaries enables scholars to focus on issues associated with a substantive problem (Levine 1995, 290–94). With respect to education, they make possible a shift from inducting the young into academic specialties and professional career lines to a priority of focusing on specified educational objectives. The university educators at Chicago instinctively understood that *it is virtually impossible to sustain a focus on cultivating a broad grasp of human knowledge or a broad range of human powers without engaging colleagues from different scholarly fields and constraining them to shift their usual perspectives.*

Like the turn to a fresh definition of the undergraduate curriculum, the institution of interdisciplinary teaching bodies involved a shift that gathered momentum in the 1920s and took off with explosive force thereafter. Under Dean Wilkins, some faculty pursued the idea of offering students a grand synthesis of human knowledge. This notion led to a notable multidisciplinary course, The Nature of the World and of Man, organized by an energetic professor of zoology, Horatio H. Newman. This course took shape as a sequence of lectures presented by specialists from astronomy, geology, physics, chemistry, microbiology, zoology, evolutionary biology, ecology, physical anthropology, embryology, physiology, and psychology. After offering the course, the specialists collaborated to publish their lectures in a book proudly authored by "Sixteen Members of the University of Chicago Faculty" (Newman 1926). Similar multidisciplinary initiatives were taken with courses in the humanities (The Meaning and Value of the Arts) and in the social sciences (Man and Society).

In the 1930s, the pace of interdisciplinary curricular work quickened, thanks largely to ideas and arrangements promoted by President Hutchins, who stressed the need for cooperation among departments and professional schools. In autumn 1930, the University's governing bodies approved a plan to organize clusters of arts and sciences departments into divisions, each headed by a dean. In place today, this structure has done much to foster communication among departments within, respectively, the Divisions of the Biological Sciences, Humanities, Physical Sciences, and Social Sciences. Colleagues from various departments collaborated in the construction of four new general education sequences representing each of those four divisions, sequences sometimes referred to as a quadruplet offspring of Newman's grand survey course. This development coincided with increased interdisciplinarity in Chicago's graduate programs — four interdisciplinary graduate programs organized by Dean Richard McKeon in the Humanities Division and four in the Division of the Social Sciences under Dean Robert Redfield.[25] This range of interdisciplinary programs was unparalleled. Although the divisional structure posed some obstacles to cross-divisional communication, later the University took steps to overcome those barriers. These steps have included, from the late 1960s, a handful of interdivisional common core sequences and a number of interdivisional concentration programs within the New Collegiate Division; from the 1980s, graduate workshops in the humanities and social sciences established during the presidency of Hanna Holborn Gray; and lately, buildings devoted to interdivisional research between the biological and physical sciences and between biology and psychology.[26] What is more, the professional schools supported fruitful linkages with their colleagues in the arts and sciences faculties with, for example, notable courses and programs between medicine and sociology and between philosophy and law.

At Chicago, faculty from various departments convene for teaching purposes in four distinct forms. One is through meetings of those who teach sections of a *multidisciplinary staff-taught course,* as when colleagues from anthropology, divinity, history, political science, psychology, and sociology assemble to discuss common readings in a yearlong sequence such as Self, Culture, and Society, or from English, history, and philosophy in order to teach Form, Problem, and Event. Such experience

25. In the humanities, these interdisciplinary programs were coordinated by the Committee on the History of Culture, the Committee on Language and Communication, the Committee on Comparative Studies in Art and Literature, and the Committee on the Analysis of Ideas and the Study of Methods. In the social sciences, the interdisciplinary committees included the Committee on Human Development, the Committee on International Relations, the Committee on Planning, and the Committee on Social Thought.

26. Two interdivisional core sequences—Liberal Arts I and Human Being and Citizen—were taught collaboratively by faculty from both the humanities and the social sciences. The aforementioned interdivisional sequences—Evolution and Form and Function in the Natural World—were cotaught by faculty from the biological and physical sciences.

broadens scholarly specialists, challenging them to expose themselves to materials over which they cannot possibly possess the same degree of mastery as over their research specialties. Louis Wirth, a professor of sociology who helped construct one of these interdisciplinary courses in the 1930s, wrote, "Each of us who has participated in the general education courses . . . has acquired an acquaintance with a number of other disciplines which have extended his range of vision, of interest, and of knowledge. Each of us has at least begun to see interrelationships of which hitherto he was more or less oblivious" (1934, 29). Daniel Bell, recalling his own teaching experience at Chicago in the late 1940s, wrote that debates about course materials were thus "lively and provocative" and "the courses . . . were extraordinary intellectual adventures for the teaching staff" (Bell 1966, 32). A later analyst of the era was told that the weekly staff meetings produced "high faculty morale and solidarity," and one of his informants exclaimed, "Why, we even visited one another's discussion meetings, though we didn't have to" (Severson 1972, 22).[27]

A second form of interdepartmental teaching takes place when colleagues from two or more departments join forces to *co-teach a particular course.* Thus, David Bevington (English Department) and Ellen Harris (Music Department) collaborated in Shakespeare at the Opera, studying plays and operatic versions of the Verdi Shakespeares and others including *Romeo and Juliet* (Gounod), *Antony and Cleopatra* (Barber), and *Measure for Measure* (early Wagner). In a course called Dependency and Disrepute, Margaret Rosenheim (Social Service Administration) and Edward Rosenheim (English Department) joined forces to examine attitudes toward underprivileged strata by looking at statutes, court decisions, research reports, fiction, drama, and lyric poetry. Since the 1990s, the genre of Big Problems courses, which treat "matters of global or universal concern that intersect with several disciplines and affect a variety of

---

New interdivisional research buildings were created along the University's major east-west axis, 57th Street—in 1998 the Bio-Psychological Research Building, designed to facilitate frontier work on the relationship between behavior and the neural and endocrine systems; and in 2005 the Center for Integrative Science, designed to enhance collaboration among biological and physical scientists in fields of exceptional complexity, from condensed-matter physics to synthetic chemistry to complexity theory.

27. David Riesman corroborated: "Not all the staffs shared the reverence for the classics. What they did share was a belief that pedagogic issues were of vital importance. They were willing to argue about such issues and to collaborate in a staff-taught course with colleagues of strong views and different persuasions, despite the compromises this necessitated" (Jencks and Riesman 1977, 495).

interest groups," has attracted scholars from disciplines even farther afield. The idea of teaching about problems for which solutions are crucially important but not obviously available has brought together scholars from economics and biology (World Hunger); linguistics, philosophy, and anthropology (Language and Globalization); and humanities and biology (Evil).

A third form of cross-departmental instruction involves collaboration on a *course sequence,* each component of which comes from a separate department, as when faculty from astronomy, biology, chemistry, geophysical sciences, and physics collaborated on the curriculum for two-year sequences on evolution and on systems, or when colleagues from computer science, mathematics, and statistics collaborated on a novel course in quantitative studies.

A fourth mode occurs when a faculty group creates an *interdepartmental baccalaureate degree program.* Following the Levi reforms of the mid-1960s, numerous "concentrations" of this stamp arose, ranging from PERL (Politics, Economics, Rhetoric, and Law) and FIAT (Fundamentals: Issues and Texts) to HIPSS (History, Philosophy, and Social Studies of Science) and Environmental Studies. Like interdisciplinary general education courses, these concentration programs afford opportunities for faculty from diverse fields to convene regularly, thereby gaining experiences as educational for themselves as for the undergraduates they serve.[28]

THE CULTIVATION OF HUMAN POWERS Besides directing the Junior College curriculum to provide general culture, Harper offered foundational language for what became the hallmark of the University of Chicago's curricular tradition. Against the view of college education as preprofessional training, Harper also directed Junior College work to cultivate "systematic habits" and "control of intellectual powers" (Harper 1905, 272–73).

28. The list of interdepartmental concentration programs created by the College faculty since the 1960s includes African and African-American Studies; Arts and Sciences of Human Medicine; Biological Chemistry; Biological Sciences; Cinema and Media Studies; Civilizational Studies; Conceptual Foundations of Science; Disciplines of the Humanities; Environmental Studies; Fundamentals: Issues and Texts; Gender Studies; General (now Interdisciplinary) Studies in the Humanities; General Studies in the Social Sciences; History and Philosophy of Religion; History, Philosophy, and Social Studies of Science; Ideas and Methods; Law, Letters, and Society; Medieval Studies; Philosophical Psychology; Politics, Economics, Rhetoric, and Law; Public Policy Studies (formerly Public Affairs); Religion and the Humanities; and Tutorial Studies.

Discourse about mental habits and intellectual powers had figured prominently in nineteenth-century educational thought. However, two philosophers closely identified with the University of Chicago inspired much of the development of the 1920s and beyond: Aristotle and John Dewey. Dewey's psychology and ethics informed the thought of many educators who worked at Chicago, including Henry C. Morrison, an influential specialist in secondary school curriculum and longtime superintendent of the university's laboratory schools. Specification of intellectual powers or virtues formed a key portion of Aristotle's ethics, which entered Chicago curricular thinking largely through Wilkins and then through Hutchins and McKeon.

Picked up again in the 1920s, this language provided the wedge for a radical attack on the question of how to constitute an undergraduate curriculum. Key innovators here were Wilkins and Morrison. In 1924, they and their colleagues presented a Report on the Future of the Colleges that broke new ground in the discourse on curricular objectives.[29] The report began by rejecting any definition of the aims of general education tied to length of time spent or "any definition in terms of units, courses, majors, any standards of mechanical measurement such as grades and degrees." Instead, it demanded a definition of aims couched in terms of human powers. The report describes those powers not in terms of preprofessional preparation but as "the three types of power necessary to a proper adjustment of the individual to modern society." It enumerated them as follows:

A. As essential to the attainment of independence in thinking:
    1. Ability to conceive the past as a process of evolution.
    2. Generalized control of the thinking processes.
    3. Ability to think in simple mathematical terms.
    4. Ability to use the simpler fundamental concepts of the sciences of (a) general biology, (b) chemistry, (c) physics, (d) geography, (e) geology, (f) astronomy, (g) economics, (h) politics, (i) human psychology.
    5. (a) Ability to use the vernacular correctly and clearly.
       (b) Ability to use non-vernacular languages as a means of understanding the racial habits of thinking employed by other peoples, and as a means of access to the materials of learning and culture.

29. Report of the Commission on the Future of the Colleges, 1924, Harold Swift Papers, Box 34, Folder 7, Special Collections, Joseph Regenstein Library, University of Chicago, Chicago.

(c) The attainment of a linguistic sense, and of an appreciation of the phenomena of language as a means of inter-communication and as an expression of human thought.

B. As essential to the attainment of aesthetic independence:

1. The power of appreciating literature.
2. The power of appreciating music, and the pictorial and plastic arts. In neither case is creative production the primary object in the stage of general education.

C. As essential to the attainment of moral independence:

1. Rational apprehension of the principles of ethics.
2. A consciousness of the obligations which the individual owes to society, and active fulfillment of such obligations.
3. The acquisition of those habits under the control of which men live together advantageously in social groups and which are commonly classified as good breeding.
4. The acquisition of habits conducive to the intelligent maintenance of physical well-being.[30]

This bold enumeration injected new life into the Chicago tradition. It offered a benchmark for the many later efforts to organize curricula not around the memorization of facts but on behalf of promoting identifiable human capacities. It would find resonance in the *definition of an educated person* offered by Hutchins; in the *objectives of the College curriculum* specified by Clarence Faust; in the *measurable objectives of educational programs* tested by Benjamin Bloom; in the *rationale for teaching by discussion* offered by a committee of College faculty; and in the *new forms of arts and disciplines* proposed by McKeon.

Clarence Faust strained to connect courses in the College's general education program with the cultivation of specific powers, particularly in the humanities courses. Thus, the three-year humanities sequence, first offered in 1942–43, focused on cultivating (1) the powers of appreciating music, painting, and poetry; (2) the arts of interpretation needed to understand historical, rhetorical, philosophical, dramatic, and fictional works; and (3) the arts needed to articulate critical assessments of works of art and the powers needed to understand and assess alternative critical viewpoints. Faust pointedly contrasted these courses with a straightforward chronological journey through Western civilization, which had constituted the humanities core requirement up to that point. He transfigured

30. Ibid., pp. 2–3.

the teaching of foreign language, viewing modern languages not merely as instruments of trade or conveniences of travel but as offering material for grasping the very nature of language (including English), for increasing a student's capacity for expression (oral and written), and for providing direct contact with the literature and culture of other nations and peoples (Frodin [1950] 1992, 75).

In its first systematic articulation of the value of teaching by discussion, the College announced: "The end of education to which the means of the discussion technique is adapted is that of developing the inherent powers of human agents" (Axelrod et al. 1949, 14). This conclusion was hard won. Although Harper, like Woodrow Wilson, had praised small-scale interaction as crucial for learning at the collegiate level—"The Professor having his whole attention directed toward a single subject, and a small class of [students], is enabled to know them for the time being, in the most intimate way"[31]—only in the 1930s did the College faculty explore ways and means of teaching by discussion in small groups. Faculty documents from that time testify to continuous experimentation with this novel mode of pedagogy.[32] The key figure in extending this pedagogical practice into the natural sciences, Joseph Schwab, analyzed the relevance of teaching by discussion to the cultivation of powers in these words:

> Discussion, by itself, does not constitute an education. There are many things it cannot do or cannot do well. It cannot teach the whole art of reading well. It cannot do much toward teaching a student to write with clarity and to the point. It cannot efficiently give one the statements of fact or the experience with concrete things which knowledge and wisdom must sooner or later in-

31. Harper to Trustees, p. 156.

32. For example, one professor wrote to Dean Boucher: "A discussion leader has almost to be a dean. I mean he has to get acquainted with his students in more ways than an intellectual one. You have to hold your students and interest them. There is much greater frankness between students and instructors than there ever was under the old system. The discussion leader has to be a propagandist for the material of the course; he has to appeal to the human rather than the intellectual side and then has to get the students started. The only way he can maintain discipline is through the stimulating of interest" (E. N. Anderson to Dean C. S. Boucher, 22 May 1933, p. 4, DC Box 7/2, Dean of the College Records, 1925–58, Special Collections, Joseph Regenstein Library, University of Chicago, Chicago). Another wrote: "We began with only one idea in common: that the meeting should be conducted as a discussion, not as an old-fashioned quiz section nor as a supplementary lecture. . . . We have successively made changes which, I think, have resulted in improvement. We began by assigning in advance a narrow and definite topic for discussion; this tended to cut down windjamming on the part of instructors and class. We further improved on this by pointing the discussion as often as possible to one particular piece of literature . . . " (J. L. Cate to Dean C. S. Boucher, 7 June 1933, p. 4, DC Box 7/2).

clude. It cannot substitute for the solitary labor of organization and memory which underlies knowledge. Nor is it the place for the work of lonely creation which crowns knowledge if one is lucky. . . . In a curriculum, however, which aims to impart intellectual arts and skills and habits and attitudes, as well as bodies of information, discussion is not simply efficient or powerful but indispensable, for the same reason that the act of swimming is indispensable to teaching that art and practice on the piano indispensable to learning that. Discussion is an engagement in and a practice of the activities of thought and communication. (Schwab [1954] 1978, 105-6)

The course in Observation, Interpretation, and Integration was designed by McKeon and Schwab to equip students for distinguishing different types of problems that they would encounter as human beings and as citizens and to help them determine the appropriate methods needed for solutions. Dean Ward offered one of his own formulations in this vein when introducing a book of readings for one of the social science courses, entitled *The People Shall Judge:* "If citizens are to be free, they must be their own judges. If they are to judge well, they must be wise. Citizens may be born free; they are not born wise. Therefore, the *business of liberal education in a democracy is to make free men wise*" (Ward 1949, vii; my emphasis).[33]

FLEXIBLE PACING   To set a high standard of academic performance is to put a premium on performance rather than on amount of time served. This principle became another enduring guideline of the Chicago tradition. It appeared early on, for example, in a faculty decision to reduce the number of courses required for superior students to graduate. It informed Harper's division of the academic year into quarters—initially, four twelve-week periods separated by one week, each quarter divided into two "terms" of six weeks each.[34] The quarter system made the curriculum more flexible. Students could begin study or graduate at four points in the year. The quarter system also made it easier not only for someone with

33. In a later reminiscence, Ward recalled that the College curriculum in those years was designed "to instill in students balanced habits of relevant judgment": "The overall end of this education was to teach students 'how to think.' In a free and increasingly complex society, men and women are confronted constantly by diverse statements purporting to be true, by alternative courses of action claiming their adherence, and by individual works of art inviting their admiration. The College sought to give students the knowledge and intellectual competence to choose wisely and live well in such a society" (Ward 1962, 127, 123).

34. "Too much of an innovation" for most colleges was Harvard President Eliot's judgment about the quarter system and the flexibility it gave faculty and students (Goodspeed 1916, 147). The innovation spread and was adopted by dozens of universities, including Northwestern, Stanford, and the University of California.

the requisite ability to graduate in less than four years but also for students needing more time to master required skills not to have to leave before their education was complete. The policy continues to this day, in accord with the rationale Harper forwarded: students receive their diplomas not because a certain number of years have passed and a certain day in June has arrived but because their work is finished. Whether earlier or later than the ordinary period of college education, it does not matter. The College should not be a machine.[35]

The impulse to align degree requirements with actual academic attainments of students surfaced in another radical form in the 1920s. In 1927, President Max Mason waged a campaign against the "academic bookkeeping" of American colleges, in which he indicted the custom of couching degree requirements in terms of course units and course credits. A Faculty Senate committee he appointed, chaired by Dean Chauncey Boucher, proposed to abolish the awarding of degrees upon accumulation of a fixed number of course credits. Instead, the Boucher report advocated that both the completion of the Junior College and the awarding of the bachelor's degree be based upon passing a certain number of comprehensive exams which students might take whenever they felt ready. Although President Mason's resignation killed the report, its central ideas came to be implemented under the New Plan of March 1931, whereby the Junior College certificate was awarded not through course credits but by passing comprehensive examinations ("comps"); class attendance became optional; and students could take those exams at any time. The object of such an arrangement, Hutchins once remarked, was "to permit the student to keep constantly in contact with material that is stimulating and challenging to him" (Hutchins 1936, 191). Although awarding degrees on the basis of comps was dropped in 1958, individualized pacing continues to be promoted by letting students place out of certain subjects through exams administered when they enter the College. The principle continues to this day: Chicago uniquely provides guidance conferences with professional academic advisers, including diagnosis and remediation for difficulties in reading, writing, and studying; offers tracks at varying levels of difficulty for calculus; and permits students to graduate at the end of any quarter. More recently, it is manifest in the moral support offered to those who need to spend time away from academic work—what Chicago has long defined as a "positive dropout"—and has included letting those who wish to move faster to pursue combined BA-MA programs.

35. Harper to Trustees.

ENHANCING INDEPENDENCE AND INQUIRY The intellectual powers that University of Chicago faculty sought to cultivate normally included the taste and capacities needed for independent inquiry, although the extent to which inquiry was linked to academic research has varied. Harper's University sought to socialize students in their Senior College years to acquire the habits needed to carry out professional research. In the 1920s, emphasis shifted toward developing habits of the mind that enabled students to become independent tout court. The types of power that Dean Wilkins and his colleagues deemed necessary for a proper adjustment to modern society were described as sources of independence in thinking, aesthetic independence, and moral independence.

Mason restored a bit of academic emphasis to these powers by asserting, "One of the greatest duties that we have to perform is to create . . . a university in which participation in scholarship is pleasant, looked for, and appreciated by the undergraduate body. . . . With the research background of this institution there seems to be clearly indicated a type of performance in education which it is our specific duty to try—education by participation in research" (PR, 1925–26, xiv). During the Mason years, independent inquiry enjoyed a boost in the turn toward honors work. In his magazine article "Teaching Originality in College," Professor Robert Bonner hailed honors programs as a prime means to encourage intellectual initiative in students (Bonner 1927). Commenting on the new honors courses opened to superior students, Boucher wrote, "The basic idea is to have little if any formal and perfunctory class room work; a student is to be given a problem or a really big assignment—one fit for the best student; he is then to be put on his own resources to a large extent and allowed to show his originality and the utmost extent of his powers" (Boucher 1927, 78).

Although the general education curricula prescribed under the New Plan of 1931 and the fourteen-comp College of the 1940s may have seemed to stifle initiative, their announced goals were to stimulate personal inquiry. Syllabi for each course included bibliographies intended to promote independent work. These standardized curricula were taught by methods designed to promote independent thinking, a goal to which the conventional priorities of transmitting facts and covering material were defiantly subordinated.

The Project 1984 curricular review included two task forces that dealt with the issue of individualized work. The Task Force on Course Electives examined current practices and student responses and recommended clarification of College policy and some strategies that could be used to protect elective space. One outcome of the curricular reforms of 1985 was accordingly an expansion of the opportunity for students to include electives in their degree programs, an opportunity enlarged somewhat for many students in 1998. The Task Force on Research and Guided Inquiry recommended ways to integrate student research and guided inquiry in the undergraduate curriculum. In response to their report, the College established an ongoing publication, the *CROP* (College Research Opportunities Program) *Directory,* which continues to direct a hundred or so students each year to participate with faculty in research projects.

RESEARCH ON CURRICULUM AND TEACHING   University of Chicago faculty who pushed for a fresh approach to general education sensed they were entering uncharted territory—domains that seemed to call for a new order of professional knowledge. Voicing this awareness, President Burton encouraged research on the educational process and cited as one reason for the University not to abandon collegiate teaching the need to maintain a setting for such research.[36] Hutchins followed suit, virtually demanding that Chicago's faculty pursue investigations in undergraduate education. Hutchins's brief text mandating the University's reorganization by divisions, which the University Senate approved in October 1930, assigned to the College the task of doing "the work of the University role in general higher education" and defined it as a key aim of that reorganization "to open the way to experiments in general higher education."[37]

Faculty troops jumped to the challenge. Introducing the New Plan of 1931, the College Curriculum Committee advocated bold experimentation in preparing course syllabi and devising methods of instruction. Pursuing that charge, some of the finest minds at the University labored to create or transform undergraduate courses. They forged complex syllabi that contained rationales for each of the courses, sifted reading lists, compiled supplementary bibliographies, and devised sample comprehensive examination questions. Organizing broad fields, such as those of the natural sciences or of the study of entire civilizations, required serious intellectual innovation. Another sort of intellectual ability was called upon to identify and edit—often enough, to translate for the first time—original

36. PR 1922–23, xv–xvi; President's Papers, 1923, Special Collections, Joseph Regenstein Library, University of Chicago, Chicago.

37. University Senate Minutes, 22 October 1930, Special Collections, Joseph Regenstein Library, University of Chicago, Chicago.

works suitable for leading students toward deep engagement with key issues in those fields. These curricular labors claimed energies on the level of major research projects.[38]

When the four-year general education curriculum came to fruition in winter 1942, the College Policy Committee held fourteen long meetings during six weeks in which a report was drafted (Frodin [1950] 1992, 65). Soon after, a Committee on Evaluation of the College was established "with the specific obligation of studying the operation of the College curriculum, of reporting its findings to the College Faculty annually, and of recommending alterations in the light of these findings as frequently as seems desirable."[39] The College Evaluation Committee, chaired by noted biologist Ralph Gerard, comprised eleven subcommittees. These subcommittees investigated student opinion and faculty opinion regarding the newly reorganized College. They examined teaching evaluations, faculty contributions to students, and the opinions of alumni, employees, and parents. After its first year of deliberations, the committee concluded, "There is bitter need for evaluation, for objective, extensive, continuing measurement, of the achievements of the American college. Only as educational hypotheses and methods are tested by their results can they be subjected to rational experimentation and progressive modification. This is the scientific way."[40]

38. Boucher described the effort to concoct syllabi for the four general education courses mandated under the 1931 New Plan as entailing "immense amounts of time, careful study, pointed discussion"—and, indeed, nontrivial inconveniences, since the curricular work required them to postpone research projects and change residence plans for the summer (Boucher 1935, 38). Some of the work that went into this daunting curricular effort was reported in the volume edited by then Dean F. Champion Ward, *The Idea and Practice of General Education*, published in 1950 (and reprinted as a centennial publication of the Press in 1992). Richard McKeon and Joseph Schwab, two of the key progenitors of those curricular structures, also produced seminal papers on the principles involved in such educational programs (see chapters 6 and 7).

39. Memorandum for Meeting of Subcommittees of the College Evaluation Committee, 1 April 1944, p. 1, Dean of the College, Records, 1925–58, Box 17, Folder 9, Special Collections, Regenstein Library, University of Chicago, Chicago.

40. The statement continued: "The College at the University of Chicago offers highly favorable conditions for such an evaluative study. It does possess a clear and consistent educational philosophy which can be assessed. It possesses a faculty collectively informed in, working towards, and exploring with these ends and the methods of attaining them. The University is devoting an important fraction of its resources—administrative, educational, and financial—to furthering its new educational experiment. Most immediately, the College has already initiated just such an evaluation study of its workings and achievements and is prepared to apply its findings" (ibid.).

Of all the projects sponsored by the committee, the most consequential was carried out under Benjamin Bloom, professor in the Department of Education. Working with Ralph Tyler and others in the Subcommittee on Testing, Bloom investigated ways of assessing the extent to which curricular practices of the new College attained their stated objectives. Before long, he expanded his study from its original goal of examining the Chicago College only to studying three groups of matched students elsewhere. Bloom's studies culminated in a *Taxonomy of Educational Objectives,* perhaps the most famous schema ever devised for this purpose. His taxonomy arranged "classes" of "educational behaviors" on a hierarchy from simple to complex:

1.00 Acquisition of information
2.00 Comprehension
3.00 Application
4.00 Analysis
5.00 Synthesis
6.00 Evaluation

Studies using this schema found that as much as 90 percent of college instructional time went into instilling "knowledge"—to the detriment of helping students cultivate more complex skills such as analysis and evaluation (B. Bloom et al. 1956; Anderson and Sosniak 1994).

Student writing was investigated intensely. Several techniques were tested in a yearlong course on writing, which promoted standard expository patterns and sensitivity to elements of good style. The experimental spirit of the enterprise was foregrounded: "There is no easy way in which so complex an accomplishment as writing well can be imparted without labor and occasional failure" (Ward [1950] 1992, 210). Teaching practices were monitored incessantly. Instructors maintained contact with what went on in other courses; at one point a committee consisting of Henry Sams, Robert Streeter, and others investigated how the very writing styles of students tended to vary according to subject matter. Over the years, other committees on writing have pursued this charge further. The Project 1984 Task Force on Writing carried out investigations of its own. The enterprise soared when Joseph Williams and colleagues created the Little Red Schoolhouse (LRS), a program for training graduate students to help undergraduates improve their writing skills. Since its founding in the 1970s, the LRS has carried out a number of systematic investigations, for example, examining the features of hundreds of student papers divided according to whether they were assessed as honors or mediocre or whether they were written by first-year or fourth-year students.[41]

During the latter part of the Hutchins era, the College faculty experimented with a technique of instruction that differed from the lecture format which had dominated course work during the 1930s. They called this new technique the method of "structured discussion" to distinguish it not only from "shooting the breeze" but also from discussions in which students merely ask questions to clarify or to challenge something an instructor has said. In 1949, Joseph Axelrod and four colleagues reported on a two-year investigation of this approach to teaching, based on independent observations and tape recordings of hundreds of class discussions. Their *Teaching by Discussion in the College Program* set forth (1) a formulation of the parameters of the problem; (2) a statement of the ends of a general education program; (3) types of student behavior in the learning process;[42] and (4) techniques of teaching by discussion linked with those types of behavior. In consequence, dozens of College faculty requested resources to record and analyze discussions in their own classes.

Responding to complaints about undergraduate student malaise, Dean Ward invited sociologist William Bradbury Jr. to investigate adjustment problems among Chicago undergraduates. The Bradbury report of 1951

41. The former study found the principal marker of the papers by honors students to be the amount of space and quality of thought that went into the framing of the paper's central problem. The latter study discovered that first-year students were reluctant to present differing opinions, fearing that to do so might undermine their argument, while fourth-year students commonly presented opposing views because they understood the need to do so in order to strengthen their own arguments (J. Williams 1999). In yet another study, the LRS solicited responses from more than a thousand alumni of their program to determine its long-term benefits.

42. These types of behavior were arranged in order of the extent to which they required students to organize their learning independently:

1. The student listens to the instructor expound a point.
2. The student asks questions in order to clarify in his own mind what the instructor has said.
3. The student challenges the instructor's statements.
4. The student propounds his own solution to a problem and has it approved or corrected by the instructor; if corrected, he listens to the instructor's reasons for modifying or rejecting.
5. The student propounds his own solution to a problem and is led by the instructor to elaborate and to defend it against attack, to relate it to other ideas, to modify it, if necessary, in the light of the attacts [*sic*], etc.
6. The student *participates* in a *group effort* in which #5 is done by other students as well as by himself. (Axelrod et al. 1949, 24, original emphasis)

analyzed sources of emotional distress experienced by many students in the College. It then proposed an array of institutional reforms regarding faculty practices, College facilities, the advising system, and student peer culture — proposals that guided administrations over the succeeding decades in making numerous improvements affecting the quality of College student life.[43]

Research on curriculum and teaching practices peaked during the Hutchins years, but the notion that Chicago's College is especially suited to experimentation never died. In the 1970s, two yearlong studies carried out under Dean Jonathan Z. Smith scrutinized systematically the College's array of concentration programs and then the Common Core sequences. In the 1980s, the College created a Center for Curricular Thought, which sponsored several initiatives including conferences on issues in liberal learning; ways to improve the teaching of natural sciences to undergraduates; ideas for the teaching of foreign languages; and ways to teach courses on civilizations. In Project 1984, under my deanship, eleven task forces spent a year examining a dozen aspects of the College program, from the freshman year and foreign language instruction to physical education and creative work in the arts. In the late 1980s, Isaac Abella offered lectures on physics to faculty in other disciplines, with an eye to exploring the differential effectiveness of varied presentational techniques. The curricular review of the mid-1990s, from 1995 to 1998, was based on retreats funded appropriately enough by the Robert Maynard Hutchins Memorial Fund.

Codification and dissemination of what had been learned about effective teaching took a number of forms. The University's Center for Continuing Studies developed a series of institutes on teaching and learning for faculty members as well as a series of seminars for invited faculty from several colleges in the Midwest. A University-wide Council on Teaching joined the College in developing a Chicago Teaching Program, which organized materials on teaching for the benefit of graduate student instructors and conducted weekend workshops and forums designed to build skills in lecturing, leading discussions, and focused writing assignments. Several departments established teacher training programs for their graduate students.

43. These proposals included, for example, orienting faculty to transcend a "jealously exclusive valuation of intellectual activity" by expressing whatever genuine interest they feel in other pursuits (Bradbury 1951, 104–7); providing opportunities for students to anchor themselves in real-world pursuits, such as jobs and internships (129); bringing interesting adults from outside the University to live in the residence halls (109–13); and encouraging student contributions to decision making through student participation in curricular and extracurricular planning groups with faculty and administrators (119–20).

The controversial decision of summer 1996 to phase out the University's historic Department of Education by no means signaled the end of the University's commitment to research on curriculum and pedagogy. It showed, rather, the depth to which focused attention to educational questions was rooted in the University's culture; a string of initiatives took shape in the wake of that decision. Another yearlong review of curricular requirements took place under Dean John Boyer in 1998. A Center for Teaching and Learning was established in 1999 to carry out a wide range of functions, including compilation of studies on good teaching practices, production of materials to aid beginning teachers, information technology training for faculty, support for faculty wanting to experiment with new courses, and workshops that feature best-teaching practices in various areas.[44] Relatedly, the College also formed a Society of Fellows in the Liberal Arts, a multidisciplinary organization of senior and junior fellows dedicated to promoting liberal arts teaching and scholarship in general and to maintaining a high standard of teaching in the College in particular.

In January 2006, the University inaugurated a campuswide Committee on Education, under the direction of a distinguished new appointment, Stephen Raudenbush. The committee seeks to improve the quality of public education in the country at large. Its faculty roster includes professors of economics, psychology, public policy, human development, mathematics, social service administration, and sociology—manifesting once again the University's long-standing commitment to multidisciplinary collaboration and research on education.

PLURALISM OF AND IN THE CURRICULUM   Thanks to Dean Marion Talbot, whose notes preserve the only extant report of the faculty assembly that opened the work of the University, we have a record of the ringing words with which President Harper sought to inscribe the ethos of the institution he was helping to found. "The question before us," he intoned, "is how to become one in spirit, not necessarily in opinion."[45]

The notion of forming a kindred assemblage constituted by diversity of opinion became the guiding maxim for the University and its College, and a studied diversity of outlook has indeed been the hallmark of the place

44. Additional information on the center may be found online at http://teaching .uchicago.edu/site.html.

45. Marion Talbot, Notes Taken at the First Faculty Meeting, 1 October 1892, Marion Talbot Papers, Box 1, Folder 12, Special Collections, Joseph Regenstein Library, University of Chicago, Chicago.

since day one. Paul Shorey, head of the Department of Greek, noted this feature of the University when it was still only in its second decade:

> The University is neither a sectarian school nor a hot-bed of infidelity, though the Carnegie trustees pronounce it the one and the rural brethren are sometimes suspicious that it is the other. It is neither a college of socialist propaganda nor the hired advocate of capitalism, though the sapient reporter often sets it down as both. (Shorey 1909, 240)

Just as many departments made it a rule to secure a balance of diverse viewpoints and methodological approaches among their research faculty, so in their continuous efforts to clarify and articulate the aims of undergraduate education the Chicago College faculty never closed ranks behind a single exclusive principle of curriculum construction. Mindful of the need to recognize a diversity of educational objectives, Harper distinguished objectives of the first two years of college from those of the last two; "no greater mistake is being made in the field of higher education," he warned, "than the confusion which is coming to exist between [junior] college and [senior college] methods of work" (Harper 1905, 339). His own formula for junior college work, noted earlier, included emphases both on acquiring knowledge of the past and on developing disciplined habits of mind. Similarly, the curricular innovators of the 1920s were concerned both with the cultivation of human powers and with sufficient knowledge of the world to enhance adaptation to the environment. Their successors in the 1930s also sought to balance a plurality of objectives: knowledge useful for citizens of a democratic society, acquaintance with great works of Western thought, and cultivation of human powers.

It was also a continuing concern, we have seen, to find ways to balance a program of general education, however defined, with opportunities for elective work and independent inquiry. In addition, except for the years when the baccalaureate was awarded solely for completion of work in general education (1942–53), the faculty paid due respect to the demands of specialized concentration programs.

Even when consensus about the aims and scope of general education prevailed, the door remained open for debating those principles. Throughout the 1930s, vigorous debate about curricular principles set the tone for campus discourse. And long after those debates were apparently settled with the establishment of the Faust curriculum, Paul Diederich, a central figure in the Faust College, penned a lengthy critique of what he considered the hegemonic principle of promoting powers of the mind.[46] It remained for Joseph Schwab, in work to be considered in chapter 6, to articulate the necessity and the value of acknowledging pluralism in any curricular enterprise.

The reorganization of the College that followed the Levi proposals of 1964 ushered in a host of curricular innovations under the banner of pluralism. It appeared in the very organization of baccalaureate programs under five collegiate divisions, each of which mandated its own second year of general education of courses in addition to the year in common. It was apotheosized in the New Collegiate Division, formed in 1966 as a protected place for programmatic diversity, including the extreme form of a wholly student-designed program in Tutorial Studies. Moreover, the crystallization of concentration programs, as a later systematic review of them determined, involved not the incarnation of a common skeletal grid but a studied diversity of forms of specialized learning.[47]

If pluralism was encouraged regarding discourse about curriculum and in curricular structure, it was enshrined a fortiori in the content of the College's courses in general education. In the humanities, social sciences, and natural sciences and in integrative courses, students were systematically exposed to courses that exhibited a plurality of analytic and interpretative perspectives. The College faculty asserted resolutely that the teacher's task was never to provide a singular philosophy of life, human nature, and society, stating, "This is as it should be in our present society in which variety of doctrine and opinion rather than agreement and unity of view are characteristics" (Axelrod et al. 1949, 11–12). The College achieved what Hutchins once proclaimed as the objective of a utopian university: "*making the consideration of philosophic diversity the primary concern of educational philosophy*" (Hutchins 1953, 67; emphasis mine).

FOR ENFOLDING STUDENTS IN A COMMUNITY OF SCHOLARS
Harper's quest for a community whose members would be "one in spirit" became a leitmotif of the Chicago tradition. Generation after generation, talented University spokesmen sought to define that spirit. Paul Shorey devoted a spring convocation address to extolling it, which he defined as the "spirit which values a man for what he is, not for what he is not; which has many preferences but few exclusions, which recognizes diverse and

46. Diederich sought to substitute what he called an ethical conception of general education, in which educators would seek to promote "the essential elements of a good life" (1947, 6).

47. Report of the College Curriculum Committee 1979, University Archives, Special Collections, Joseph Regenstein Library, University of Chicago, Chicago.

even contradictory kinds of excellence, and eschews all rigid and peremptory judgments. And thence arises that indefinable sense of freedom which those who have long enjoyed it here miss bitterly when they go away. . . . The University of Chicago is the freest place in the world . . . a place where a man may work out his own destiny and *be* the thing he will" (Shorey 1909, 240, 242).

The way President Burton defined the spirit of the University was in standing for "the ideal of a symmetrical and well-balanced life . . . a place for hard work . . . [where individuals are] truly members of a community, parts of a social organism."[48] The Committee on the Theory of Education under Dean Wilkins issued a formal report enjoining the colleges (and graduate schools) to be pervaded by "the university spirit," which they defined as "the combination of the desire and the ability to participate in the advancement of knowledge or in the application of knowledge, as it advances, to the development of human welfare."[49] Hutchins defined it with different accents at different times but always emphasized that "spirit of inquiry with which the University opened," a stance of determined independence through free inquiry, a spirit of enthusiasm, and a commitment to the notion that, above all, "the object of a university is intellectual" (Hutchins 1932, 77–81). In a more prescriptive vein, he observed that while the pursuit of truth for its own sake constituted the common aim of all parts of a university, such an aim was too vague to hold the university together, and therefore, "real unity can be achieved only by a hierarchy of truths which shows us which are fundamental and which subsidiary, which significant and which not" (Hutchins 1936, 95). Richard McKeon found the genius of the University in its penchant for maintaining "a problem-oriented attitude in research, and it has tended to subordinate erudition and information to inquiry and the questioning examination of positions and arguments in its teaching" (McKeon 1972, 71).

President Levi not only celebrated the University's special spirit but also stressed the importance of symbols to represent that spirit. Levi's discourse begins by calling attention to moments of teacher-undergraduate collaboration "in which the faculty member is also challenged to try to point a path through a subject matter . . . [and where] students and faculty together can explore the uncertain area of the application of competing

48. Ernest DeWitt Burton, Anniversary Chapel Address, 1 October 1923, Presidents' Papers.

49. Report on Theory of Education, January 1927, p. 1, Dean of the College, Records, 1925–58, Box 14, Folder 5, Special Collections, Joseph Regenstein Library, University of Chicago, Chicago.

general principles for purposes of practical decision" (Levi 1969, 95). He portrays the College as "a generalizing influence within the institution, a way of restating advances of knowledge in the simplest terms, which may be the most difficult and significant terms, and a way of thinking through problem areas, with the advantage of seeing the same problem change its content and meaning as it is handled by different disciplines" (95). He depicted the collegiate divisions then forming as microcosms of the larger university,

> communities with something of an existence of their own. They must become areas where communication is established between faculty and students, where ceremonies and events reaffirm the ideals of the community, and where the concern of the faculty, which is actually easily aroused, for the education of their students will give rise to those informal pressures that guide and induce faculty participation. The colleges must take hold to help develop educational and cultural programs that are outside the curriculum, and that do not take the form of courses or any formal work, but nevertheless, or perhaps on that account, can add immeasurably to the life of the students. (98–99)

What, one might ask, has all this celebration of community to do with curriculum? Simply this: permeation by a common spirit lends meaning to the requirements of a curriculum and lends coherence to an exceedingly complex structure. In its finest moments, the College at the University of Chicago realized this. And when, as often happened, it fell short, the notion remained as a regulative ideal, ever calling its best defenders back to work.

The Chicago Tradition of Liberal Learning

Harper's University took shape as a high-powered research institution, with nothing on the horizon that might have been expected to engender Chicago's notable tradition of liberal learning. Ironically, its commitment to high scholarly standards entailed a certain institutional logic that led to a uniquely powerful system of liberal education. If an undergraduate college were to flourish in a place geared to research and graduate training, and if the University were to be animated by a single spirit, then the University had to find ways to incarnate that spirit in the college.

Even so, the principle of high standards could not in itself suffice to have engendered that powerful tradition of liberal learning. A contrasting principle had to be invoked, and this was the classic and Renaissance principle of education for the sake of producing a cultivated person. Ironically, the same ancestral figure who inspired Harper's commitment to the modern research university, Wilhelm von Humboldt, also provided a point of departure for those nineteenth-century educators who devoted themselves to the ideal of *Bildung,* or cultivation.

Edward Shils has called attention to the seminal role of Humboldt's 1910 memorandum on the organization of higher academic institutions in shaping the ethos of modern research universities. The principles that Humboldt enunciated in that memorandum became guiding maxims of German universities throughout the nineteenth century. The "Humboldtian University," as Shils calls it, in turn became the model for Harper and the scholars he recruited to found the University of Chicago.

What is less commonly known is that that same Humboldt authored a contrasting text two decades earlier, a text that became a point of reference for academics who wanted to shape modern universities in a very different spirit. In that earlier work, a long essay on the limits of state power, Humboldt drew on emerging German idealism to affirm the humanistic priority of forming cultivated autonomous individuals. In that essay, he propounds the doctrine that man's goal is "the highest and most harmonious development of his powers to a complete and consistent whole" (Humboldt [1791] 1993, 10).

Among proponents of a university organized by that doctrine, John Henry Cardinal Newman has long stood as a charismatic figure. In *The Idea of a University* of 1852, Newman evoked the vision of an academic institution devoted to cultivating general powers of the mind. The time of the University's founding—the cresting of the German-inspired university movement of the 1890s—was propitious for an institution based on the Humboldtian research model. The same kind of intellectual energy was then in place for the cresting of a very different kind of movement for academic reform, that inspired by the general education movement. It was the University's alertness to cutting-edge academic developments that disposed it to absorb these ostensibly opposing traditions so enthusiastically (Levine 2000).

In breeding a sort of Newmanian university in its College, the University of Chicago felt constrained to proceed in accord with its fundamental commitment to its highest academic standards. This meant

1. finding ways to implant high standards of academic achievement: tougher admissions requirements; concentrated course work; distinctive focuses for the academic and university colleges. That meant

2. defining the Junior, academic College as a place for a distinctive curriculum that would complete the pregraduate's general education, and that involved inventing a coherent two-year program of instruction.

3. To do justice to the mission of the Junior College meant appointing faculty devoted to the task of instructing undergraduates at that level within a coherent curriculum.

4. Since coherence could not be achieved simply by relying on the offerings of disparate academic departments, faculty from different disciplines had to collaborate.

5. In order to organize such collaboration, the participating faculty had to form a reasonably clear conception of the educational objectives of their program. Although the objective of introducing students to the universe of human knowledge about their world never disappeared, the philosophy of education that triumphed at Chicago focused on cultivating a range of human powers suited for all members of a democratic society.

6. A focus on quality of student performance and on training human capacities meant finding novel ways to assess those capacities and thereby enabling students to move through the program at their own pace.

7. Since the goal of the programs was to enhance intellectual independence, it involved finding ways and means of encouraging students to undertake independent work alongside or after their prescribed general education.

8. In order to pursue these educational objectives effectively and be responsive to the investigative ethos of the university, research on curricular and pedagogical questions became important.

9. Collaboration among high-powered academics from diverse backgrounds meant accepting a certain degree of pluralism in their approaches to education and incarnating a good deal of pluralism within the curriculum.

10. In order to motivate all concerned to partake in such a demanding program, and to balance the perpetual drift into specialisms and parochialisms, it was important to clothe the whole enterprise in a common spirit and sense of community.

Such are the themes that emerged from a century of *reflect, experiment, reflect, revise*. They continue to stimulate educational thought, at the University of Chicago and beyond. Although important features of the Chicago tradition have been irretrievably lost, parts of it survive and may continue to develop. In any case, one can still learn a great deal about those themes by recovering contributions of the figures who brought that tradition to its greatest heights. In that regard, none soared higher than John Dewey and Robert Maynard Hutchins and their especially creative colleagues Richard P. McKeon, Joseph Jackson Schwab, and Robert Redfield.

4

Dewey and Hutchins at Chicago

The purpose of school education is to insure the continuance of education by organizing the powers that insure growth. JOHN DEWEY (1916)

The object of a university is to emphasize, develop, and protect the intellectual powers of mankind. ROBERT MAYNARD HUTCHINS (1934)

What is needed for free minds is discipline, discipline which forms the habits which enable the mind to operate well. Nothing better can be said on this subject than the concise statement of John Dewey. "The discipline," he said, "that is identical with trained power is also identical with freedom."
ROBERT MAYNARD HUTCHINS (1943)

The University of Chicago's contribution to the general education movement took place over the course of a century. At the heart of the educational tradition that developed there, one finds the convergent ideas of John Dewey and Robert Maynard Hutchins.

This claim must seem odd to one who knows something about their personal differences and public hostilities. Prior to the culture wars fueled by Allan Bloom's provocative 1987 book, no curricular controversy captured the American public's attention so dramatically as that between those two towering innovators. In the one corner, an engaged philosopher, embodied, drawn to aesthetic epiphanies, conciliatory to a fault—the grand prophet of concrete experience; in the other, an administrative celebrity, solitary, standing in the West, aloof, aesthetically indifferent if not tone-deaf—a grand apostle of abstract intellection.

Beyond differences of character, they found themselves as head-on antagonists in academic politics. As incoming president of the University of Chicago in 1929, Hutchins sought personnel changes in the Department of Philosophy. His initiatives immediately antagonized the department's leadership, then in the hands of Dewey's old close colleagues, James Tufts and George Herbert Mead, both about to retire. Hutchins's proactive efforts to bring Mortimer Adler, Scott Buchanan, and Richard McKeon into the department upset both Tufts and Mead and fostered the perception that Hutchins was antagonistic to Mead and to the work of the pragmatists more generally.[1] Although Hutchins wanted to palliate these tensions, particularly with Mead,[2] the conflict left lingering animosities, especially since it led to Mead's spending the final year of his life in distress.

This episode may have contributed to the famous flare-up between Dewey and Hutchins half a dozen years later, despite Hutchins's subsequent praise for Dewey's work ([1934] 1936, 39). In two successive issues of the *Social Frontier* starting in December 1936, Dewey leveled a critique of Hutchins's book *The Higher Learning in America* that drew much attention. His review faulted Hutchins for (1) his alleged "contempt for science"; (2) divorcing the higher learning from contemporary social life, and divorcing intellectual work from experience; (3) insisting that the elements of human nature are fixed and constant and that the truth is everywhere the same; (4) relying so heavily on Plato, Aristotle, and Aquinas; and (5) for a conception of rationality that assumed the existence of "fixed and eternal authoritative principles as proofs that are not to be questioned" (Dewey 1937a, 1937b).

1. Although Hutchins, Adler, and Dewey had very high regard for one another's intellectual powers, a certain ambivalence did color their relations from time to time. As early as 1924, when Adler was Dewey's student at Columbia, Adler read a paper at a philosophy conference in which he criticized Dewey's conception of philosophy for leaving out the suprahuman dimension of experience. On that occasion, Dewey uncharacteristically pounded his chair and abruptly left the room. Even so, three years later, Dewey went out of his way to write a complimentary review of Adler's first book, *Dialectic* (Adler 1977, 49); and, at various points, both Hutchins and Adler expressed their admiration for the work of the pragmatist philosophers (e.g., Adler 1941, 379–80; Hutchins [1934] 1936, 39).

2. When Mead and others threatened to resign, Hutchins responded that "he fully recognized the right of a department to pass on its personnel," that he would not keep Adler or Buchanan in the department if the others wished, and that he would raise department salaries according to Tufts's recommendations. When shortly thereafter Mead resigned and fell ill, Hutchins told Mead he was distressed by the latter's resignation and had delayed communicating the resignation to the board of trustees, hoping for a reconciliation.

With characteristic wit, Hutchins pleaded, "Mr. Dewey has stated my position in such a way as to lead me to think that I cannot write, and has stated his own in such a way as to make me suspect that I cannot read" (Hutchins 1937, 137). In short compass, Hutchins proceeded to cite passages that handily refuted the charges of being against science, of promoting withdrawal from the world, of authoritarianism, and of relying too much on Plato et al. Dewey in turn accused Hutchins's response of adopting the method of legal forensics, thereby evading what Dewey claimed was the central critical issue: "the place of experience, practical matters, and experimental scientific knowledge in the constitution of authentic knowledge, and consequently in the organization of the subject matter of higher education" (Dewey 1937b, 167).

It must be said that the animus in the exchange originated with Dewey's distortions of Hutchins's position.[3] Hutchins *never* endorsed the view of truth as a fixed body of doctrine that was secured by an elite and imposed dogmatically upon hapless students. He consistently upheld the values of science and scientific observation, the notion that what was considered true was subject to continuous change, and, as he expressed it in *Education for Freedom,* the assumption that intellectual principles, "like all knowledge, are derived from experience [and] are refinements of common sense" (1943, 62).

Allowing for Dewey's manifold misreadings and Hutchins's slight evasiveness, both men had a point, insofar as neither clarified the misunderstandings that produced their ostensible differences of opinion.[4] What is more, on one important issue they appear to have truly polarized: on the

3. Knowledgeable persons have expressed wonderment at this uncharacteristically contentious outburst by Dewey, who in nearly all other engagements was the very model of a pacific, unruffled, gentle man. Indeed, this contentiousness persisted in subsequent exchanges with Hutchins and his defender Alexander Meiklejohn through 1945 (Martin 2002, 452–58). Beyond some lingering feelings about the 1931 episode with the Philosophy Department, the following seem pertinent to account for it: the fact that the two universities Dewey had been most closely tied to, Columbia and Chicago, were in the forefront of what was seen as a return to traditional forms of liberal learning; the instigation provided by Dewey's young followers at the journal *Social Frontier,* a medium for radical, progressive educators associated with Columbia's Teachers' College; and possibly Dewey's lifelong struggle against religion triggering an aversion to figures Hutchins quoted such as Augustine and Aquinas. Issues regarding the appropriate intellectual defense of democracy, discussed later in this chapter, probably aroused the most passion. These plausible interpretations were suggested by Philip Jackson in oral communication, March 3, 2003.

4. The exaggeration of differences and the escalated antagonism between Dewey and Hutchins may be taken as a case in point to illustrate how hard it is even for brilliant and well-educated people to engage in undistorted communication, even when the parties in question are prominent proponents of the value of dialogue.

question of the philosophical basis for defending democracy, each of them viewed the other's position as dangerous. Interpreting Hutchins's call for attention to a value hierarchy as a way station toward authoritarianism, Dewey peppered his otherwise civil critique with insinuation by denial: "I would not intimate that the author has any sympathy with fascism" (Dewey 1937a, 104). For his part, Hutchins attacked positivistic naturalism, which many readers took to be an indirect attack on Dewey, as an abandonment of reasoned discourse in support of democratic values, thereby presenting a relativistic way station toward fascism. In all this back-and-forth, the perception of antagonism was heightened by the fulminations of Hutchins's erstwhile comrade Mortimer Adler, who famously accused academics like Dewey of promoting a kind of morally bankrupt position more dangerous to democracy than Nazism—a serious distortion from the other side, since Dewey himself attacked empirical naturalists no less severely for abdicating the need to ground moral judgments on rational discourse (Westbrook 1991, 519–23).[5]

In fact, however, the two were much closer than Dewey allowed. They shared numerous assumptions and commitments. Both of them were passionate advocates of democracy; they even opposed U.S. involvement in the looming World War II precisely on grounds of the threat it would pose to democratic freedoms.[6]

On a number of other issues, moreover, differences between the two educational philosophers amounted to very little. Although Dewey objected to Hutchins's assumption of a universal human nature, his own *Human Nature and Conduct* (1922) presumed a certain universality. Although Dewey famously criticized Hutchins for looking to Plato, Aristotle, and Aquinas, he himself (as Hutchins noted [1937, 137]) had praised the same three authors for their exemplary grasp of the science and social affairs of their times. What is more, insofar as they ostensibly differed in their views of the relative educational importance of concrete experience

5. For a discussion of the broader context of the democracy debate, see Ciepley 2001.

6. Both appealed to the disaster of World War I chiefly by citing the effect it had on eroding democratic freedoms. "It is quite conceivable that after the next war in this country we should have a semi-military, semi-financial autocracy . . . [and] the suppression of all the democratic values for the sake of which we professedly went to war" (Dewey 1939, 11). "When we remember what a short war did to the four freedoms [freedom of speech, freedom of worship, freedom from want, freedom from fear], we must recognize that they face extermination in the total war to come" (Robert Hutchins, "Untitled, re: Our present society," 10 March 1940, Folder 4, Box 25, Robert M. Hutchins Papers, University Archives, Special Collections, Joseph Regenstein Library, University of Chicago, Chicago).

and intellectually challenging texts, this difference may be linked in part to Dewey's virtually exclusive preoccupation with primary school grades—contrary to Harper's hope that Dewey would extend his experimental educational work into the high school—and Hutchins's preoccupation with the early collegiate grades.

What is more, with respect to their more general educational visions, whatever remained of apparent differences between them appeared trivial. Indeed, the ideas they had in common generated a continuous tradition of academic reforms at the University of Chicago, an institution with which both developed intense emotional involvements.[7] In Dewey's rejoinder to Hutchins's defense, he praised Hutchins's book as being highly significant for its "vigorous exposition of the present confused state of education in this country" (Dewey 1937b, 167) and for raising a basic issue in the philosophy of education. Had he been able to reflect on the University's first full century of curricular development, he might have appreciated the extent to which he and Hutchins had been pursuing a similar radical and visionary quest for educational reform.

Dewey as Educator

Both Dewey and Hutchins came to Chicago from the East, where virtually nothing in their early work suggested the kinds of iconoclastic positions they would come to espouse there. Dewey's Chicago sojourn ran from 1894 for a decade, during which he completed the transition, started at Ann Arbor, from trying to straddle three interests—neo-Hegelian idealism, physiological psychology, and political activism—to a formulation of pragmatist philosophy and social psychology whereby those three elements contributed to an emerging synthesis. The Chicago Laboratory Schools formed a principal outlet for this synthesis, embodying Dewey's view that student learning, institutional reconstruction, and civic democracy are mutually constitutive.

At Chicago Dewey came to formulate the educational ideas for which he would become famous. His work there became a gathering point for fresh departures in educational thought, for which the innovative university founded by William Rainey Harper provided a benign milieu. Like

---

7. Biographical parallels between their relationships to the university include the youthful age at which they came to it—Dewey at thirty-five, Hutchins at thirty; the aura of special excitement that surrounded their arrival at the University; and the traumatic circumstances of their departure (Dewey after eleven years, Hutchins after twenty-two), when those who had opposed or offended them tried strenuously to keep them from leaving.

Dewey, Harper pioneered ideas and arrangements that were at odds with academic conventions, and he went out of his way to support the lab school experiments. Although Harper never had the budget he needed to provide adequate support for the lab school (or anything else, for that matter), he tried his best to help; when in spring 1899 the school faced a deficit of one-tenth its annual costs, Harper made a special appeal to potential donors and contributed $100 of his own (equivalent to about $2,300 in 2006 dollars).[8]

Dewey's educational philosophy embodied a pointedly sociological vision. It was not by accident that three of his students—Charles Horton Cooley, Robert E. Park, and William I. Thomas—went on to become three of the foremost figures of American sociology of the early twentieth century. All four of them voiced concerns about the levels of social disorganization engendered by the rapid changes associated with modern science, technology, industry, and urbanization. For Dewey, these concerns issued in a lifelong project to reform the learning experience at all levels.

One may condense Dewey's complex concerns about the links between education and modern society into two points. For one thing, the unparalleled growth of objectified knowledge and technical skills led to objectified programs of training that were increasingly in danger of being split off from connection with one another and with the experience of everyday activities. For another, the expansion of society and the eruption of novel social problems created unprecedented demands for individuals educated for thinking and communicating about these problems in democratic forms. Both sets of changes meant that conventional modes of instruction, in which students were passively lectured at and required to memorize by rote, had become dysfunctional.

For Dewey, the reconstruction of society and the reconstruction of education were aspects of the same process. The capacity to solve social problems required intellectual habits needed to perceive problems, identify their features, and entertain in imagination diverse options for their solution. In order to promote such habits at all levels of learning, Dewey maintained that new forms of teaching were needed, forms in which curiosity and imagination were awakened through direct encounter with puzzling experiences. Thus, instead of being confronted with formal lectures about the abstract properties of substances, students would engage

8. Harper's support for Dewey has been hidden under the perception of an antagonistic attitude that led to Dewey's departure. In fact, what upset Dewey was an administrative misunderstanding regarding his wife's lab school appointment for which Harper was not responsible, and Harper tried ardently to get the Deweys to stay at Chicago.

in spinning and weaving, activities through which they would run up against questions that would prompt them to investigate such properties. Performing such investigations again and again would afford the discipline that led to the development of robust powers. In Dewey's words, "Since really to satisfy an impulse or interest means to work it out, and working it out involves running up against obstacles, becoming acquainted with materials, exercising ingenuity, patience, persistence, alertness, it of necessity involves discipline—ordering of power—and supplies knowledge" (Dewey [1915] 1990, 37).

The powers so developed could not be gained in isolation. They could be acquired only in social settings that did not suppress impulses but instead directed those impulses into creative channels. The structuring of this learning was constituted by forms of communication that were open, mutually respectful, and mutually responsive. Learning thus deeply relied on powers of communication, the same powers that were requisite to public deliberation in a democratic society. Beyond that, he argued, the very process of communication itself has an inexorably educative effect on all parties involved.

Regard schools at all levels, then and to a great extent now, and you will find precious little of this sort of learning going on. Over much of the educational world, Dewey's plaint written in 1915 still applies: "Why is it, in spite of the fact that teaching by pouring in, learning by passive absorption, are universally condemned, they are still so entrenched in practice?" (1915, 38). That is because those who support, direct, and teach in these schools have been habituated to inherited patterns, whereby each generation unthinkingly reproduces the paradigm of teaching—a process of delivering facts—that it grew up with. This pattern has now been reinforced by the plethora of standardized tests that determine students' futures, tests that today are increasingly being prepared for by forced attention in the classroom and by commercially packaged and seductively propagated supplementary programs.

Dewey's antidote for such archaic systems, which mindlessly pursue goals frozen in yesteryear, consists of an effort at reconstruction wherein educators subject their programs to searching reviews. These reviews consider afresh the goals of each educational program, in the context of the entire trajectory of educational programs, and work to find the best means for attaining those goals. This is a never-ending process, since both the stock of knowledge and societal conditions are continuously changing.

What is more, innovation in one part of a program may require adaptation in other parts. This becomes evident only when attention is focused

FIGURE 2 Dewey's chart of the school system
Clusters represent component parts of the school system. Blocks within each
cluster indicate the time students spend in each stage. Shaded blocks denote an
overlap of time and subject matter. Captions show historical periods and ruling
ideals. The line bridging the first two clusters indicates continuity in pedagogy
(Dewey [1915] 1990, 65).

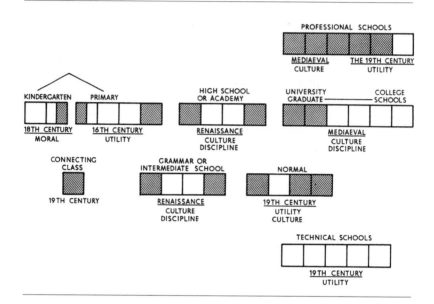

on curricular coherence. For Dewey, no piece of the curriculum should be
considered in isolation, either synchronously or over time. This approach
contrasts with the curricular bricolage whose pieces derived randomly
from different genealogical eras, a state that Dewey depicted in the remarkable chart reproduced as figure 2. To rid schools of rampant waste,
educators need to replace all parts that impair coherence.

In Dewey's account, the kindergarten emerged as a site for moral instruction; primary school reflects the practical, skills-based priorities of
the sixteenth-century "popular movement"; grammar school originated
to teach Greek and Latin, for acculturation more than discipline. Technical and normal schools arose, respectively, in response to changing business conditions and the related need to train teachers. The resulting
system is disjointed. Its parts arose in distinct periods for the sake of different goals and "have never yet been welded into one complete whole"
([1915] 1990, 70).

Dewey urged a turn toward coherence in curricular planning along two dimensions. Along the horizontal dimension, he wanted to make school an "organic whole" rather than a composite of isolated parts: "All studies arise from aspects of the one earth and the one life lived upon it. We do not have a series of stratified earths, one of which is mathematical, another physical, another historical, and so on" ([1915] 1990, 91).

He sought to connect academic studies with everyday life, so what the student learns at school willy-nilly reflects the unity of lived experience.

Yet more daunting, he envisioned coherence along a vertical dimension, so that educational programs formed a continuous progression from kindergarten through graduate school. This meant identifying developmental stages, adapting curricula to what is appropriate to each period of personal growth, and fitting the curricula to one another in a coherent manner. Thus, stage one (four-to-eight-year-olds) involves material connected to immediate social and personal interests informing immediate motor outlets — teaching through "play, games, occupations, or miniature industrial arts, stories, pictorial imagination and conversation." Stage two (eight-to-twelve-year-olds) involves material connected to "rules of action — that is, of regular means appropriate to reaching permanent results" rather than merely personal ends, while the third stage involves specialization through the use of independent powers and skills in "distinctive studies and arts for technical and intellectual aims" (Dewey [1915] 1990, 106–15).

In addition to his emphasis on attuning curricular materials more finely to what was appropriate to each developmental stage, Dewey also stressed the fact that no two students are identical. Each one presents a particular profile of needs, interests, blockages, and talents. For this reason, education for autonomy, creativity, and community must find ways to address individual differences. It cannot rely on standardized inputs that are applied mechanically to an entire cohort. It cannot set up objectified goals — whether preparation for a remote future, an unfolding of presumed native faculties, an instillation of specific disciplines, or a recovery of some canon of past achievements — that depart from the essential goal of education: enabling individuals to reorganize their current experience in ways that equip them to direct the course of future experience (Dewey [1915] 1990, chaps. 5–6).

None of the issues in question is simple or easily decided. They require the same kind of energized thought that any tough investigative problem entails. That is why, Dewey argued, an important part of the mission of a great university must be to conduct programs of research and evaluation regarding all aspects of educational technique and content. All educational programs mounted by a university, from kindergarten through doctoral, must become experimental in a nontrivial sense.

As the massive changes in society require changes in how students are educated, and these changes in turn require changes in systems designed to educate them, so the reconstructed teaching institutions will entail changes in the larger society. An attitude of openness to learning, support for ability to define problems and imagine alternative solutions, communication about them in a mutually respectful discursive network, and the enrichment of experience that all this entails will form the lineaments of the new democratic society. These goals would require public support for a restructuring of universities in several respects: precisely the reconstruction that Robert Maynard Hutchins pioneered. It would, in words that Hutchins celebrated, become a "learning society."

Hutchins as an Unwitting (?) Deweyan

The academic reforms Hutchins pioneered after becoming president of the University of Chicago in 1929 and the rhetoric with which he sought to promote those and other reforms look as though they were derived straight from Dewey's educational theories. Like Dewey, Hutchins initiated his discourse on American education by attacking its lack of clear direction and its discordant and wasteful organization: "The most striking fact about the higher learning in America is the confusion that besets it" (1936, 1). The forces that directed American education appeared to consist of commercial pressures, consumerist whims, professorial predilections, and public opinion. The system appeared rampantly disordered because it lacked an ordering principle. This situation was doubly tragic, Hutchins thought, because it deprived students of the possibility of developing their human powers and deprived society of citizens equipped to facilitate intelligent social change.

In order to help students cultivate those powers and to prepare them for promoting informed social changes, universities would have to devote special resources and energies to the task of creating a program designed for those purposes. The key ingredients had to include faculty dedicated to the task as well as materials and methods organized to accomplish it. Instead of letting professors teach whatever they chose, they would be expected to teach in a program designed with specific educational goals in mind. Instead of letting students sign up for whatever courses they wished, they would be expected to follow a carefully constructed, coherent course of study. Instead of following the old custom of offering students textbook summaries of facts, faculty would offer them serious texts that engaged their intelligence and forced them to think. Instead of following the custom of teaching through lectures that more or less repeated the textbook packages, teachers would engage students in stimulating discussion of problems.

In pursuing the ideal of a coherent program of study suited for students in accord with their developmental stage, Hutchins sought to institute a curriculum of general education that would run from the beginning of the junior year of high school to the end of the sophomore year of college. This curriculum would be self-contained, such that it could mark the end of formal instruction for most students. The materials of this curriculum would be books that have attained the stature of classics — the best books we know, books that raise perennial questions and are contemporary in every age. These books are essential to general education because they are needed both to understand the foundations of all subjects and to comprehend the contemporary world. In order to read such books intelligently and critically, students would also learn the arts of reading, writing, thinking, and speaking by means of the study of grammar, rhetoric, logic, and mathematics. Given a curriculum of this sort, which is serious, coherent, and comprehensible, students would be expected to find it attractive if teachers could be found to present it as such. And young students would not find it intimidating or inaccessible; reporting on his work in teaching classics to young people, he quipped, "Mr. Adler and I have found that the books are more rather than less effective the younger students are. Students in University High School have never heard that these books are too hard for them. . . . They have not had time to get as miseducated as their elders" (1943, 15).

Like Dewey, Hutchins did not imagine that creating such a curriculum would be simple or easy. For one thing, little is known about the best way to organize the curricular materials and the best ways to teach them, taking into account the differences among students. To provide such understanding, universities would need to establish programs of focused research regarding education, as he proclaimed already in his inaugural address of September 1929. "If this were not so," he observed soon after, "I should recommend [the College's] abolition. . . . [For] few institutions in our area can do what we can do in collegiate education, and that is to experiment with it with the same intentness, the same kind of staff, and the same effectiveness with which we carry on the rest of our scientific work" (Hutchins 1930, 12; 1931).

Even with the best of information, moreover, such a curricular project would face serious resistance. Much of it would stem from the persistence of old habits among the teaching faculty: not many professors of today, he complained, are ready to change the habits of their lives, and meanwhile, they are bringing up their successors in the way they were brought up, so that the next crop will have the habits they have had themselves. And the love of money, a misconception of democracy, a false notion of progress, a distorted idea of utility, and the anti-intellectualism to which they all lead conspire to confirm their conviction that no disturbing change is needed.

It was with such ideas in mind that Hutchins proceeded, in the first two years of his presidency, to restructure the university in such a way as to support initiatives to design a coherent curriculum and a faculty especially devoted to creative teaching; to separate administratively the undergraduate college as a division distinct from the divisions devoted to research and graduate training; and to support initiatives to carry out focused research on learning at this level.[9] Over the next two decades, the faculty of the College would engage in extraordinarily creative work in designing such a program of liberal learning, as the following chapters will show.

After leaving the University in 1951, Hutchins continued to develop his ideas about learning in a democratic society. At a time of growing public nervousness, he spoke out boldly against attempts to curtail the University's rights to free expression and inquiry. At a time of growing anti-intellectualism and of the stupefying effects of television, he articulated afresh his vision of the ideal university and the ways in which it could promote and enhance the elements of a "learning society."

In these and other ways, the critiques and the visions of Hutchins and Dewey appear remarkably similar. The parallels between them become transparent when presented in the form of a schematic concordance, as shown in table 3.

The Hutchins-Dewey Debate

Given the consensus between Dewey and Hutchins on so many key points, their well-publicized antagonism of 1936–37 becomes all the more remarkable. Indeed, some truly striking differences in their views about education never really came to the fore. In two areas not mentioned in the

9. In 1929 Hutchins secured a sizable grant from the General Education Board to pursue such research.

TABLE 3 Dewey-Hutchins concordance

Points of convergence	Dewey	Hutchins
Critiques of American education	a. Confused (1937b, 167) b. Degraded by mindless conventions ([1922] 1988) c. Hodgepodge curriculum ([1915] 1990, chap. 3) d. Remote from life experience ([1915] 1990)	a. "Beset by confusion" (1936, 1) b. Corrupted by "materialism" (1943, chap. 3) c. Curricular incoherence d. Fails to prepare students for life (1936, 109)
Societal need for educational reform	a. Need for adaptation to changed conditions (1916, chaps. 1, 3) b. Sustaining democracy (1916, chap. 7)	a. Need for social change directed by intelligence (1935, 130–31) b. Support for democracy (1943, chap. 5)
Pertinent reforms	Eliminate waste ([1915] 1990, chap. 3) Reconstruct through adapting means to ends	Don't squander two more years of college than other countries have; squeeze out waste, water, and frivolity (1943, chap. 4)
Aims of education		
a. Powers	a. Independent use of powers ([1915] 1990, 113–55)	a. Development of human powers (1936, 58; 1943, 44)
b. Freedom	b. Plato on the slave as one whose actions express another's ideas, not his own ([1915] 1990, 23)	b. Freedom as condition for knowing and achieving the order of goods (1943, 87ff.)
c. Moral improvement	c. Moral conduct as unifying and culminating end (1916, chap. 26)	c. Enhanced morality (1936, chap. 3; 1943, 44, 91)
Means		
a. Don't just transmit information	a. Information as such is not meaningful ([1915] 1990, 99)	a. Mere information obsolesces fast (1936, 28–29; 1947, 54)
b. Engage students actively	b. Active experience instead of passive absorption (1916, 38, 132; [1915] 1990, chap. 2)	b. Active engagement with issues to replace textbooks, listening to lectures (1936, 78)

(continued)

TABLE 3 *(continued)*

Points of convergence	Dewey	Hutchins
c. Give experience in solving problems	c. Focus on searching for solutions to genuine problems ([1915] 1990, 37–40)	c. Give practice in thinking about problems, vocational skills in on-the-job training (1936, 53)
Coherence of curricular structure	a. Integrated learning: coherent general curriculum ([1915]1990, 92–94) b. Integrated learning: coherence across the life cycle ([1915] 1990, 105 ff.)	a. General education curriculum contra anarchic elective system (1936, 92) b. Student completes solid general education in sophomore year (1936, 91)
"Progressive" education as license is harmful	Valorize impulsivity, but only to reconstruct habits ([1922] 1988, chap. 8; [1915] 1990)	Locks up the growing mind in its own whims and difficulties (1943, 89)
Sociality of education as means	Education a social process, not a function of isolated individuals ([1915] 1990, chap. 1)	Education as participation in dialogue (1969, 126)
Sociality of education as end	Communication as both means and end of education (1916, 119–21; [1915] 1990, chap. 4)	Education as way to promote social consciousness, conscience (1943, 28–30)
Respect for young students	Celebrates abilities, powers of the young (1916, 50; [1915] 1990, 181–209)	Freshmen can do independent work (1936, 187); liberal education can be completed by college sophomores (1936, chap. 3); young students like to tackle tough classics (1943, 15)
Individualized programs	Important to tailor educational structures to situation of individual students ([1915] 1990, chap. 2)	Individualized education affordable if schools allocate resources wisely (1936, 186)
Conduct university research on education	Use precollegiate schools as laboratories for university study ([1915] 1990, chap. 3)	Need for focused research on education in a great research university (1930, 1931)

TABLE 3 *(continued)*

Points of convergence	Dewey	Hutchins
		Scholarship should aim to reveal highest human powers (1936, 32)
Toward a learning society	Learning in school as continuous with a learning society (1916, 50)	Universal learning as the highest goal of democratic society (1943, chap. 5)
Chicago as exemplar	Chicago's lab schools as model ([1915] 1990)	Chicago's 1942 BA as a lodestar (1943, chap. 4)

Social Frontier debate, one can identify marked differences of emphasis if not position in their beliefs about education. Soon after their debate, Hutchins achieved notoriety by abolishing football, which led to the famous image of his antipathy toward athletic activity, whereas Dewey emphatically affirmed the educational value of attention to bodily well-being.[10] The educational tract that was the object of Dewey's critique proclaimed Hutchins's conception that the University should cultivate intellectual powers and not focus on powers of artistic creativity,[11] while art formed a central part of Dewey's curriculum and later philosophical discourse. One could still play up the different roles they assigned to reading books, with Dewey much more disposed to emphasize a certain amount of hands-on practical experience.

When these distracting points are bracketed, points of difference between them reduce to different formulations of broadly similar positions.

10. Here as elsewhere, differences between them have been subject to exaggerations that distort their true beliefs. Dewey quite objected to conventional physical education as practiced in the United States (see chap. 11 of this volume); Hutchins, while publicly disdaining physical exercise, was himself an avid tennis player. Beyond that, the "Hutchins College" developed some distinctive forms of athletic work. In its famous Humanities 1 course, it also gave students distinctive opportunities to create paintings, poetry, and music (Ward [1950] 1992, chap. 3).

11. Hutchins insinuated that making music, sculpture, or painting did not qualify as a "university discipline" (1936, 93–94).

Despite the notorious polemics between them, it proved possible for educators who aligned themselves with both Dewey and Hutchins to develop educational ideas that embodied the convergent principles they espoused. This was conspicuously true of two of the foremost educators at Chicago during the heyday of the Hutchins presidency, McKeon and Schwab, whose achievements we shall examine in succeeding chapters.

This is not to say that the University of Chicago has remained staunchly true to the ideals of Dewey and Hutchins. Forces of the market, which both of them decried as inimical to education, have made serious inroads against the gains that they promoted. Ironically, whereas for Dewey the subject of geography should stand at the center of precollegiate learning, in 1986 the University revoked the departmental status of its historic Department of Geography. Moreover, whereas for both of them a crucial component of the University's work should be carried out in its Department of Education, in 1996 the University decided to dissolve its historic Department of Education. And whereas for both of them, granting a monopoly to consumerist appetites remains one of the most insidious obstacles to liberal learning, the University of Chicago subsequently became publicly identified with the hegemony of economistic thinking. Both of them decried the lack of coherence in curricula at all levels. The University's College has found it increasingly difficult to strive for curricular coherence, without which "the course of study goes to pieces because there is nothing to hold it together" (Hutchins 1943, 26).

During the first century of its existence, however, the University created an unparalleled wealth of resources for the enterprise of liberal learning, and it has by no means squandered all of them even today. This is a story that must be told, again and again.

5

Richard McKeon:
Architecton of Human Powers

No one at the University of Chicago or anywhere else in the twentieth century advanced the discourse about human powers as far as did Richard McKeon. Arriving on the Chicago scene at a critical moment in the 1930s, McKeon decisively shaped the undergraduate curriculum even as he reorganized graduate work in the Humanities Division as dean. Following the deanship, McKeon entered a profoundly creative period in philosophical work in tandem with generative work for UNESCO. In philosophical investigation as in the international arena, McKeon labored to show that people of diverse cultures or philosophical positions can be unified in communication and cooperation without needing consensus in a common ideology. In that vein, he promoted international scholarly communication by linking American thought with European traditions and then by working during the Cold War to erect bridges between Western scholars and colleagues in the Soviet bloc.

In the mid-1960s, McKeon returned to questions of undergraduate learning. He participated in fresh debates over the college curriculum and issued a series of radical statements on the philosophy of liberal education. Those statements resemble many of his other writings which, Walter Watson (2000) suggests, appear to have been written for future readers as much as for his contemporaries. They continue to pose challenges to those who care about the future of liberal education.

Entering the Fray

McKeon was one of the scholars whom Hutchins himself recruited. On trips from Yale to Columbia, Hutchins met McKeon through Mortimer Adler, who was then participating with McKeon and Scott Buchanan in a group to discuss Aquinas's *Summa Theologica* and other philosophical works — a "holy triune," Hutchins called them (Ashmore 1989, 104). McKeon seemed an attractive ally in Hutchins's campaign to find ways to spark philosophical awareness within the University and to transfigure the liberal arts curriculum in particular.

The initiative encountered difficulties at both ends. Comfortably perched in the Philosophy Department at Columbia, McKeon seemed perfectly content to remain there. Although he visited Chicago in 1932 as external examiner of students taking the Great Books course taught by Hutchins and Adler, he flatly turned down Hutchins's invitation to resettle. Hutchins changed McKeon's mind by asking him how he would feel if he were not at Chicago while educational history was being made.[1] McKeon was also moved by the ability of Chicago's bright undergraduates to discuss Great Books.[2]

On the other end, McKeon's presumptive home department at Chicago was less than welcoming. When Hutchins broached McKeon's appointment to the Department of Philosophy, enough objections were raised that for some time McKeon refused to let himself be considered further, although he continued to visit Chicago to examine students. When he did finally come to Chicago in 1934, it was through a visiting appointment in the Department of History. In 1935, McKeon became dean of the Humanities Division, with appointments in the Departments of Greek and Philosophy.

1. Richard P. McKeon Interview, 3 June 1975, Robert M. Hutchins and Associates, Oral History Interviews by George W. Dell, 1958–78, Box 2, Folder 7, Special Collections, Joseph Regenstein Library, University of Chicago, Chicago.

2. "I must confess that I was surprised at the familiarity and understanding shown by the high-school juniors of books that are far from easy reading. I might even, if I had been asked beforehand, have expressed some hesitation concerning the feasibility of setting students of that age to reading Thucydides, Aristotle, Cicero and Augustine. . . . The college students were no less a surprise with the richness, diversity and depth of their understanding" (McKeon to Hutchins, 1 July 1934, Richard P. McKeon Papers, University Archives, Special Collections, Joseph Regenstein Library, University of Chicago, Chicago [hereafter cited as McKeon Papers]). Following his first visit, McKeon had observed that the better sophomores at Chicago were equal to the best seniors in general honors at Columbia (McKeon to Hutchins, 13 June 1932, McKeon Papers).

For the next decade or so, McKeon was one of Hutchins's closest allies. Hutchins sent him advance copies of virtually every speech and article as well as copies of every written attack that he received by mail. Hutchins sought McKeon's advice on his public statements and on how to handle his increasingly precarious position at the university.[3] McKeon first intervened publicly in the Chicago curricular debates in a riposte regarding Hutchins's 1936 volume *The Higher Learning in America* where, after gently questioning the way Hutchins uses the category of "metaphysics," he applauds Hutchins's remedy for some commonly cited defects in general education by means of training in disciplines needed for "precise, pondered, and appreciative reading of books" (McKeon 1937, 370). With a wry aside to the book's academic critics, McKeon observes that "for those of us to whom textual interpretation is still a serious enterprise it is sometimes difficult to find the passages in *The Higher Learning* on which to construct the dogmatic, antiquated, asocial, and unscientific philosophy which its expositors have found in it" (370–71).

McKeon's discussion here focuses on the place of principles that inform the arts and the sciences. In pointed rejoinder to a 1937 critique by Charner Perry, of the Hutchins book, McKeon clarifies and defends what Hutchins advocated, "not the introduction of metaphysics into an educational and scientific system to which it is foreign, but the recognition of a philosophic activity in a system in which it is already present" (McKeon 1937, 372). McKeon faults Perry for misrepresenting Hutchins's recommendations for general education as so many sterile and premature exercises in metaphysics. Instead, McKeon presents Hutchins's program more accurately as one designed to enable college graduates "to write correct, expressive, and fluent English; to understand arguments and demonstrations [and] to formulate rational grounds on which to defend their own positions; to organize the sequence of their thoughts clearly, order them relevantly, [and] present them persuasively" (375). McKeon goes on to articulate his own view of the aims of education:

> Whether or not principles are thought to determine the sequence, a student should emerge from such a general education with a knowledge of how problems, whether of life or of science or of art, have been treated, and with some

3. McKeon so thoroughly revised Hutchins's draft of an article on Whitehead for the *Atlantic Monthly* that Hutchins quipped, "[Your revision] is so much better that I am afraid my friends, to say nothing of my enemies, will recognize that it is ghost-written" (Hutchins to McKeon, 8 September 1936, McKeon Papers).

insight therefore into how problems may be treated; and, joined to that knowledge, he should possess an ability to understand positions other than his own, to present his own convictions relevantly, lucidly, and cogently, and finally to apply informed critical standards to his own arguments and those advanced by others. . . . [The student] should be taught to use materials in accordance with principles, and their presence should be indicated not by metaphysical jargon in his conversation but by the quality of his thought, his speech, and his ordered information. (377)

In further defense of the Hutchins proposals in *The Higher Learning,* McKeon endorses the former's aspirations to have students move beyond reams of facts; to shun textbooks for the great works of the past; and to organize learning sequentially, so that work in early courses provides foundations for subsequent training. In his contributions to transforming the humanities curriculum in the College, McKeon had a golden opportunity to put these aspirations into practice.

Changing the Humanities Course

McKeon began teaching at Chicago while the 1931 New Plan of the first Hutchins College held sway. Under this plan, students earned a certificate—later, an Associate of Arts title—after two years of general education. Their work was assessed through comprehensive exams covering four yearlong courses in general education, corresponding to the four divisions of humanities, social sciences, biological sciences, and physical sciences; an additional year of work in two of these divisions; and competence in writing, mathematics, and foreign language.

The New Plan's yearlong course in humanities took shape as a grand course in European civilization. The renowned culture-historian Ferdinand Schevill was brought out of retirement to create it. Schevill's course was divided into three segments—Mediterranean, middle, and modern periods—which were subdivided by focusing on "great movements which have agitated humanity." A dense, typewritten text supplied a chronological framework for the course, and within each unit, students were expected to read classic texts such as the *Iliad,* the *Annals* of Tacitus, Dante's *Divine Comedy,* or Goethe's *Faust.*

The launching of the new humanities course stirred a good deal of enthusiasm. One young colleague waxed eloquent about its potential for liberally educating teachers as well as students, and Dean Chauncey Boucher, lapsing into the vernacular, called it a "wow." McKeon himself later described Schevill's humanities sequence as a "pioneering course," one "widely influential in American higher education," and even, despite the radical changes it underwent in the 1940s, the basis of discourse about the Chicago humanities course well into the 1950s (McKeon [1953] 1990, 19).

Even so, the course provoked numerous criticisms. Instructors in the course objected both to the length of the syllabus — it kept growing and became so large that by 1939 the course spread across three years — and to a lack of continuity among guest lecturers. They complained that students were getting lost in details and failing to see connections among the course's components. They felt that too few students enrolled in honors sections. One criticized the course for containing a "lamentably meagre" amount of history, another for containing too much history. One felt it suffered from ignoring historical Judaism, another for failing to treat the rise of democracy. Some thought the course needed to be coordinated with the three other required general education courses. Schevill himself withdrew from the humanities course after a few years, observing that the range of subject matter was "so excessive as to be unmanageable," that the proportion of three lectures to one discussion section was imbalanced, and that it contained too many facts at the expense of directive concepts.[4]

In the end, it was McKeon's criticism that proved decisive. As dean of the Graduate Division, McKeon played no official role in undergraduate curricular discussions; but in 1937 the members of the College Curriculum Committee invited him to join their deliberations on how to revise the College's general education curriculum. They never knew what hit them.

As McKeon later recalled, "the [Schevill] course raised many problems, among which one had a recurrent and fundamental character." Because it followed the historical sequence of cultural developments in the Western world, "the humanistic disciplines required for the appreciation and interpretation of arts, letters, and philosophy, tended to be lost in the story, while the story tended to be accepted uncritically" ([1953] 1990, 19). The committee then planning the new humanities curriculum thus recommended the separation of a course in humanities from a course in history, with the proviso that the two courses be closely related.

In the ensuing discussion, McKeon argued that once the problem of constructing a humanities course is separated from questions of "covering" the history of art, literature, and philosophy, one could deal directly with determining the contribution which the humanities might make to

4. A number of pertinent documents are contained in University of Chicago, Joseph Regenstein Library, Special Collections Department, Dean of the College, 1923–58, Box 7, Folder 2.

contemporary life. He went on to suggest three major objectives which such a course might pursue:

> The development in the student of taste and broad acquaintance with the arts, literature, history, and philosophy . . . ; the formation of the abilities which are necessary to the recognition and appreciation of artistic, cultural, and intellectual values, as opposed to the random associated reflections which frequently accompany the attentive attitude and proper remarks that pass for appreciation; and, finally, the analytical abilities needed to integrate taste and interest, on the one hand, and critical judgment and discrimination, on the other hand, into the context of the principles . . . which are particularized in the character and attitudes of a man, and universalized in the philosophies and cultural communities men share. ([1953] 1990, 20)

McKeon's suggestions carried the day. He thereby supplied the rationale for transforming the humanities course from a curriculum providing knowledge of the past to one geared to cultivating civilized powers of the mind.

Reconfiguring the Liberal Curriculum

The transformation of the humanities course took place in the context of a radical recasting of the entire College curriculum. The New Plan, although exciting in many ways, was vulnerable on two counts. One was Hutchins's dissatisfaction with its content; the other was the wish of Hutchins and other educators to merge the first two undergraduate years with the last two years of high school. Both elements came to a head in 1937.

Hutchins wanted to recast the liberal curriculum by organizing it around the reading of Great Books. In 1936, with funds from a wealthy supporter, Hutchins assembled a group of like-minded educators—Stringfellow Barr, Scott Buchanan, and others together with McKeon and Adler—to explore that curricular idea.[5] Hutchins persuaded McKeon to lend this group, called the Committee on the Liberal Arts, some status in his division so they could meet on campus. Forty years later, McKeon reminisced about the committee's fortunes:

> We then began meeting and it turned out that what we thought was possible was quite different. I began by saying, "Let's get away from the medieval liberal arts.

---

5. Three of McKeon's graduate students from Columbia University—Paul Goodman, George Kimball Plochmann, and William Barrett—were invited to join the group.

Let's get away from the Great Books. . . . The [Great Books] grew out of community circumstances and we merely glorify them. Let's take a look at what the
liberal arts are today." I lost that argument, and I said, "If we're going to do
something on the model of the traditional liberal arts let's not do it by reading
books." I lost that argument. "If we are going to read books, let's read modern
books and not Greek books." I lost that. "As long as we're reading Greek books,
let's not read Aristotle." We began with Aristotle's *Poetics*.[6]

More divisive than the choice of text was disagreement about how to
read a text. McKeon later recalled that the main point of disagreement on
the committee was that the others believed that there was one defensible
way to read the classics, whereas McKeon argued that there were essentially plural ways to do so. Adler's recollection supports this point. He
traced their disagreements to philosophical differences that had emerged
after their days together at Columbia. Faulting McKeon's disposition to
accommodate conflicting positions, Adler wrote Hutchins around the
time of the meeting that "Dick is today taking the position which I took in
Dialectic eight years ago, and which I now think is nothing but clever
sophistry. It is simply a way of avoiding the obligation to take sides and
take the chance of being wrong" (Adler 1977, 176).

Disagreements proved so fundamental and tenacious that the Committee soon disbanded, to Hutchins's enormous distress.[7] Buchanan and Barr
left to establish the Great Books curriculum at St. John's, and Hutchins
failed to secure the curriculum he wanted at Chicago.[8] Years later, when

6. Conversation with the author in dean's office at University of Chicago, February
1984.

7. Amy Kass's searching account records yet other lines of disagreement, including
McKeon's preference to start by considering the problems of the modern university rather
than texts (Kass 1973, 26).

8. Buchanan's recollection describes that fateful meeting as one that "will never be forgotten by any of those present. It was one of those occasions of recognition that mark the
crises in tragedies and comedies. Although there was good will and agreement on the
problems set by poetry and mathematics, or the liberal arts, and in spite of many inter-
changes of lectures and papers, McKeon, Adler, and I, each of us, had constructed and
complicated quite different universes of discourse which reached into deep matters of
method and metaphysics. The three worlds separately had absorbed and accumulated the
energies of our associates. They also carried within them the stresses and strains in our
chaotic intellectual culture. Brought into proximity the three worlds discharged their energies at each other. Heat and light became thunder and lightning. There was never another general meeting of the whole committee. We agreed to disagree and to pursue our
separate courses" (Buchanan 1962, 27–28).

Hutchins decided to resign from the University, he gave as his prime reason the fact that what he had wanted to do most—establish the curriculum of his dreams—he could not accomplish at Chicago. All he had succeeded in doing, he mused, was effect some changes in organization.

Nevertheless, those changes were momentous. They meant, first, giving the College its own dean, budget, and power of appointment, changes that took effect in 1930. Then, in November 1932, the University Senate approved the idea of constructing a four-year program of general education that would include the last two years of high school. Two months later, the Board of Trustees approved that action, and a College Curriculum Committee was appointed to prepare a plan to implement that decision. In 1937, the committee, chaired by Acting Dean Aaron Brumbaugh, issued an ineffectual report that nonetheless signaled the institution's continuing commitment to a college program for student years 11 through 14. Finally, following a decade of tumultuous debates on the matter, the senate in 1942 authorized the College to award a Bachelor of Arts degree upon completion of this program. (The proposal was carried in a vote of 58 to 58, in which Hutchins cast the deciding vote.)

Between 1937 and 1942, the faculty had progressed toward the novel curriculum of the "Second Hutchins College." This curriculum took shape as three series of three-year courses in the natural sciences, social sciences, and humanities, followed first by one, then two, capstone integrative courses. The generative principle of this curriculum was the assumption that the scientific, moral, and aesthetic domains involve irreducibly distinct intellectual powers. In the experience of the College, that principle can be traced back to the 1924 statement of Wilkins and Morrison about the three categories of powers cited in chapter 6: independence in thinking, moral judgment, and aesthetic appreciation. In McKeon's personal experience, it could be traced back to his master's thesis on Santayana, Tolstoy, and Croce, whom he viewed as representing, respectively, naturalistic, moral, and aesthetic perspectives on art and literature (McKeon [1953] 1990, 6). In the thought of the framers of the program of the Second Hutchins College, it tended to be associated with Aristotle's differentiation among the theoretical, the practical, and the poetic (or productive) sciences.

The rationale for this program was spelled out in McKeon's 1949 paper, "The Nature and Teaching of the Humanities." The paper begins by noting the grounds for the recurrent criticism of educational practice—that education has ceased to be relevant to life and that it has failed to make adequate use of knowledge newly available. It concludes by enumerating ways in which the cultivation of the humanities can contribute to resolving conflicts by which the world is riven: by honoring humanistic aspects of diverse cultures; examining the logics that unite and divide people; seeing human values as resources for escaping the twin perils of authoritarianism and relativism; and deploying arts of thought and expression to move and instruct humankind.

The paper proceeds by clarifying ways in which disciplines such as the humanities have been delimited. Refusing to define disciplines in terms of either a single subject matter or a single method, McKeon advocates the use of problems as a basis for organizing the disciplines. "If education is approached in terms of methods or arts adapted to the solution of problems," he observes in a crucial passage, "it is apparent that methods are not uniquely adapted to things but that any subject matter is susceptible of treatment in a variety of ways and according to a variety of methods. . . . So conceived, education is concerned properly with three sets of arts adapted to three kinds of problems" (1949, 295).

This idea became foundational for the College curriculum under Deans Faust and Ward. It informed the organization of the general education curriculum into its three main divisions of natural sciences, social sciences, and humanities. The central idea behind this organization was to conceive those disciplines as defined not by distinct subject matters but by three distinct sets of problems and arts. Each of those arts was conceived as manifesting distinctive human powers. Accordingly, the place of the natural sciences in general education was determined by the arts required to analyze problems, validate knowledge, and communicate statements about natures and things. The place of the social sciences in general education was determined by the arts required to deal with problems concerning associations set up by humans to achieve common values. The place of the humanities in general education was determined by the arts required to analyze the great achievements and products of human creativity when considered with respect to their formal structure. All three of these arts, McKeon insisted, are applicable to all subject matters. For example, a great work of science, such as Newton's *Principia* or Darwin's *Origin of Species,* is subject to scientific, social, and humanistic analysis. A program of general education is unified, McKeon argued, when these three sets of arts supplement one another in the treatment of related problems.

With this formulation, the faculty of the College proceeded to construct the general education sequences as instruments for developing three kinds of powers in courses of study that built upon one another. Concretizing the general objectives just summarized, McKeon (1949) went on to describe the three humanistic arts that constituted the sequence of three courses in the transformed College humanities program.

The first he glossed as *appreciation*. This art was to be cultivated by having students directly encounter a selection of great works of literature, philosophy, science, art, and social speculation.

The second major art, *analysis,* gives students the power to distinguish the characteristics to which they respond in a work of art and to choose significant characteristics for attention. Thus, for example, analysis "substitutes for that enjoyment of music in which sounds form a background for trains of reflection on other matters—interrupted by nervous starts when the music intrudes on attention—an ability to distinguish the characteristics of harmonic, melodic, and rhythmic development which constitute music" (McKeon 1949, 299). Similarly, analysis of pictures or poems or novels would help distinguish elements in them that are pleasant because they recall scenes of youth, reinforce favorite prejudices, or stimulate unexamined bodily reactions from qualities through which great art is differentiated from what is merely tolerated or accepted.

The third humanistic art, *criticism,* enables students to become aware of the criteria by which they judge human products, provide resources for articulating them, and become acquainted with the assumptions behind other critical systems. The variety of critical systems in question includes those that focus on the potentialities and uses of a given medium; the significance supplied by cultural contexts; the values achieved through their forms; and the ideas they embodied.

Around the same time that the new humanities sequence was being offered, in the fall of 1943, McKeon and his colleagues unveiled a capstone course that had no equal anywhere else—Observation, Interpretation, and Integration (OII). The course was designed "to clarify for students the relationships of the subject matter of the general courses in which they have been working." Among other things, the course's designers intended OII to enable students "to analyze and compare the methods of acquiring and testing knowledge in the natural sciences, the social sciences, and the humanities"; to consider the "history of the relations between the various fields of human knowledge"; and "to prepare students to distinguish clearly the differences in the nature of the manifold problems they will encounter as individuals and as citizens" (College Announcements, 1943–44, 64).

This course emerged from discussions among the entire College faculty. McKeon describes the hothouse atmosphere in which the course came into being:

> All of this four-year program was worked out in meetings of the entire faculty of the College. The College had become a RULING BODY, and it welcomed a

program that was intelligible to all members. I have never in my entire teaching seen an entire group meeting—sometimes twice a week . . . and fighting over all the issues. There were about 100 faculty all told. One of the teachers of biology—a man whose father was on the faculty—said that there ought to be some way of pulling the bundle together and it ought to be one in which the students were given the skills of observation, interpretation, and integration. A committee was formed—Joe Schwab and I were members of that committee—to plan such a course and all four graduate divisions were represented. We decided that that name was as good as any we could think of. . . . I think that it was one of the best courses which the College organized. . . . The committee that taught the course met for a full year before the course went in.[9]

Although a number of colleagues had some say in the creation of this course, McKeon's powerful mind tended to prevail in debates about its content.[10] However much the originating impulse had been to focus serially on observation, interpretation, and integration, and however much the rhetoric about the course stressed its function as both linking the earlier courses and empowering public citizens, as the course emerged, it came to reflect three rather different kinds of interest. The first concerned the diverse ways in which various philosophers had thought about the *organization* of the domains of knowledge. Plato, Aristotle, Aquinas, Bacon, Kant, and Comte were the key figures in this lineup. Carefully selected excerpts from their works gave students direct entrée into the ways in which they separated or joined theory and practice, reason and faith, percepts and concepts, nature and convention. The second kind of interest concerned the diverse ways in which philosophers and scientists thought about the *methods* of inquiry. The third concerned the operation of *principles* in diverse domains; the issues treated typically had to do with the role of different ways of construing such commonplaces as pleasure, justice, or causality. Since these McKeonesque interests in fact dominated the course and constituted the titles of the booklets of selected readings, after several years the OII course became de jure OMP: a course in the Organizations, Methods, and Principles of the Sciences.

Besides transforming the College humanities program and helping to

9. McKeon Interview.

10. As Joe Schwab later recalled, "Dick and I were the most active members of the committee called first Organization, Interpretation & Integration, later called Organization, Methods & Principles of the Sciences. We were pretty continuously at opposite ends of the pole, and on the whole he won. So OMP in its first form could have been said to be virtually his" (Schwab 1976).

create the OII course, McKeon weighed in on discussions affecting the new History of Western Civilization course. This side of his curricular work has been less visible, since McKeon was never publicly associated with that course. What is more, in the curricular debates of the 1940s and their aftermath, McKeon was often portrayed as an enemy of history — an amazing portrayal, considering McKeon's almost obsessive concern with thumbnailing the history of virtually every single topic he wrote about, including human rights, the idea of responsibility, honors programs, and, not least, the liberal arts. The fact is that McKeon not only supported the decision to recast the Schevill courses into two different ones, a humanities course and a history course, but he actually came to serve on the committee that recommended the creation of the History of Western Civilization course.

In authorizing the new history course in December 1946, the Faculty of the College stated: "The proposed course has two major aims: (1) to acquaint the student with the history of Western Civilization from the River Civilizations to 1938; (2) to provide an historical interpretation of the College curriculum" (Review Committee for History 1948, 1). According to one witness, the very idea of such a course was a rallying point for McKeon's opponents and anathema to his most ardent followers, who considered the fact of historical change inconsistent with the eternal truths they were supposedly called on to disseminate. In any case, "the great man himself entered the fray" (McNeill 1991, 130, 152–54). Engaging such noted historians on the committee as Louis Gottschalk, Christian Mackauer, and Sylvia Thrupp, who favored a Schevill-like course on the succession of cultural epochs, McKeon suggested an alternative mode of constructing history. It was what he came to call "disciplinary" or "problematic" history, which treats the "development of ways of posing problems and of means of resolving them in the arts and disciplines" (Review Committee for History 1948, 4). Following an intense, protracted controversy, the faculty reached a compromise decision, resulting in a course that was mainly epochal history but interlarded with the treatment of historically evolved problems such as the concepts of space and time, from Aristotle to Whitehead, and the treatment of perspective in painting, from Alberti to cubism and surrealism.

The three-year humanities sequences and the two integrative courses were innovative, coherent, and distinctive features of the Second Hutchins College curriculum. All of them reflected the pioneering philosophical thought of Richard McKeon, and through them the influence of his ways of thinking permeated far and wide, generally without the bearers having any consciousness of the director of their thoughtways.

The Return in the 1960s

In the immediate postwar years, McKeon disengaged from developments at the University. This detachment reflected his growing alienation from Hutchins, due to the latter's authoritarian tendencies and behind-the-scenes criticisms of McKeon. It did not help when Hutchins asserted in a speech early in 1944 that the faculty still needed to "figure out what a liberal education is," not long after McKeon and associates had completed work on what was arguably the flagship program of liberal education of its day.[11] Growing estrangement between the two led McKeon to resign from his deanship in 1947 (although McKeon was among the numerous faculty who in 1951 pleaded with Hutchins not to resign).

McKeon's withdrawal also reflected a turn to activity in the international arena that had germinated during the war years, when he directed the Army Specialized Training School for language and area studies on campus. Immediately after the war, he served on the University's Committee to Frame a World Constitution and played an active role in the early years of UNESCO.[12] He became a founding member of the International Institute of Philosophy, work which took him to meetings all over the world and involved him in deliberations that pertained to the composition of the 1949 Universal Declaration of Human Rights.

Thus McKeon had little to do with curricular matters in the 1950s beyond developing his own sequence of courses on concepts and methods in the various disciplines.[13] Indeed, some colleagues faulted him for remaining silent when the College curriculum he had done so much to create came under attack in 1953. So while College faculty were licking wounds from the abolition of an independent College following the retirement of

11. Robert Maynard Hutchins, speech at Trustee-Faculty Dinner, South Shore Country Club, Chicago, January 12, 1944. In a letter written following Hutchins's remark, McKeon wondered "what are the conditions . . . which justify the President's assertion," and countered, with no little pique, that he himself had clear "convictions as to what the liberal arts are or may be made to be and as to what good advanced training in them involves" (McKeon to Redfield, 17 April 1944, McKeon Papers).

12. This role included McKeon's involvement in preliminary meetings on the formation of UNESCO, service as adviser to the U.S. delegations to the General Conferences of UNESCO in 1946–48, first acting counselor on UNESCO affairs attached to the U.S. Embassy in Paris, and member of the U.S. National Commission on UNESCO.

13. These courses were recorded on tape by unknown parties in the 1960s. The course on Natural Sciences was edited by Daved B. Owen and Zahava K. McKeon and published by the University of Chicago Press as *On Knowing: The Natural Sciences* (McKeon [1963] 1994). Companion volumes on the social sciences and the humanities have yet to be prepared.

Hutchins and the protest resignation of Dean Ward, McKeon concentrated on a schema for articulating the constitutive elements of various philosophical positions.[14] At the same time, he gravitated to problems of the world community, attending conferences to explore the possibilities of world unity at a time of glaring ideological differences. Central to both projects was his pluralistic conviction that the truth is one but necessarily captured in divergent, mutually irreducible systems of thought that differ in their constitutive principles, their methods, and their modes of interpretation. Indeed, McKeon argued in his "spiritual autobiography" that, viewed in retrospect, his engagement with problems of philosophical scholarship, educational practice and administration, and international and intercultural relations "may be described more nearly accurately as three approaches to the same problem" ([1953] 1990, 5).

In the mid-1960s, however, McKeon turned once again to foundational problems regarding the liberal curriculum. This renewed attention reflected his growing suspicion that "one of the fundamental philosophic problems of our time must be a reconsideration of what is usually called the liberal arts" ([1963] 1994, 1). To some extent it was connected with the revived interest in curricular issues attendant on the reorganization of the College under Provost Edward Levi and Dean Wayne Booth. This interest found expression in a quartet of papers composed between 1964 and 1969 (McKeon 1964a, 1964b, 1967, 1969). Although their formulations differ on certain points, these papers share the supposition of a need to reinvent ways of thinking about the liberal arts.

McKeon composed the first of these papers for a 1964 volume of essays honoring Hutchins, *Humanistic Education and Western Civilization*. His essay begins by recalling that Hutchins was wont to remind us that "the liberal arts are the arts of freedom," and so to be free one must understand the arts of freedom (McKeon 1964a, 159). With a nod to the book's title, however, McKeon quickly joins that theme with a focus on the "arts of humanity," noting that to be truly human, one must understand what has been and what can be accomplished by human arts. Building on this conjunction, he suggests that the history of education has involved an interplay between conceptions of freedom and conceptions of value and that "general education" was "the name given to a revolution in education designed to rediscover the arts to make men free and the arts to discern and under-

14. This remarkable schema became known as his semantic matrix. For an introduction to this matrix, see McKeon 1990, chaps. 7 and 8. Watson 1985 offers a more accessible introduction. Its evolution is discussed in Plochmann 1990. See also Levine 2000.

stand the problems men must face and the values they might achieve" (159). This point introduces an analytic history of the liberal arts since Hellenic times, which culminates by stating four respects in which the liberating and humanizing arts are "general." They are general in the senses of (1) being applicable to all subject matters; (2) embracing all fundamental skills; (3) developing the whole person; and (4) being suited to all human beings.

Taking off from this fourfold scheme, the paper launches into a ringing criticism that general education no longer performs those liberating and humanizing functions: "We have proceeded for the most part by addition and subtraction. We set up distribution requirements to be general; since they are general and superficial, we add specialization requirements to be proficient and profound" (McKeon 1964a, 173). What we need instead is a fresh effort to discover what arts in the present world situation are truly liberal and humanizing. And we must do so taking account of the enormous changes in the four spheres associated with the four meanings of "general":

1. Regarding subject matters, the profusion of knowledge calls for new modes of selectivity in liberal learning.
2. The multiplication of technologies indicates a need for reconceiving what are taught as basic skills.
3. The fragmentation of life makes it harder to formulate what it takes or means to become a "whole person."
4. The implosion of cultural contacts makes it harder to represent what is suited to all humans.

Because of these changes of scope, new fields and new disciplines must be identified. McKeon proceeds to lay out an astonishing new liberal curriculum, one constituted by four new fields of humanistic education and four new liberating disciplines. He defines the four fields as (1) *invention,* or coping with new problems through creative discoveries; (2) *recovery,* or recognizing objective evidence; (3) *presentation,* or techniques used to affect action and art; and (4) *commonality of action,* or unifications and pluralisms that open up intelligible meanings and practical programs.

In order to cope with changes in the universe of knowledge, skill, valuation, and contact among peoples, new lines of differentiation are needed to transcend the disciplinary demarcations of the old system of liberal arts. McKeon identifies these disciplines as

· canonics, which sets forth simple forms of general expressions, and is useful for relating tradition to innovation;

- hermeneutics, which interprets actions and facts as well as documents and texts, and is useful for relating facts and values;
- homiletics, which deals both with sequences and consequences, and is useful for relating particulars and universals; and
- systematics, which achieves insight into coherences of experience, value, and knowledge, and thereby serves to relate parts and wholes.

In another paper of the same year, created for a conference on the liberal arts (McKeon 1964b), McKeon focused exclusively on the qualifier "liberal." He begins that presentation by analyzing the cycles through which schemes of liberal arts become created and then ossify. This analysis leads him to stake out a set of new liberal arts that are responsive to the novel problems of our times. Since the emphasis here is on the emancipatory character of liberal learning, McKeon looks for ossifications from which the arts can liberate us. They liberate from passivity by removing false problems that distance us from inquiry and action and by clarifying true problems that open inquiry and action. Thus, *rhetoric* is the art of inducing new opinions by arguments that lead to agreement rather than to submission or hypnosis, and it serves to liberate us from the opposition between tradition and innovation; *grammar* combines description of the facts of the case with expression of cultural values and so liberates us from the opposition between facts and values; *logic* examines structures of consequences in processes and in discourse and consequences of particular things (perception) and of universal laws (criticism), thereby liberating us from the opposition between particulars and universals; and *dialectic* combines literalness and productive ambiguity and combines increased individual spontaneity with increased complexity of environments, thereby liberating us from the opposition between parts and wholes.

McKeon launched yet another attack on this problem at a conference in 1966 on approaches to education for character. In this context, he looked for, on the one hand, ways in which the liberal arts can contribute to solving problems of modern fragmentation, and, on the other, how their cultivation can lead to desirable character traits. Once again, he divides the liberal arts into four categories; the names parallel those in the first (1964a) paper. By virtue of their necessarily interdisciplinary character, all of the arts serve to overcome fragmentation. And each of them leads to specific virtues.

1. Discovery or invention leads to curiosity and disciplined originality.
2. Recovery promotes disciplined sensitivity.

3. Practicing the art of presentation promotes disciplined coherence and open-mindedness.
4. Systematization generates disciplined purposiveness.

Although McKeon's ideas for reconstructing the liberal arts did not get incorporated into the Chicago curriculum, they did stimulate an interesting initiative. Soon after McKeon's 1964 papers appeared, the College Executive Committee, under Dean Wayne Booth, created the blueprint for an entirely new way of organizing general education at Chicago. This new structure took the form of a four-year "vertical" curriculum to house what had just been authorized as a year in common for all students before they headed into collegiate divisional specialties. The curriculum consisted of a double course taught across the three quarters of the first year, called simply Liberal Arts I, to be followed in each of the three succeeding years by two-quarter sequences, Liberal Arts II, III, and IV. The first year's course was to focus on arts of discovery and invention, the second on critical judgment, the third on practical decision making, and the fourth on intellectual integration. Although the novelty of this conception aroused so much anxiety among the faculty that the plan never even came to the floor of the council for deliberation, Booth and several colleagues did create the Liberal Arts I course, which was taught for half a dozen years (and arguably became the template for a later double-course sequence, Human Being and Citizen).[15]

Richard McKeon's last formal statement on education was a talk prepared for the National Collegiate Honors Council at the University of Arkansas in 1976. He used the occasion to differentiate two strands of what is usually traced as a single history of liberal education in the twentieth century: the history of general education and the history of honors studies. The former question—what program provides an appropriate education for all people associated in a community, or humanity, to enable

15. A more durable curriculum based on McKeon's new ideas has been created by a former student of McKeon, Richard Buchanan, at the Carnegie Mellon University School of Design. In this program, students majoring in communication design, industrial design, design studies, or human-computer interaction are expected to complete 35 percent of their work in a general education program. This program includes a vertical curriculum organized to enhance "discovery" in the first year, "concentration and development" in the second and third years, and "integration" in the fourth year. In addition, Buchanan has produced a graduate course, Concepts and Methods of Interaction Design, which creatively embodies the whole gamut of McKeonesque categories as well as his schematization of the new liberal arts.

them to develop their individual capacities and to participate in their communities—moved in programs devised to answer it from the Amherst of Alexander Meiklejohn to Columbia, St. John's, and Shimer. The question of honors studies—how talented students are recognized and provided with opportunities to pursue studies adapted to their interests and talents—moved from the Swarthmore of Frank Aydelotte to the Inter-University Committee on the Superior Student to the National Collegiate Honors Council. McKeon went on to discuss criticisms leveled against each type of program, namely, the metaphysical assumptions underlying them and the ways they conjoin to form a double ideal. This double ideal of education for all and education adapted to the abilities and values of each was institutionalized at Chicago in the "Levi College" of the mid-1960s. McKeon also noted the changes needed to extend this double ideal to newly liberated nations and underprivileged peoples and classes and to reconfigure general education so that it draws on the culture of humanity rather than on a particular culture of the Western world. The talk concludes with the same ringing challenge that informs McKeon's entire discourse about the liberal arts throughout the 1960s: "What are the new disciplines, in the sense of subjects of inquiry, that are brought to our attention by considering the culture and problems of mankind? What are the new disciplines, in the sense of arts and abilities, that will contribute to knowledge, art, community, and communication by transforming them and making them relevant to a developing world culture and to an altering organization of arts and science, technologies and polities?" (McKeon 1979, 16).

These brief summaries can only hint at the complexities of papers that are enormously dense; they simply offer an invitation to consider the provocative implications of so radical an approach to reconstructing the liberal arts. Enough has been said, however, to reveal two notable respects in which McKeon's later construction of the liberal arts curriculum differs from his formulations of the 1940s. A steadfast differentiation among the arts of theory, practice, and production, congruent with the Aristotelian division of the sciences, has given way here to a differentiation of arts based on the Roman and medieval arts of rhetoric, grammar, and logic. This new typology appeared at a time when McKeon was especially active in recovering the discipline of rhetoric for the academic world.[16] McKeon notes the prominence of rhetoric in the Roman conception of liberal arts

---

16. Six of the eight essays on rhetoric reproduced in McKeon 1987 date from the period after 1955.

and the Renaissance conception of humanism, and he likens their concerns to the contemporary interest in communication.

For those wishing to secure a definitive schematization of the arts as formulated in this period, McKeon's penchant for altering his schemata with each new presentation is perplexing. For each situation, he altered his schematization according to whether, for example, he was attending to humanization, emancipation, or character formation. It is only by accepting those shifts that one can come to terms with what was so empowering—as well as so maddening—about McKeon as a teacher.

McKeon as Teacher

From his earliest forays at the University of Chicago, McKeon revealed a particular interest in questions regarding the techniques of teaching as well as the substance of what was to be taught. Some of his thoughts on pedagogy appear in the 1949 essay on the humanities, which concludes with a section on teaching that reflects ideas incorporated into the curricular practice of the College under Faust and Ward (and summarized by McKeon's devoted colleague Russell Thomas in *The Idea and Practice of General Education;* Thomas [1950] 1990).

For one thing, McKeon notes, insofar as attention is centered on human works, the dangers incident to poor classroom performance are minimized: "However bad the teaching or tangential its purposes, if the student is brought into contact with great works of literature, philosophy, science, art, and social speculation and contrivance, he will be started on that movement to the more human which is the mark of humanistic education. Plato, Aristotle, Dante, Shakespeare, Newton, Mozart, and Cézanne are teachers in their works, and the dangers to humanistic education are to be found in the obstacles that are placed in the way of their teaching" (McKeon 1949, 302).

Although lectures are useful to inspire appreciation, stimulate interest, or supply background information, their evil effects outweigh their advantages, especially when they are most interesting, for they inhibit the students' progress in discovering values in works on their own. Explicating texts in classroom discussion, on the other hand, helps discover and remove the difficulties that students experience in interpreting works; and discussions also serve to facilitate exploration of issues in criticism of works. McKeon's own teaching manifested the value of getting students to avoid the conventional "isms," which he considered shibboleths, and to become aware of differences in the meanings of words as they appear in different passages of original authors and become prominent in secondary sources (Plochmann 1998, 60). Finally, the paper advocates that "the training by which a student learns to express correctly what he has to say, to adapt his statement to circumstances and purposes, and to organize his arguments clearly and cogently should be closely related to his analyses of the qualities which make great works clear in statement, effective in presentation, and sound in demonstration" (McKeon 1949, 302). Commenting on the qualities needed for fine undergraduate teaching, he elsewhere affirmed that "there can be no satisfactory teaching of liberal studies at the College level except by people who have genuinely inquiring minds and who have been systematically trained by experts in the particular methods of analysis and research proper to these subjects." [17]

Other dimensions of McKeon's concern for pedagogy can be gleaned from consideration of his own remarkable style of teaching. This style rested on paradoxes that evolved along with the substance of his own philosophy. By the 1950s, McKeon had produced a highly differentiated analysis and defense of pluralism without parallel in the history of Western thought. It yielded the first paradox of his teaching: his penchant for embracing philosophical doctrines that that are nontrivially opposed to one another. Students who followed his magisterial expositions of these oppositions, however, came away convinced that he had illuminated an enormous amount of cognitive territory. "The keys to the kingdom!" were not atypical words. [18] The other paradox, however, was that McKeon was quick to belittle or deprecate you if you used his schema to make sense of the world. He fed you a powerfully seductive framework and then objected when you used it.

Elder Olson, one of McKeon's erstwhile students who went on to pursue a distinguished career in the field of English literature, reflected on McKeon's paradoxical pedagogy as follows:

> [McKeon] wanted no one to come away from his lectures or writings with a fixed mind—a mind, that is, moving in channels which he had pre-cut. He detested parroting; if a student played parrot, he would instantly challenge him, questioning the very statement he himself had made only moments before.

17. McKeon to Redfield, 14 April 1944, McKeon Papers.

18. Professional colleagues encountering McKeon for the first time sometimes had a similar reaction. Max Horkheimer, who visited the university in the mid-1950s, accompanied me once to an ordinary course lecture by McKeon. Afterward, Horkheimer exclaimed to me, "This man has made sense of the whole of Western philosophy for the first time in my life!"

There was an extraordinary trio of lectures on William of Ockham. In the first of these he portrayed Ockham as a simon-pure, thoroughgoing Aristotelian. In the second, he showed him to be anything but that. In the third he pointed out both the Aristotelian and the non-Aristotelian elements in Ockham. Dumbfounded like the rest of us, one student demanded, "*What* are we supposed to think?" Smiling, McKeon said, "You are supposed to *think.*" He preferred hints to flat-out statements; he wanted to activate intellect and imagination rather than memory, though he thought the last faculty has been much undercultivated in modern education. (Shils, 1991, 304)

And that is why Walter Watson's recent analysis (1999) of the unity of McKeon's thought proposes that McKeon's philosophy is "not a doctrine but a power." It is a power, he adds, that manifests itself through the deliberate employment of paradoxical formulations; that has appeared inseparable from the man himself, and so scarcely reproducible; and that the character of the man was like that of a bully, for he typically responded to those who tried to restate his views by saying that they had not understood him.

If Watson's profile is right, it raises a provocative question. What kind of a personage is it who presents not a doctrine but a power; who speaks in paradoxes; who offers a virtually inimitable exemplar; and who is hard on his disciples? It is difficult to avoid identifying this figure as that of the religious prophet. That done, one brings to mind Max Weber's famous distinction between two kinds of prophets, which he called emissary and exemplary prophets. As Weber portrayed them (1978, 447–49), the emissary type of prophet addresses a set of ethical demands to the world. In emissary prophecy, the devout experience themselves as instruments of a god, frequently that of a supramundane, personal, loving, demanding, punishing lord of creation. In contrast to the emissary prophet stands the kind of prophet who points out the path to salvation by exemplary living, usually by a contemplative mode of life. The supreme being of an exemplary prophet is an impersonal being, accessible only by means of contemplation. Generally speaking, Weber associated the religious virtuosos who took the form of emissary prophets with the West and those who took the form of exemplary prophets with the East.

Watson's characterization of McKeon leads to an association with exemplary prophetic figures from great religious traditions. Not preaching a doctrine, but exemplifying a special salvific power; relying on the pervasive use of paradoxes in their teaching; holding themselves up as models to be imitated; and responding to disciples in critical and reprimanding manner—these features of McKeon's profile so insightfully formulated by Watson are precisely the features one associates with the gurus, the masters, and the sensei of India, China, Korea, and Japan.

Consider McKeon's Japanese contemporary, Morihei Ueshiba, the founder of the discipline of aikido. To his followers, Ueshiba is known as O Sensei, or the Great Teacher. Although Ueshiba occasionally verbalized his philosophical ideas, what he tried to convey to his students was a power, not a doctrine. The power rests essentially on paradoxes. For example, aikido is a martial art whose medium is love; it embodies a repertoire of techniques whose goal is the absence of technique; it is a power of concentrating on one's own inner self in order to become connected to the whole of the universe. What is more, as is true in most traditional Japanese arts, the teacher holds himself up as a model to be emulated. He was proverbially hard on his students, as befits an Eastern sage or master, and even used language almost identical with that ascribed to McKeon. For example, in one public demonstration where some of his most outstanding students brilliantly demonstrated the art of aikido he had taught them, Ueshiba is said to have remarked: "That's okay, but what they are doing is not what I do."

It is not just through personal style that McKeon resembles the great teachers of the Asian traditions. However much they differ among themselves, the Asian traditions seem to share a disposition to discourage attachments to particular cognitive forms. Fa-tsang, author of the sutra that inspired the tradition of Hua-yen Buddhism, made the point by declaring that all of the following are true: A is true; not-A is true; the statement that A and not-A are contradictory is true; and the statement that A and not-A are not contradictory is true. Mahatma Gandhi, another Great Teacher, justified his espousal of ahimsa, or nonviolence, on grounds that violence was inconsistent with the pursuit of truth, since violence implied the absolute verity of one's position, and any single human's purchase on truth was necessarily partial.

With that in mind, one could say that McKeon showed a way to bridge the millennial chasm between Eastern and Western thought. If Eastern philosophies present conceptions of unity with relatively little attention to cognitive forms, and Western philosophy a rich multiplicity of forms standing in mutually discordant relations, McKeon discovered a way to incorporate both the diversity of forms and the experience of unity. This makes him a master indeed.

If that is so, then McKeon's place in the history of Western philosophy may be unique. One might in this respect compare him with other great philosophers who tried in various ways to sum up the lessons of the Western tradition. Hegel used the resources of Western philosophy to attempt a grand synthesis of their ideas and methods. Marx, Dewey, and Heidegger used the resources of Western philosophy to declare an end to traditional philosophy. McKeon used the resources of Western philosophy in a way that neither integrated them into a single synthetic doctrine nor repudiated them as historically outmoded formations but respected their integrity while transcending them.

What is one to do with such a teaching? Can one do more than confront the paradox that McKeon offers himself as an exemplar to be imitated, but no one, however sincerely dedicated, can be expected to reproduce the model? Here again, Watson offers us a fruitful formulation, when he says that "the usual effect of McKeon on his students is that each takes from his philosophy what he will and makes use of it in his own way, and this, it seems to me, is an appropriate mode of influence for a philosophy such as his" (2000, 26). That, again, is precisely the message of a teacher like Morihei Ueshiba, who urged his students to take the power of his teaching and make it their own.

And that is the ultimate achievement of a teaching program designed to energize powerful habits of mind.

6

Joseph Schwab's Assault
on Facile Teaching

The ideal of liberal education does linger. It might be that a conception of education that associates itself with . . . sociability, civility, and self can be restored. And, if such restoration comes to pass, Schwab's essays and books will play an important part in the rediscovery of the meaning of these notions. He articulates a way of thinking which lets us see more clearly than does the way of any other contemporary thinker what thought about education *might* be and how it *might* be possible to give visions meaning. The burden of his work is an invitation to the reader to participate in the search that he ventured. IAN WESTBURY AND NEIL J. WILKOF (1978)

At age twenty-seven, armed with a master's degree in zoology, Joseph Jackson Schwab seemed destined to make his mark as a biologist. Protégé of renowned biostatistician Sewall Wright,[1] Schwab had engaged in genetics research and published on the effect of raised temperature on inherited changes in diverse regions of *Drosophila* chromosomes (1935). He was

1. Sewall Wright, professor of zoology at the University from 1926 to 1954, was an eminent exponent of the application of mathematical techniques to the analysis of genetic processes. His mature work focused on theoretical formulation of gene frequencies in natural populations in an effort to model fundamental patterns of evolution (Swift 1991).

primed for a fellowship year at Columbia University's Zoology Department, where his research on *Drosophila* genes would deepen, earning him a dissertation and a twenty-one-page paper in *Genetics* (1940). At the time, however, the prospect of making educational history during the Robert Maynard Hutchins presidency at the University of Chicago attracted Schwab as it had Richard McKeon. After earning his doctorate, Schwab decided to drop a promising research career for another vocation: the reconstruction of general education.

In the event, Joe Schwab became a prime mover behind Chicago's three-year sequence in the natural sciences — a curriculum which has captured the attention of science educators ever since. He helped create the famed course in Observation, Interpretation, and Integration (OII), which he taught for nearly two decades. As pedagogue, he was legendary; students invariably recall him as one who made learning in the second Hutchins College electrifying. A key player in the University Examiner's office, he broke new ground in creating evaluation instruments geared to specific goals of liberal learning. One of the rare natural scientists accomplished in humanistic learning as well, he was eagerly embraced by Hutchins and Adler in their extension programs for teaching and publishing the Great Books of the Western World. Following these germinal achievements during the Hutchins years at Chicago, Schwab went on to address a national audience with provocative essays on the liberal curriculum and pedagogical practice.

Genesis of an Educator

The sketch that introduces some 6.5 linear feet of Schwab materials in the University's archives begins:

> Joseph Jackson Schwab was born on February 2, 1909 in Columbus, Mississippi, where he attended a private elementary school that served as a practice school for the prospective teachers of the local women's college. After the sixth grade, Schwab entered the public schools where he discovered science. As Schwab was virtually alone among his classmates in his interests in science, the principal of the high school, who was a former science teacher, encouraged his creative license by giving him free rein in the school laboratory. Schwab became fascinated with the poisonous snakes and other animals kept there and delighted in setting off homemade gunpowder by pounding it with an ax. He finished high school in three years and in 1924, at the age of fifteen,

he set off by train for the University of Chicago where he was to remain for almost fifty years.[2]

No biography mentions the stormy years that followed. Frustrated by his father's philistine opposition to higher education and exasperated by a scene where his bigoted father was beating his closest Negro friend, the strong-minded fifteen-year-old ran away, albeit to a city with supportive maternal relatives.[3] He gave university authorities a fabricated Hyde Park address for his parental residence. Aspiring to become a physicist, his passion for science was deflated by weak performance in math and by the standard mode of science education: memorize findings. In consequence, young Schwab's grades in math and science averaged C- during his first two years; after five quarters, he simply stopped taking such courses.[4] But his performance in English literature was not much better, he earned Ds in courses on Shakespeare and poetry. Awed by the University's intellectual culture, the young teenager stayed up nights discoursing with bright older students instead of attending to conventional academic requirements. At age seventeen he returned to Mississippi for two years, selling shoes.

On his return to the University of Chicago campus, his record improved only slightly; in spring 1929 he was put on academic probation. That action prodded him to show what he was capable of; his grades surged to straight As. More important, he found in James Weber Linn, with whom he took courses in composition and English literature, the kind of teacher he had been looking for.[5]

In December 1930, Schwab completed his baccalaureate with a major in English literature. In the third year of Hutchins's presidency, he returned to science as a graduate student. For the first time since arriving at the university, his appetite for creative scientific inquiry began to be satisfied, as he got caught up in swarms of research on the genetics of fruit flies.[6] At the

2. Schwab Biographical Sketch, from Finding Tool, Joseph J. Schwab Papers, University of Chicago Special Collections, Joseph Regenstein Library, University of Chicago, Chicago.

3. Not the first time he ran away; ten-year-old Joe had run off on a freight train, an incident he recounted decades later (Schwab 1976).

4. Standard biographical sketches err in having him graduate with a BS in physics.

5. According to his daughter Jill Schwab, to whom I am indebted for much of the biographical detail in this paragraph, in later life he always spoke with enormous affection of Linn.

6. In at least one respect, however, his empirical work proved frustrating: he had ruined a pair of eyeglasses with scratches from the microscope eyepieces while trying to view

same time he found, in the teaching of botanist Merle Coulter, a model for fostering critical discussion of scientific texts in small groups. At some point, he sat in on one of the Hutchins-Adler Great Books seminars, an experience that initiated a lifelong friendship with Hutchins. Strong interests in both natural science and humanities coupled to shape the driving forces of Schwab's career: a drive to humanize the teaching of natural science and a drive to apply the intellectual rigor of scientific work both to the classroom discussion of texts and to the evaluation of educational growth.

In the late 1930s, two experiences nurtured these interests: a formative year at Columbia University and the formation of ties with three mentors at Chicago: Hutchins, McKeon, and Ralph Tyler.[7] McKeon, whom Schwab regarded with awe,[8] radically deepened Schwab's grasp of curricular principles in general and mediated Schwab's acquaintance with Aristotle and Dewey in particular. Tyler, who came to the University in 1938, nurtured Schwab's interest in the testing process and served as a mentor and patron for Schwab's growing preoccupation with all aspects of the educational process.

After returning from Columbia in 1937, Schwab reconnected with Coulter and became an instructor in the Biological Sciences sequence.[9] What he found was a course that, despite its talk about science as a special way of discovering principles, solving problems, and enriching students' lives, merely walked them lockstep through a survey of facts—about seedless plants, seeded plants, metabolism, invertebrates, vertebrates, animal reproduction and development, heredity, evolution, and ecology, and then,

---

different specimens from exactly the same distance and angle for repeatable measurements, and so swore off drosophila research ever after (personal communication from Janice Spofford, 2002).

7. On a science education fellowship at Teachers College in Columbia in 1936–37, besides pursuing his doctoral research in one of the zoology labs, he studied educational testing and measurement under Irving Lorge and worked with senior colleagues to produce a monograph on the teaching of genetics (Laton et al. 1939).

8. Schwab repeatedly referred to McKeon as the greatest mind of the twentieth century. Just after McKeon died, Schwab wrote, "Dick's was a great mind. The greatest I have known. And it was he who taught me more than any other person" (Schwab to Wayne C. Booth, 23 April 1986, private collection). He maintained this respect despite McKeon's later occasional mistreatment of him and despite his own misgivings about what he viewed as McKeon's tendency to confound the philosophical and scientific levels of enquiry.

9. The general education program of the late 1930s required three years of science, distributed as students chose between two courses titled Biological Sciences and Physical Sciences. For this purpose, both a one-year and a two-year version of each course was provided.

in its second year, human anatomy and physiology, with special emphases on disease and the nervous system.[10]

Things changed after Schwab's arrival. A year after he began to teach the sequence, the course staff issued a fresh declaration: its new aim was "to improve the student's ability to think scientifically and to strengthen his habit of thinking in this way" (Coulter 1939, iii). What is more, the staff now openly criticized the teaching of science through lectures. To provide direct experience in scientific thinking, Coulter, Schwab, and the other staff members produced handouts, titled Thought Questions, which required students to reorganize findings and ideas and apply them to novel contexts. They confronted students with such questions as:

Compare heat production in a muscle with heat production in a combustion engine.
How would you go about proving that the islets of the pancreas secrete a substance which is essential for normal carbohydrate metabolism?
One gene may affect several parts of the organism. . . . True or false, and [why?][11]
Which is more "fit," a fish or a bird?

Such questions forced students to engage in genuine scientific discourse, which they carried out in the sectional conferences, now renamed discussion sections. A year later, the Thought Questions were compiled and published as a required text accompanying the syllabus, with the announced goal of strengthening *habits* of scientific thinking (Coulter 1940).

In three postdoctoral papers, Schwab went on to articulate the guiding concerns of his dual interests in science and humanistic education. These papers manifest what came to be his characteristic style of expression in classroom, committee, and corridor: a sparkling stream of defiant energy contained within banks of granite integrity.

The first graced a collection of papers on new frontiers in collegiate education delivered at an institute for university administrators in 1941. Assigned to represent the natural sciences, Schwab moved from biology to ethics and politics, claiming that confinement to their subject matter led science educators to perpetuate a dysfunctional system. The paper belittles

10. Materials for the two-year Biological Sciences course were prepared by John Mayfield, who later would join the committee that founded the Natural Sciences sequence and become one of its first staff members. This course description comes from the 1938 version of the syllabus he edited (Mayfield 1938).

11. This question reflected a key problem in Schwab's own doctoral dissertation.

training normally given to science teachers; if that training makes for good scientists, he writes, "unless supplemented, such training makes for irresponsible citizens and educators" (Schwab 1941a, 36). Since the training of scientific specialists focuses exclusively on their circumscribed subject matter, they receive no training in the ideas and methods needed for providing general education. In consequence, education "gets grudged time and little thought" (37). In practice, the objectives they support in undergraduate education become (1) to satisfy the professional jealousies of the staff members by including as much of each one's special field as the time allows; (2) to make the course sufficiently technical and detailed as to satisfy other scientists in the university that the course is indeed a "science" course; and (3) to make whatever concessions are necessary to keep repercussions and complaints from the dean of students' office at a safe minimum (37).

The narrow outlook and poor training of most research scientists unfits them for being good college educators. They begin as "sulky traditionalists," confused and insecure, who get by through duplicating courses they took as undergraduates. The best they can do for college students is "to teach everybody a little of everything for a year or so—and then a lot about some one thing" (1941a, 39). They may try to improve things by adopting new media, such as visual aids and streamlined textbooks. Only when bothered by conspicuous omissions in their syllabi do they face a need to utilize criteria of selection. Those criteria, however, are inconsistent and contradictory; they lack a coherent rationale to justify what should be included and excluded. Such teachers have paid attention to the subject matter of education but ignored its purpose: the education of a human being (42).

To find proper criteria for what should be included and excluded, Schwab continues, one must consider the species characteristics of humans. In this effort, he would focus on their social character, their capacity for "syntactical communication," and their quest, beyond mere survival, for a state called "happiness." He further observes that the clients of our educational system are "potential citizens of a democratic state" who need to be taught how to deliberate wisely about technologies based on science. However, "to choose thoughtfully *among* several technological methods requires a certain kind of knowledge of them all, not of one" (1941a, 45). This fact poses a burning dilemma for science educators: "It is not knowledge of the subject matter of one specialty which permits reasonable choice of methods and means; it is knowledge of all specialties. And no man can master the content of all the sciences and technologies" (45).

This problem appears most acutely when one beholds specialists striving to understand one another. "Under the present system of training specialists, the effective cooperation, say, of an entomologist, an economist, and a mechanical engineer in the solution of a national problem . . . is literally impossible" (1941a, 45). Their communication requires the guidance of an additional person who is not a specialist but who possesses "knowledge of what the sciences are, not knowledge of their content" (46). It is not the content of the sciences, then, but their natures that the citizen must know—"what they are good for and what their methods are" (46). In biology, for example, such a curriculum would not teach the classification of invertebrates from phylum to order but would instead invite the student to consider the act of classification as one of the basic activities of the human intellect.

The paper goes on to name other educational targets: promoting wisdom in the selection of *ends* of action; promoting justice and equity; assessing sources of information. It also names rhetorical skills: discerning the character of an argument when reading; expressing oneself with clarity, persuasiveness, and civility; and thinking analytically and critically. Finally, it includes a set of moral virtues: justice, temperance, prudence, courage, and wakefulness. The mandate to cultivate these powers, Schwab concludes, presents "not *oughts* or *shoulds,* but *musts* if a democratic human society is to survive" (1941a, 52).

While the 1941 curriculum paper focused on the failure of science education to impart the nature of several sciences, a companion piece in *Bios* that year stressed the failure of biological education to impart the ingredients of rational value judgments. This piece faults science survey courses for not showing the inadequacy of the materials of science as guides to human action. After making a clear-cut distinction between knowledge of means and knowledge of ends and showing that the expertise of science is limited to the former, Schwab reviews a series of inadequate theories held by scientists regarding the evaluation of human goods. One, the "PROTOPLASM THEORY OF ETHICS," holds that all activities can be judged the same way that protoplasmic movements are made, as positive reactions to sources of energy and adjustments to reduce environmental irritants to a minimum. A second, the "YOUR OPINION IS AS GOOD AS MINE theory, or the *Democratic Evasion,*" refuses to give humans credit for having any better machine for making ethical judgments than a monkey has. The third theory follows the phrase, "the greatest happiness for the greatest number"— in Schwab's words, "it is a good phrase . . . but unfortunately, it goes no further. It does not constitute a workable ethical principle because it still leaves us with the problem of defining happiness and choosing between conflicting ideas of what constitutes happiness" (1941b, 91, 93).

The paper sums up these surveys with three points:

1. Ethical judgment is essential for all action.
2. Direct observational data have not (and probably cannot) supply a basis for an ethical principle.
3. Ethical judgments, to be useful and defensible, must be articulated and assessed on a rational, not intuitive or emotional, basis. (1941b, 94)

From these points, Schwab sketches a four-part schema for college biology courses. First, he asserts, they need to deflate the "ain't science wonderful" balloon by puncturing the invidious notion that science is a body of verified facts while philosophy is merely armchair speculation, which means conveying

> the plain truth about science—that the most useful aspect of scientific knowledge lies not in its body of organized fact, but in its generalizations and its well-constructed and well-tested theories. These generalizations and theories depend upon the body of fact, but they also depend (and equally) upon intellectual tools which are common both to science and philosophy. (1941b, 95)

Second, Schwab explains, biology courses can convey this truth by replacing an authoritatively presented compendium of findings with descriptions of experiments, letting students learn the roles of imagination, deduction, and generalization for themselves. Indeed, give a student the data, but let the student work out the conclusions. Then, "give him the conclusions, but let *him* work out the appropriate generalizations. Let *him* apply generalizations . . . to the end that he discover for himself the value—and the dangers—of the generalization" (1941b, 95).

Third, instead of evading opportunities to handle matters of controversy, Schwab argues that biology teachers should present controversial issues in the classroom, on such topics as state-controlled programs of soil and water conservation or eugenic programs. Analyze those matters with the student to reveal "that such programs of action involve both data as to means and judgments as to ends, to let him see what ethical principles must be used to decide the issue, and to give him an opportunity to deduce *for himself* the appropriate application of those principles to the particular problem" (1941b, 96).

Finally, Schwab contends, courses in biology should devote more attention to the study of the human species itself, with a focus on the distinctive characteristics that make humans unique, including the capacity for reason.

The following year the country was at war. This development fortified Schwab's commitment to reconstructing collegiate education to support democracy. A bold statement in the *Atlantic Monthly,* "The Fight for Education," attacked the problem directly and presented the Chicago Plan of 1942 as a worthy attempt at solution. The article harks back to the early American college for having sought to provide students with experiences that would yield habits to serve them in their quest for happiness and their efforts to promote the common good, and it bemoans its passing: "The American college has been engulfed by the backwash of an American version of the German ideal of exhaustive, factual, and specialized research" (1942, 727). Specialist teachers have taken over the college, dictating a curriculum predicated on the twin vices of the free elective system and the major sequence, the latter being "specialization at a close approach to its worst" (1942, 728).

> Domination of the American college by these two curricular devices spells time-serving for the student and disaster for the nation unless stopped or counteracted. In a college run on these twin principles, the judgment of an adolescent—inexperienced, ignorant, and swayed by winds of momentary publicity and prestige—determines what education he shall get. (Schwab 1942, 728)

By this point, the aims of Schwab's program to transform the teaching of science were in place. They stemmed from the conviction that a proper science education was essential for participation in a democratic society. For one thing, the habits of mind instilled by intimate contact with scientific work formed a bedrock for rational discourse about the pressing problems of modern society. Moreover, given the prominence of science in the modern world, Schwab deemed it essential for future citizens to grasp how science works in order to make wise policy decisions involving science.

Those desiderata fueled Schwab's long-standing personal animus against the standard methods of teaching science, especially the recitation of a potpourri of scientific findings through textbooks and classroom lectures. Schwab solidified his conviction that to attain the stated goals of science education meant a radical shift in pedagogical means—from lecture to discussion and from textbook conclusions to texts that recorded the process of original inquiries. In 1942, as the great threat to democracy posed by the Axis powers intensified, he found an unprecedented opportunity to realize this aspiration.

Transforming the Natural Science Curriculum

Soon after the "14-comp College" curriculum was approved, Dean Faust formed a committee to reconsider the place of science in general education. For three years this committee[12] deliberated, planned, and experimented—a moratorium of sorts, during which Schwab published nothing, and the Biological Sciences syllabus, revised annually the preceding decade, stood still.

The committee members agreed on devising a course to impart nontrivial understanding of scientific method, so they were startled to discover that they held radically disparate views of what they had assumed to be a common methodology in natural science. At such a juncture, others could readily have abandoned the quest. "The level of goodwill was so high in the group, however, that rather than beg the question of the nature of science or disband in mutual dissatisfaction," Schwab recalled, the committee members proceeded to engage this difficulty as an interesting problem in the philosophy of science (McGrath 1948, 71–72).

Their explorations, carried on for months, brought them the following insights regarding methodological statements:

1. "Many statements which had earlier appeared to us as meaningful now became visible as mere aphorisms, or as statements so general as to be largely meaningless without extensive qualification and specification."
2. "A great many other statements were seen to be true if carefully restricted, but to be grossly misleading if taken as sole truths, or as referring to the whole or the most important part of science. Conspicuous among them were statements which characterized science as: the classification of facts (Pearson); knowledge of antecedent-consequent relations (Mill); precise measurement (Kelvin); laws of

12. Veterans of the old general education courses in Physical Sciences and Biological Sciences, the committee members included Malcolm Correll, Benson Ginsberg, John Mayfield, and Aaron Sayvetz; Schwab was appointed chair.

nature or empirical generalizations (nineteenth-century physicists); knowledge of sufficient and necessary causes (Bernard); knowledge of forces as 'causes' of phenomena (Newton); knowledge of the parts of the whole under investigation (Mill, other neo-Comteans, and other adherents to the doctrine of a 'natural order' of sciences always read in one direction only, namely, social science, psychology, biology, chemistry, physics, mathematics)."

3. "There is not one scientific method, but several, differing certainly from field to field, and even, in many cases, from problem to problem."

4. "Even a thoroughgoing and systematic single doctrine is misleading or meaningless unless taken in conjunction with a number and variety of examples. Examples if sufficient in number and variety, can indicate limitations of the doctrine by exhibiting exceptions to it."

5. "No one doctrine on the nature of scientific method, known to us, is sufficiently complete and multidimensional as to include all others." (McGrath 1948, 72–75)

The committee's second big discovery was that the "method" of science consisted of conceptual *content* as well as activities. Continued reading of scientific papers disclosed what they came to call, by analogy with laboratory instruments, "instruments employed by the mind." These instruments consisted of "particular, explicit ideas which the long-term experience of each science had found especially fruitful as tools for the solution of its kind of problem. This notion of ideas as an aspect of method consists in seeing that scientists do not merely 'form hypotheses' in an unqualified sense." Rather, when formulating a hypothesis, scientists do not look everywhere for an idea; they look first at the possibility of specifying certain familiar ideas of proved value. The pedagogical import of this insight is that "a view of method in a science is not complete without knowledge of the principal notions which have been fruitful in hypotheses in that science" (McGrath 1948, 75–77).

Returning to the question of aims for a science program in general education, Schwab's committee rejected such commonplace slogans as "information useful to the student as man and citizen" as vague or inadequate or both. Seeking to conjoin criteria reflecting the scientist's view of what is important in science with political and ethical considerations, the committee members reframed their goal: to help students "*understand something of science as a mode of investigation, and understand some aspects of the living and nonliving world*" (McGrath 1948, 79; emphasis in original). That formulation, too, proved a nagging embarrassment since, "unlike the case of method, however, we were not then able, nor are we able now, to formulate a systematic, responsible, and defensible statement of our view of 'understanding'" (79).

The most the committee could do—and a great deal it was—was to (1) describe in general terms the behavior of one who possesses understanding in contrast with one who does not; (2) identify an apparently indispensable component of the process of acquiring understanding; and (3) cite examples of questions designed to discover its presence or absence in a student. Regarding the first of these, Schwab wrote that "a person *understands* a theory if and only if he can, *himself* criticize it, accept or reject it with reasons deemed cogent by an expert, or, if tendered an alternative theory with its defense, choose one over the other or state the impossibility of choice, with reasons deemed cogent by an expert." As an indispensable component of acquiring understanding of a scientific statement, the committee identified the need of participating in some form "in the process of examining the data, selecting and rejecting alternative notions, trying and testing, which went originally into the production of the theory" (McGrath 1948, 79–80).

The committee's deliberations held clear directives for how to pursue these goals in the curriculum. The committee's view of scientific method as pluralistic required that it be represented by varied examples of work that reported on scientific investigation. The committee's view of method and of "understanding" required that the student be given the data of scientific work and expected to synthesize them and to test alternative formulations—for which papers representing the progress of a scientific investigation were optimal materials.

These views led the committee to explore whether several series of scientific papers could be selected and edited such that each series "simultaneously:

1. Presented intelligible pictures of varied scientific attacks upon a variety of scientific problems.
2. Displayed the development and varied application of several of the conceptions which have proved fruitful in hypotheses in the several sciences.
3. Unfolded a coherent statement of current or near-current views on the scientific problems treated.

4. Constituted, in respect of vocabulary, adequacy of description of phenomena treated, syntax, and so forth, materials intelligible to the student, yet sufficiently rich and complex to be appropriate to the process of 'participation.'" (McGrath 1948, 82)

The committee proceeded to conduct a library search for such materials and subjected them to trials for two years. Some materials were found successful enough to warrant further search; others were abject failures. Testing and replacement continued for two more years; the first preliminary edition of papers was initiated in 1945. Writing in 1948, Schwab noted that "the search for replacements goes on" (McGrath 1948, 83).

The course that emerged from these deliberations departed radically from the customary science course by dispensing with lectures and textbooks entirely. In their place it substituted three hours per week for discussions and two for laboratory work. For course materials it substituted research papers, monographs, and chapters that represented the sciences by means of problems. It also provided a set of queries and problems designed to draw the papers together and to show students how to pursue inquiry in natural sciences. The experiment in a proto-Natural Sciences course continued until Dean Faust convened a new committee in 1945 to assess the damage.[13]

The 1945 committee, which ran for two years, continually grilled Schwab and other staff members on the progress of the natural science experiment. The committee assessed the curriculum in two areas: its contribution to the goals of general education and its "adequacy as predivisional instruction leading to professional work" in the two natural science divisions. Schwab later acknowledged that the 1943 program provided excellent training in particular examples of problems solved by scientific method, but it did so at the expense of an understanding of method in general. Students were not showing the ability to apply the methods to new problems. The students' difficulties were aggravated by a piecemeal introduction to the specific problems of individual scientists, for the absence of textbook materials had left students without unifying ideas in biology or any of the broader categories of science.

As a solution to these problems, the 1945 program began to combine the fittest genetic material of the 1930s program to that of the 1943 program.

---

13. Dean Faust chaired the committee, whose other members included W. C. Johnson, E. P. Northrop, M. Iona Jr., and F. J. Mullin. Later, Iona left the university, Vice President R. G. Gustavson joined the committee, as did H. Zachariasen, and Mullin became chair.

While the two-year Biological Sciences sequence (years 13–14) continued to evolve on its own, the three-year Natural Sciences sequence (years 11–13) was reconfigured. Limited but vital textbook materials were provided to unify and provide structure to the isolated scientific papers, but the papers and methods therein remained the focus of the course. Natural Sciences 1 consisted primarily of short papers or excerpts, beginning with Archimedes on the lever and proceeding through more detailed accounts of elementary physical mechanics. Natural Sciences 2 was devoted to biology, and Natural Sciences 3 offered equal measures of physical and biological science.

Throughout these modifications, Schwab kept insisting that the sequence be neither a preprofessional initiation nor a survey of conclusions and that the courses focus not on topics but on problems. The content of scientific knowledge was to hold a status approximately equal to questions about the way such knowledge was obtained, because the goal was to produce a liberal education in the natural sciences rather than scientists. Schwab also stressed that a primary object of college courses in biology was to provide students with conscious scientific knowledge of themselves as investigators. He wanted to expose students to a variety of scientific methods, inferences, and experiments, while encouraging an appreciation of the relationships between one scientific field and another. He insisted that students learn methods not as sociological reflections, exercises in the history of science, or alternatives to be read in a textbook; the laboratory experiences and papers were to provide experience *with* methods.

Natural Sciences 1, for example, proceeded from ideas of chemical and physical change, through molecular and atomic theories, to a construction of the periodic table of the elements. Then it turned to astronomy, "a new start which appears, at first, to the student to be unrelated to the earlier unit. From the treatment of astronomy, however, the problems of motion develop, and as solutions to them, the various conceptions and relations of classical mechanics and dynamics are expounded. The concept of energy is thereby introduced and, with it, the kinetic molecular theory. This is then seen as a solution to a number of unresolved problems deriving from the phenomena of chemical change examined in the first semester" (Schwab [1950] 1992, 151). Thus students were to gain an appreciation of the "unifying function of scientific inquiry" (151).

Natural Sciences 2 was designed around three unanswered questions central to the biologist's activity, meant for continual examination: (1) What is causation? (2) What kind of understanding is obtained by studying wholes through their parts? and (3) How can a biologist critique the representation of individuals as members of particular classes?[14] The curriculum identified three substudies in biology: ecology in systems, evolution of species, and development of individuals.

The Natural Sciences 2 sequence began with Harvey's classic on the circulatory system, followed by increasingly sophisticated accounts of the same subject. A segment called Syndromy traced increasingly knowledgeable accounts of glandular disorders. Other segments focused on specific and general topics within the substudies, such as papers on the embryonic development of the eye and on animal differentiation in general. The final segment studied theories of evolution beginning with Mendel and Darwin. Natural Sciences 3 continued in this pattern, on the physical side with a protracted study of the evolution of theories of light from Newton through Roentgen and Einstein, and on the biological side with a capstone study of human beings, including readings on psychology and perception.

The Natural Sciences sequence as a whole was designed to fit within the broader College program of liberal education. It sought to promote understanding of the sciences as vehicles of prediction and control for practical purposes. It utilized a variety of subjects and inquiries in order to yield an inductive understanding of "science as a process of inquiry" (Schwab [1950] 1992, 160). It instilled appreciation for limitations of circumstance and accuracy, and for diverse standards of "verification"—a sophistication that would serve students in their other studies as well. The student "learns to recognize *types* of problems, *kinds* of data, and *modes* of formulation of knowledge" and to evaluate their advantages and disadvantages (167).

Teaching a course of this sort could not be easy. All concerned were aware that for this kind of curriculum to be successful, it "must have more competent and experienced teachers than are required for advanced courses in restricted fields of specialization." What is more, "the staff should not only be interested in problems of general education, but should also be able to give future students of science the correct start in their scientific education."[15]

So much for the intellectual background needed for trenchant teach-

14. This third question built on Schwab's 1939 work on genetics as a mechanism for teaching social tolerance (Laton et al. 1939).

15. R. G. Gustavson, W. C. Johnson, F. J. Mullin, E. P. Northrop, and W. H. Zachariasen, "Report of the Committee on the Natural Sciences 1 Course in the College," 1947, p. 4, Dean of the College Papers, Special Collections, Joseph Regenstein Library, University of Chicago, Chicago.

ing. Beyond that, Schwab analyzed a wholly different set of desiderata for the exemplary teacher, qualities that he manifested in his own teaching practice.

Transforming Classroom Pedagogy

Students in the Hutchins College were scarcely aware of the key role that Schwab played in constructing their curriculum. Most of them, however, were keenly aware — at first, second, and even third hand — of his prowess as a pedagogue. As one of his former students has recalled, Schwab's "pedagogical imprint was pervasive, profound, and lasting. No student could ignore his impact; no student could ever forget his pedagogical power. He eschewed the lecture, though he could be a fine lecturer when he wished. His teaching was superbly Socratic in the classical sense. He posed problems for students" (Shulman 1991, 455).

It was indeed his talent for posing problems that turned Schwab into such an electrifying teacher. He applied this talent at every turn: in homework assignments, in classroom interrogation, and in formal examinations. As early as his first ventures into teaching in the late 1930s, he created the daunting Thought Questions described earlier. In class, he rarely contented himself with parsing particular texts. Instead, he startled the student by raising large, unexpected questions. He would ask not what the author is saying, but, as a former student recalls, " 'What is the author doing?' . . . The student would attempt a response. Then Schwab would begin his relentless questioning, pressing the student to reflect on his answer, to apply it to examples, to examine the inconsistencies among his responses" (Shulman 1991, 455).[16]

When Schwab asked, "What is the author *doing?*" he was presuming

16. As Lee Shulman recalled, "I will always remember a morning in one of his classes . . . I was nineteen. Schwab asked me to read aloud the opening passage of Book 2 of Aristotle's *Physics*. 'Of things that exist, some exist by nature, some from other causes.' . . . 'All right, mister, what is the author doing in that sentence?' I provided a careful paraphrase of what Aristotle had said. 'I didn't ask what he was saying. What is he doing?' I remember feeling tense. It took what seemed like half an hour — probably no more than ten minutes in reality — for me to understand the difference between what the author said and what he was doing that made what he said appropriate. Now, more than thirty years later, I have not forgotten the distinction, nor the strategy of critical reading that yielded up its meaning" (1991, 456).

Happily, in "Enquiry and the Reading Process," Schwab published a discourse precisely on his model for teaching that very Aristotelian text by opening with the question "What is the author *doing* in the first, short paragraph?" and offering advice on how to pursue a pedagogical strategy that departs from that question ([1958] 1978, 149–63).

that the student already had mastery over what the author was saying—a presumption that sometimes paralyzed less-capable students. For those who had "done the reading," Schwab's question was an invitation to join in an often breathtaking ride whose destination no one knew in advance. In contrast to class discussions where voice flits around the room while impulses of exhibitionism, excitement, or puzzlement jump from one student to another, Schwab's classes were marked by putting one student in the hot seat for a while and working that person as thoroughly and creatively as possible. On a humdrum epistemological text by Dewey, for example, he would suddenly blare out, "Mr. X, tell us what Dewey has to say about love!" Or on a paper about the properties of a vertebrate organism, he would ask, "What conception of the organism is the author presuming, and how might such a conception be applied to human society if society were viewed as an organism?" Nothing could stop his imagination from seizing remote domains to which the underlying principles of a test could be applied.

One of Schwab's favorite terms was *radical,* understood, he always advised, as meaning "going to the roots of things." In pressing students toward the radical reading of texts, he could be said to have anticipated by half a century what more recent purveyors of "critical reading" attempt under the label of deconstructionism. However, in contrast to those who think they have enlightened students when they have led them to divine the elements of political aggrandizement, ideological distortion, sexual ambition, or cultural coloration that inform an author's expressions, Schwab's deep reading could be glossed as positively constructivist. He guided students to discern the perspective and the method that characterize a text and then to examine the very practice by which the terms, perspectives, and methods employed in the work can be identified and how their effect upon the scope and quality of a solution can be estimated and understood (Schwab 1978, 132).

If such a learning agenda was not sufficiently intense in itself, Schwab's high-strung temperament made it downright sizzling. As Lee Shulman recalls, using different predicates, "sitting in Joe Schwab's classes fostered clammy hands, damp foreheads, and an ever-attentive demeanor" (Shulman 1991, 455). Indeed, classes from which students left the room weeping, albeit infrequent, were notorious. To some colleagues, Schwab's teaching style amounted to a sadistic practice that set out to trample on the feelings of students. That was simply not the case. Although such a pattern might at times be attributed to McKeon, for Schwab it does not hold. McKeon gave no quarter, and his arrogant and at times apparently heartless behavior, reflecting the impatience of an exceptional mind in the face of apparent stupidity, has been amply documented.[17] Schwab, how-ever, attuned himself to the emotional side of the learning situation. If he intimidated, he never abused. He railed against teachers who use their po-sitions to aggrandize their insecure egos, and he cautioned against commu-nicating, even if only through facial expressions or bodily posture, any sense of contempt, impatience, or patronizing patience — even as he criti-cized those who sought to flatter or ingratiate themselves with the young. Schwab fastened on students, with genuine affection, in order to draw them out and into a process of inquiry in ways that fortified their habits of listen-ing, reflecting, and conversing. He functioned like a coach determined to push all athletes to their personal best.

Such pedagogical behavior did not just happen; it was a matter of deliberate policy. In the same way that Schwab forced the issues of cur-ricular structure and pedagogical format by holding them accountable to defensible educational goals, so did he force the issue of the emotional texture of classroom work. To neglect the emotional side of learning on grounds that man is a rational animal, he stressed, is to perpetuate a gross misunderstanding of what it means to be human:

> It is a large-scale error of conception, arising in biology and carrying over into logic, concerning the meaning and relation of genus and species and applied to the notion of man as generically animal and specifically rational. The error assumes that the generic and specific exist as separate, insulated, determining agencies in the organism. . . . [This presumes that] man's specific rationality has simply been stacked upon his generic mammalarity and that, so situated, each competes with the other for man's time and energy. . . . [However,] man's actions and emotions are rife with reasonings (some good, some bad), just as his reasonings teem with consequences of his actions and emotions. . . . We may employ the emotional and active factors existent in student and teacher as means for intensifying and facilitating the process of intellectual education— or ignore them and suffer at the least a loss of them as effective aids, and pos-sibly an alienation which places them in active opposition to our purposes. (Schwab 1978, 107–8)

In accord with this nondualistic understanding—shocking in the 1950s, barely attained in our time—Schwab attempted in his teaching to

---

17. In his eulogy at McKeon's memorial service, one of his former students, Wayne Booth, recalled, "The first time Richard McKeon was mean to me . . . " McKeon's some-times destructive behavior was characterized for posterity in Robert Pirsig's *Zen and the Art of Motorcycle Maintenance* (1974).

foster what he analyzed, in "Eros and Education" ([1954] 1978), as *liking and respect*. These sentiments were to be based on experiences in which the teacher ignites a grateful warmth in the student by some special moment of personal recognition—and then, beyond that, by responding to different qualities of individuality each in its own way and degree. In pursuing this policy, Schwab worked to touch the distinctive qualities of as many students as he could and to draw on them productively in the course of navigating a classroom discussion.

Once he had locked the student's transference into his personality as a trustworthy mentor, he sought to let it disengage from his person and shift onto the beauty of the subject and the joys of enquiry.[18] Drawing on the model of successful parent-child interaction, he sought to redirect the erotic energy directed to the mentor as love object into intellectual pursuits that the teacher modeled and which they all could enjoy collaboratively. In this vein, he charted a curriculum for the development of Eros. In the first stage, the student's affectual energy for the teacher engenders a wish for the teacher's approval of what he or she does. In the second stage, the student discovers the pleasure of working collaboratively with the teacher; you may call this, Schwab suggests, "Eros for the remembered experience of 'friendship' with the parent" ([1954] 1978, 123). This stage prepares the student to surmount the competitive feeling toward peers originally experienced and to try the experience of conjoint work with them. The culminating phase of development occurs when Eros is shared with the objects of conjoint, creative action and "ultimately, in very rare instances, with the work of creation itself" (124).

Bringing love into the classroom thus amounted to a serious part of the enterprise of liberal education. Eros figures not only as an indispensable means but as an essential component of its ends: "The effect of a curricu-

---

18. Schwab preferred the spelling *enquiry* over *inquiry* but could not always persuade editors to comply. "For my own amusement and guidance, I distinguish the study of *enquiry* and the study of *inquiry*. The study of *enquiry* is study of what passes for the rational, logical, or intellectual content and patterning of efforts to solve problems. The study of *inquiry* is study of why people are not satisfied with some things-as-they-are, what things-as-they-are they tend to be dissatisfied with, and what behaviors for altering them come 'most natural'" ("The Hedonic Problem: A Scrutiny of Some Schemes for the Study of Inquiry (with an i)," n.d., Box 3, Folder 12, Schwab Papers). In a letter to Westbury and Wilkof, he added, "In years centering on 1958, some educational psychologists became interested in the strategies children use to solve problems. The psychologists called this problem-solving 'inquiry'. To ensure that I would not be mistaken for one of these psychologists, I took to spelling 'inquiry' with an 'e'. Sometimes this could be forced on editors, sometimes not" (Westbury and Wilkof 1978, 3).

lum whose end was training of the intellect, pure and simple, would be a crippled intellect." The aim of a liberal education is not "to destroy the mammal within us," but "to harness Eros in the controlling reins of reasonableness in order that we may borrow energy from her for intellectual purposes and, conversely, enjoy to the fullest the capacities for feeling and action she confers upon us. . . . An education becomes liberal only if Eros is moved from one successive object to another until it comes at last to the objects of the curriculum" (Schwab [1954] 1978, 125–26).

Transforming Pedagogy through Examinations

Joe Schwab's genius for creative pedagogy extended beyond the classroom. Work in the Office of the Examiner complemented his effort to teach students to think searchingly and imaginatively. As a graduate student, he had lived with doctoral students of the famous psychometric innovator L. L. Thurstone. Thanks to his mathematical skills, Schwab was quick to grasp the significance of Thurstone's psychometric models, which stimulated him to think further about using psychological measurement to chart educational progress.

His proclivities for this work were sensed by Ralph Tyler not long after Tyler joined the Chicago faculty in 1938 (Tyler 1984, 97). Tyler brought Schwab into the Office of the Examiner, where he remained until 1956. Schwab embraced the institution of a special examiner's office for two reasons. It fit his notion that the function of testing, like the function of teaching general education courses, could be performed suitably only by properly equipped professionals. Moreover, removing the examination function from the classroom teacher makes the latter less menacing and therefore more able to elicit the affection and collaborative friendship that Schwab attached to the teaching function.

In that office, Schwab labored to fashion examining instruments that tapped the special kinds of intellectual powers fostered by courses he had helped create. Students taking the Natural Sciences 1 exam in 1949, for example, engaged the problems of definition: "By *atom*, Leibig means . . . " They faced the problems of experimentation: "The experimental condition which Daniell alters directly from experiment 18 to experiment 19 is . . . " They put scientists in conversation with each other: "The chief distinction between Avogadro's theory of acids and Franklin's theory of acids is that . . . " They demonstrated comprehension of methods used by scientists in the course readings: "Galileo introduces his discussion of continua (page 33) in order to answer which of the following objections to his theory that finites can be composed of an infinite number of infi-nitesimal parts?" They examined the starting points of science: "In view of Pascal's description of his experiments, it seems likely that Pascal con-sidered the role of experiment as . . . " They filled gaps in argument: "Mayer's method of calculating the mechanical equivalent of heat is sub-stantiated most directly by which of the following parts of Clausius' the-ory?" In other Natural Sciences examinations, students examined an ex-periment, then devised new experiments to overcome its theoretical and methodological shortcomings.[19]

Even so, no matter how expert the examinations that Schwab and his colleagues invented, he never deluded himself that they were perfect instruments—least of all when administered by a national organization separated from a teaching institution. In a landmark paper on achieve-ment tests in 1950, he demonstrated that perfection in that domain was necessarily unattainable. For one thing, Schwab argued, a "valid" test of successful general education is a "palpable absurdity," because the end of general education is to cultivate human beings and citizens, and what good human beings and citizens are is open to so much dispute that no sharp measure can be consensually established (Schwab 1950). For an-other, the more valid a test for a particular curriculum, the less its useful-ness in uncovering inadequacies in that curriculum and suggesting possi-bilities for improving it. Furthermore, measures of specific abilities that have a prima facie validity must be seen as problematic, both because a conventionally "valid" test may literally test something other than it in-tends to and because students can produce correct answers to questions through routes different from the actual skill that an instrument is in-tended to measure. Even the enhanced efficiency that accrues to the ex-amination function by virtue of assigning it to special experts runs into problems, for efficiency in assessment is not properly measured by the dispatch with which a single component of the job is done.

Following this debut into national controversies on education, Joe Schwab would go on to spend much of the rest of his life seeking to up-grade the educational complex of the nation.

Transforming Educational Systems

The 1952 decision to abolish College jurisdiction over the baccalaureate degree sounded the death knoll for the parts of the Hutchins College on

19. Box 6, Folder 3, Schwab Papers.

which Schwab had labored so intensively, the three-year Natural Sciences sequence and the course in Organizations, Methods, and Principles of the Sciences. Schwab felt the loss keenly.[20]

Nevertheless, the demise of the Hutchins College program did not paralyze Schwab as it did some other stalwarts. Drawing on all he had learned from work on the College curriculum in the 1940s and responding to shifting societal needs and pressures, Schwab turned to the national and international arenas to make what became his most powerful and enduring impact.[21] Summarizing his agenda in 1972, Schwab wrote, "My activities arise from and are directed toward reform of American educational practice. The general target is the whole range of educational practice from pre-school to adult education."[22] This later work unfolded in a number of venues: raising educational standards to meet the complexities of a high-tech era; discerning pluralism in the work of scientific investigation; directing a nationwide Biological Sciences Curriculum Study; interpreting biblical texts; reforming educational institutions; and analyzing dimensions of pluralism in curricular thought.

The enhanced public role of the sciences in the postwar years comprised one area in which Schwab sought to sophisticate educational practice. In "Science and Civil Discourse: The Uses of Diversity" ([1956] 1978), he argued that the challenge was no longer merely to raise the average level of universal literacy. Although the grammar and rhetoric of the generalized liberal arts may have been adequate when all citizens spoke a common language, in an era of increasingly specialized languages, such a program no longer sufficed. The survival of democracy in an age of

20. The three-year Natural Sciences sequence and the course in Organizations, Methods, and Principles of the Sciences were offered for the last time in 1959. In a conversation we had in the mid-1950s, Joe swore he should have gone into business. That way, when you had built up something after working on it for twenty years (as he had the Natural Sciences curriculum of the fourteen-comp College), no outsider could come and simply legislate it away.

21. "If a gathering of North American curriculum theorists were asked to nominate the five most influential scholars of the 20th century in their field, it is a fair bet that the name of Joseph Schwab (1910–1988) would figure on most of the lists" (Reid 1999, 385). In addition to work described later in the chapter, Schwab's wider reputation reflected his work with the *Journal of General Education,* where he published in three issues and on whose board of editors he served (along with numerous other Chicago notables including Clarence Faust, Henry Sams, Milton Singer, Russell Thomas, Ralph Tyler, and F. Champion Ward) from 1949 to 1987.

22. Joseph J. Schwab, "Brief (and Confidential) Statement of My Interests," 1972, p. 1, Box 4, Folder 10, Schwab Papers.

specialists required some leaders to acquire intellectual powers to grasp working principles of the sciences and thereby facilitate, on behalf of hapless publics, communication among specialists speaking mutually unintelligible languages.

The democracy could be improved if the hapless publics were at least trained in principles of the disciplines. "If we dogmatically select one of several bodies of theory in a given field and dogmatically teach this as the truth about its subject matter," he wrote somewhat later, "we shall create division and failure of communication among our citizens. . . . It is no less divisive, however, if our future citizens are . . . barred from understanding each other by having been inculcated with different dogmatic views of the roots of human action or the origins of culture and civilization" (Schwab 1964b, 29). The alternative is to teach not only without indoctrination, but also with emphasis on the strengths and limitations of the structures of the knowledge taught as well as on the alternative structures that lead to alternative bodies of knowledge.

In developing a rhetoric to address curricular problems posed by this new challenge, Schwab drew on his understanding of the pluralistic character of scientific methodology that had grown out of the 1940s committee deliberations regarding the natural sciences. He went on to develop this understanding through pioneering work on scientific research and on building the science curriculum. After reviewing some four thousand scientific papers written by European and American scientists over the previous five centuries, Schwab identified six "decision points" that determined which of a small finite number of alternative patterns of enquiry natural scientists adopt. In "What Do Scientists Do?" ([1960] 1978), he articulated these decision points in terms of (1) what notions ("principles") set the initial direction of their research; (2) what criteria are adduced for judging work guided by those principles; (3) what terms they choose for detailed enquiries; (4) whether they opt for "stable" or "fluid" enquiry; (5) what phase of investigation they select for repeated examination; and (6) whether they set out chiefly to fill a hole in knowledge, improve an instrument of investigation, or exhibit virtuosity.[23] In a classification

23. Schwab initiated a course in 1960 called Philosophical Aspects of Biology: The Decision Points of Biological Inquiry. The course continued at least through 1970, when the third edition of his syllabus was printed. It included selections from Aristotle, John Stuart Mill, E. S. Russell, Auguste Comte, Howard Stein, and Claude Bernard, as well as scientific working papers on biological phenomena such as circulation and the thyroid gland.

worthy of the taxonomies of McKeon,[24] he classified the first set of options—the generative principles—according to whether they were what he called atomic reductive; molecular reductive; formal-material holistic; formal holistic; rational; "anti-principles" that appeal to "laws of nature," "causes," or particularities; or primitive principles. The criteria for assessing the principles of enquiry he differentiated as "interconnectivity, adequacy, feasibility, and continuity."

Working with the theoretical and methodological distinctions secured from critical scrutiny of the work of scientists, Schwab examined their implications for the business of curricular reform, as he engaged with two projects with institutional ramifications at the national level. These projects were the Biological Sciences Curriculum Study (BSCS), an initiative to update high school science programs, sponsored by the American Institute of Biological Sciences; and curricular initiatives on biblical study and programs for religiously oriented summer camps, under the aegis of the Jewish Theological Seminary.

The former grew out of his concern for teaching disciplines through analysis of their principles and methods, which made him a ready spokesman for what in the early 1960s emerged as the "structure of the disciplines" movement. In "Education and the Structure of the Disciplines" ([1961] 1978) and related papers, he asked what might be meant by "the structure of a discipline" and how teaching might benefit from grasping and imparting such a structure instead of simply conveying elementary facts or general conclusions.[25] In this enquiry, Schwab defined the structure of scientific disciplines in terms of the *kinds of questions* their practitioners ask and the *kinds of evidence* and ways of interpreting evidence they admit. He assumed further that the "reasonable curriculum maker" concerns himself or herself with imparting knowledge as well as arts and skills. Schwab then presented a detailed analysis of a textbook

24. But not directly based on them. In a 1980 letter, Schwab noted that McKeon had accused him of plagiarizing McKeon's categories, though not the names, for this set of generative principles, but Schwab denied that he had ever even heard of McKeon's schema of philosophical semantics before writing this essay (Schwab to Wayne C. Booth, 15 February 1980, private collection).

25. "Schwab did, of course, identify himself with the 'structure of the disciplines' movement, although he well recognized that there was a fundamental difference between his conceptions and those of the more conventional disciplinary scholars who also figured prominently. But, despite this difference in viewpoint, it was his hope that something might be achieved that could be recognized as more 'educative' than what had been done before" (Westbury and Wilkof 1978, 25).

passage on the movement of light and the limitations of the particle theory of light, in order to show how grasping the structure of the discipline of optics proves essential to purveying knowledge about specific properties of light.[26] Furthermore, he showed that knowing the structure of disciplines figures crucially in the task of cultivating certain desirable powers — the skills of applying the fruits learned from a discipline, skills of enquiry itself, and skills of reading and interpretation by which one discovers the meanings of statements in context.[27]

Schwab's BSCS work let him teach teachers what he had learned about transmitting skills of scientific enquiry from one generation to the next. In July 1959, he became chairman of the BSCS Committee on Teacher Preparation; meanwhile, a Committee on the Content of the Curriculum produced little except fear that the BSCS might propose a single national curriculum for biology. In April 1960, BSCS director Arnold B. Grobman dissolved the curriculum committee in order to prepare three overlapping versions of the same course, on the assumption that there did not seem to be a single best way of presenting biology to American secondary school students. These versions admitted differing emphases among "the seven levels" of biological organization: molecular, cellular, organ and tissue, organism, population, community or biological system, and world biome (Schwab 1963, 10–12). Schwab edited the three versions (Blue, Yellow, and Green) and supervised the production of the teachers' handbooks. Each version included texts, lab volumes, and teachers' lab guides. All three versions used nine unifying themes, with evolution at the head, for Schwab argued that notable features of living things are *products* of the evolutionary process, while many other features can be understood only as *means* and *mechanisms* by which evolution takes place (31). The BSCS project was doubtless the contribution of Schwab's that had the broadest impact: within two years, 1,000 teachers and 150,000 students had made use of the trial instructional materials alone.[28]

26. "First, structures permit us to discover what *kind* of statement we are dealing with—whether it is a verifiably informative statement, a statement designed to move our emotions, a statement of choice, value or decision, and so on. Second, structures permit us to determine to what degree and in what sense an informative statement is 'true.' Third, structure permits us to discern more completely or more correctly the meanings of informative statements" (Schwab 1978, 236).

27. The latter task clearly formed the heart of Schwab's own vocation; "his primary commitment," write Westbury and Wilkof, "was always with science seen as a certain kind of *habit of enquiry*" (1978, 26).

28. His impact might have been even more substantial and enduring had he completed and published the book on the teaching of science as enquiry which he had begun

In "Some Reflections on Science Education" (1961), Schwab estimated "the duration of a revisionary cycle in a median science to be on the order of fifteen years." Since most scientific conclusions worth knowing in 1960 would be obsolete by 1975, learning "science as inquiry" would inure students against the cynicism likely to follow upon finding that certain facts learned as hard truths in high school were no longer considered valid. In Schwab's revolutionary vision, science as enquiry might become as pervasive in American culture as literacy, both of which would be learned in school and continued independently.

The teachers' handbook enabled Schwab to promote this vision on a national scale. It acquainted students with science as enquiry through such tactics as making liberal use of explicit expressions of uncertainty and incompleteness; replacing a rhetoric of conclusions by narratives of enquiry; organizing lab work to convey the process of enquiry; and issuing pointed "invitations to enquiry." The handbook presented some four dozen such invitations to be used by teachers of each version. One set, which focused on regulatory mechanisms, began with an invitation to explore the workings of a thermostat. The next exercise went on to ask how an organism maintains dynamic equilibrium, through investigation of processes by which the liver controls blood sugar, asking along the way such questions as "What might account for discrepancies between expected and actual variations in blood sugar levels in samples from an animal's leg?", "How can we test this hypothesis?", "What data would we need and how could we get them?", and "If our hypothesis is a sound one, what should our data show? If our hypothesis is mistaken?" The third enquiry asked advanced students to compare the two models of homeostatic regulation just examined with an eye to finding inconsistent principles or for biological conditions that would make the models break down (Schwab 1963, 196–210).

Around the time Schwab was working on the BSCS biology project, he began to develop curricular materials for Jewish children through Camp Ramah and the Melton Research Center, two programs of the Jewish Theological Seminary. The Melton materials were designed to encourage free inquiry about biblical texts and to produce students who were freely committed to Jewish tradition. Schwab integrated the "tradition-centered component" with the "secular component" by recommending that the children pursue free inquiry into the reasons and evidence for Jewish traditions, guided and encouraged by teachers and other

---

in the late 1950s. Today, 350 pages of the never-published material languish in the University of Chicago archives.

adults who model the traditional virtues. The children would experience Jewish community by participating with the adults in rituals, recounting tales of Jewish heroes, and sharing conversations that embody culturally imparted principles of rational discussion. In addition, as a vehicle for character development in a Jewish context by means of collaborative intellectual activity, he provided sets of questions that encouraged students to interpret and apply biblical texts (Cohen and Schwab 1965, 23–25).[29]

In implementing the latter, Schwab returned continually to the book of Genesis to locate issues of ethical decision best suited for collaborative study. Students and teachers would discuss problems involved in applying general ethical precepts, resolving oppositions between ethical principles, translating the experience of "felt" goods into formulated precepts, and anticipating the consequences of decisions. Questions he posed in the Genesis curriculum resembled those in Schwab's Biological Sciences comprehensive examinations. For example, he would ask:

> At the conclusion of the Garden of Eden story, each of the three characters is punished for his or her misconduct. While the Biblical account does not specify the sins for which the punishments are being meted out, we can try to infer them. . . . Below are listed some examples of misconduct; indicate next to each example which character(s) if any in the story are guilty of that particular misconduct.
>
> 1. Silent assent to evil.
> 2. Inciting others to commit evil.
> 3. Yielding to the influences of an evil companion.
> 4. Rebelliousness toward an authority known to be just.
> 5. Ungratefulness.
> 6. Taking advantage of friendship to draw a companion to evil.
> 7. Disobeying God's command.

Following that set of questions, he would restate some of those types of misconduct in the form of imperatives and ask students to comment on

---

29. Himself not a practicing religionist, Schwab enjoyed the Jewish curriculum assignment as a pedagogical challenge. He offered comparable recommendations for a secular American curriculum, designed to root students in American history and tradition while teaching the habits of enquiry, in his essays on "Learning Community" (1975; 1976).

various ethically problematic situations by identifying the most pertinent of those principles. For the examples just listed, he provided the following principles:

a. Thou shalt not stand idly by while an evil is being committed.
b. Thou shalt not entice a companion into committing evil.
c. Thou shalt not allow thyself to be drawn into an evil act by the influence of a friend.
d. Render unto just authority the respect due it.
e. Show thy gratitude unto those who have been gracious to thee.

The scenarios he offered for comment were matched to a Jewish American campfire classroom of the 1960s:

Should Southern Negroes refuse to send their children to segregated public schools in order to make the fact of segregation known? (a, d)
Should the United States give military and economic aid to countries which aid us in fighting Communism, but, at the same time, viciously suppress all political opposition and individual liberty? (a, c, e)
What should a German citizen have done, if, during World War II, he was assigned to work in an extermination camp? (a, d)

Over the 1960s, Schwab devoted increasing attention to issues of curriculum development nationwide. The problems of student unrest provoked his sole book-length publication, *College Curriculum and Student Protest* (1969), a tract that tied irrational aspects of unrest to the failure of educators to help students learn to deal effectively with matters of practice. To counteract these deficiencies, he proposed new curricular structures and also new organizational arrangements — most notably, the then novel idea of utilizing graduate students and upperclassmen among the undergraduates in functions that at a later time would be dubbed "mentoring."[30]

30. This model was institutionalized at Chicago in the early 1980s with a program known as the Little Red Schoolhouse. Named after the custom of using more advanced students to coach their juniors, this program relies on careful selection and training of cadres of graduate students, who take a quarter-long course to develop skills in teaching ways to improve writing. Those who do well become lectors who meet with first-year students to discuss their writing both individually and in small groups.

Pluralistic Thoughtways and Communal Practice

The generative themes of Schwab's life as an educator developed more fully in his late years. These themes above all included the notions of practice, community, and pluralism, notions that reflected his indebtedness respectively to Aristotle, Dewey, and McKeon.

In a series of widely acclaimed papers on "the practical," Schwab expressed his concerns for sophisticating thought about practice and for shoring up the sense of community. A critique of the field of curricular thought formed their point of departure. He argued that the field of curriculum had become crippled owing to its reliance on principles and methods that were dysfunctional, an unhappy condition due to "inveterate, unexamined, and mistaken reliance on *theory*" (Schwab [1970] 1978, 287). It could only revive, and gain a renewed capacity to improve American education, by shifting from its misguided theoretic orientation to a resolutely practical one.

In developing this argument, Schwab drew on Aristotelian distinctions between *theoria* and *praxis* to identify four ways in which the practical mode differs radically from the theoretical mode. In their *ends,* the outcome of the theoretic mode is *knowledge,* whereas the outcome of the practical is a *decision,* a selection and guide to possible action. In *subject matter,* the theoretic pursues *universals,* while the practical deals with concrete *particulars.* The *problems* of the theoretic stem from identifying areas of ignorance as contrasted with what we already know, whereas practical problems arise from states of affairs that do not satisfy us or hurt us or deprive us of more than they confer. These differences are paralleled by an equally radical difference in *method:* theoretic methods are controlled by a principle, whereas practical problems only emerge slowly and entail deliberating about the costs and benefits of alternative means of resolving a problematic situation (Schwab [1970] 1978, 288–91).[31]

Applying these notions to the domain of curricular work, Schwab argued that to pursue curricular questions in a "theoretic" mode is not only to pursue a misguided quest for a perfect curriculum applicable in all settings, it is to employ inevitably partial perspectives for a question that requires understanding in its total, concrete particularity. To consider

31. These distinctions depart somewhat from McKeon's elucidations of Aristotle. For a representation of the Aristotelian distinctions that remains closer to McKeon's analysis, see Levine 1995, 106–11. However much McKeon's Aristotle influenced the Chicago milieu, Schwab's own appropriation derived initially from his "discovery of Aristotle in the course of doing some paid work for Mortimer Adler" (Reid 1999, 390).

curriculum in a practical mode requires us to attune ourselves to the settings and constituencies of a curricular plan and to transcend the inevitable partialities of perspectives by using arts that integrate a plurality of them.

Schwab delineates a number of such arts. The "arts of the practical" take the form of deliberation among a plurality of concerned parties. They serve to discover the problem in a situation experienced vaguely as problematic and to search for alternative solutions, the probable consequences of each, and their respective costs and feasibility. They extend, following what Schwab dubs the "the arts of the quasi-practical," to coping with situations that involve quite heterogeneous groupings of students, which preclude a single curricular solution, and to consulting with delegates from an array of relevant specialties—teachers in a diversity of fields and research specialists on such matters as educational psychology, sociology, and tests and measurements (Schwab [1970] 1978, 291–95).

Beyond these arts, Schwab identifies another set of operations, "arts of eclectic," designed to repair the weaknesses entailed by the inexorably partial character of "theoretic" perspectives. Those weaknesses are twofold: "theoretic" perspectives necessarily truncate a subject by dividing it into discrete disciplinary domains, and within each discipline, different schools or research programs entail views that are inherently partial. Eclectic operations repair these deficiencies by bringing into clear view the truncations and partializations in question, and they permit the serial (or even conjoint) utilization of two or more theories on practical problems.

Schwab's attention to social relations in schools and classrooms later ballooned into analyses of how to organize curricular deliberations. In "The Practical 4: Something for Curriculum Professors to Do" (1983), he capped his series of inquiries into curriculum with a proposal for an ideal way to constitute a committee on curriculum. It should consist, he argued, of eight or nine regular members, including an ingenious and creative teacher, a teacher who represents the area of schooling under discussion, a teacher representing an area remote from that under discussion, a school principal, a representative of the community, and a representative of the students. Coordinating these various perspectives would be a chair, whose job description and preparatory training Schwab described in luscious detail. This scheme of representation would ensure that the committee would consider each of what Schwab called the four commonplaces of education: the subject matter, the student, the teacher, and the milieu. If Schwab's charter were followed, the committee might avoid the usual pattern in which committee members take sides, each of which looks only to the strengths of a selected alternative, and so discards "any means of coming to decision except eloquence and nose-counting." Instead, they would engage in a "deliberative process in which all pool their ingenuities, insights, and perceptions in the interest of discovering the most promising possibilities for trial" (1983, 255).

With this identification of diverse perspectives held by components of the community, Schwab pushed his lifelong concern with pluralism to a new height. Starting with the discovery of methodological pluralism in his work on the College natural science curriculum in the 1940s, progressing to his analysis of pluralism in scientific research, to his mission to incorporate pluralism in curricular structures in high school biology, he had found now a modality of instantiating pluralism in the social organization of learning communities.

But Schwab was not yet done. His final project was to turn the pluralistic mode of analysis to the very conception of curricular structures themselves. This analysis was to take the form of a book of curricular thought, a project already initiated in the early 1970s. In this project, he attempted to reflect the kinds of analytic categories worked out by McKeon in his semantic matrices.[32] It amounted to nothing less than an elaborate schema for representing the universe of possible liberal-general curricula.

Schwab and the Chicago Tradition

Irascible, opinionated, often abrasive, Joseph Jackson Schwab became a towering exponent of communal values and the process of group deliberation. He loved the pun "Learning Community" (1975), with its allusion both to how one learns communal values and how one advances learning within a community. He demonstrated again and again that defensible curricula could only be created through a rightly constituted community, involving "the formation of a new public and new means of communication among its constituent members" (1978, 319).

A hardheaded analyst, Schwab's intellectuality was fired by a moral passion that burned brighter with age. In a 1981 letter he declared, "When one writes on history of education, there is, as far as I am concerned, a

32. Schwab's continuing connection with McKeon also appears in their joint effort to sketch the program for a new college of general education at the University of California, Berkeley, around 1972 (Joseph J. Schwab and Richard McKeon, Schwab-McKeon Committee Proposal for the Establishment of a New College of General Education at the University of California, Berkeley, 1972, Box 5, Folder 7, Schwab Papers).

moral demand that the written shall never be simply history; it must be history in the service of the betterment of education" (Reid 1999, 393). His hortatory testament to curricularists reads as more pertinent than ever today but less likely to be heeded:

> They would attend to what they perceive as evils and vicissitudes of our government and society. They would try to convince readers that these troubles exist, show the threats they pose, and suggest ways in which alteration of school practice might help ameliorate the conditions discussed. Such publications would, of course, depart markedly from the mores of "objective" scholarship. There might not be a correlation coefficient for page after page. The curricularists would, instead, take positions in debate, concern themselves with a variety of evils and problems, be founded on differing views of what constitutes the politically beautiful and good. As such, they would rouse thought and debate, among themselves and among their graduates. They would thus inject into the lives of educators an element of active intellectualism which is sadly wanting.
>
> Some curricularists . . . might question the ubiquity and intensity of competition in our way of life and ask how the schools might contribute to the lessening of it, or concern themselves with the inanities of television entertainment, or face the question of means by which schools could go beyond mere propinquity in lessening the xenophobias and racisms which afflict us. (Schwab 1983, 263)

At the University of Chicago, Joe Schwab was considered an idiosyncratic maverick. In the national context, however, his distinctiveness reflected his formation by and total devotion to the University; his achievements are unthinkable without a number of features that distinguished Chicago during his half century of work there. Of some of these, he himself wrote in a letter discussing reasons for "the remarkable collegiality which existed at Chicago": "It was, above all, *small,* by American university standards (5000 students, not forty-thousand). A second collegial factor was the residence of virtually all of us in the immediate University neighborhood. A third was the tradition of reflexion on our methods and principles—and a further tradition of rebellion" (Reid 1999, 390).

Beyond that, his work required an independent College that could support the investment of high-powered thought on the undergraduate curriculum. His later work also required the support of a Department of Education that nourished such investigations. These influences fused through the high-energy crucible of his communications with colleagues and students, causing him to radiate ideas that still illuminate terrains known and unknown.

7

What Is Educational about the Study of Civilizations?

In December 1985, following two years of deliberation, the College Council at the University of Chicago adopted a new baccalaureate curriculum. This curriculum included a novel requirement, one that was unprecedented at Chicago and to my knowledge not replicated anywhere else: completion of one of the university's three-quarter sequences in civilization. The course catalog described this requirement as "an in-depth examination of the development and accomplishments of one of the world's great civilizations through direct encounter with some of its most significant documents and monuments." Courses available to fulfill the requirement included:

> African Civilization
> America in Western Civilization
> Civilizations of East Asia
> History of Western Civilization
> Islamic Civilization
> Judaic Civilization
> Latin American Civilization
> Religion in Western Civilization
> Roman Civilization
> Russian Civilization

Science, Culture, and Society in Western Civilization
South Asian Civilization

Subsequently, the following courses were added to the list:

The Ancient Mediterranean World
History of the Ancient Near East
Near Eastern Civilization

That requirement was remarkable in many ways. For one thing, it pre-supposed that any of a dozen civilization sequences was just as valid for fulfilling that requirement as any other. That is, Russian Civ or African Civ or South Asian Civ were taken to serve the same educational purpose as a sequence in Western Civ. What is more, although presumably some important educational benefit was to be gained by taking one of those sequences, the requirement was mandated without any specification of what that benefit might be.

How was it that such a requirement came into being in the first place? What rationale might have justified a requirement for taking a course on one of the world civilizations? What considerations might pertain to such a rationale in the future?

"Civilization" in Educational Discourse

Civilization is one of those terms—like *liberation, literacy, empowerment,* or *virtue*—that functions as a motivating symbol for liberal educators. How deny a claim that students ought to have some acquaintance with the experience of civilized peoples or nations? The very first university catalog at Chicago took as self-evident that "no student is qualified to assume the high social standing, which is awarded to the college graduate, who is ignorant of the progress of the leading civilized nations of the world" (*Annual Register,* 1892/3).

The term lent luster to what was perhaps the most famous course in the history of American general education, the Contemporary Civilization course at Columbia University. Since it appeared in 1919, Contemporary Civ has served as the flagship course in Columbia's influential program of general education. The course emerged through the confluence of several factors (Bell 1966, 13–16). A *general education* component was driven by a reaction against academic specialization and the excesses of the elective system, manifested in John Erskine's General Honors course which started a few years before. Erskine's course reflected a more general discontent with excesses of the elective system. Courses in contemporary civilization emerged elsewhere during the late 1910s and early 1920s, including Alexander Meiklejohn's American Civilization course at Wisconsin and Irving Babbitt's course at Harvard. All these initiatives shared the notion of civilization as an organizing construct that countered the elective system by bringing coherence to undergraduate general education through allowing a broad range of inquiries to be woven into a single narrative.

A *civic* component was driven by the need to educate children of immigrants and, through a War Issues course which preceded it in 1918, to indoctrinate citizens about American aims in World War I. This civic component, too, reflected concerns that had been animating the general education movement for some time, concerns about preparing all members of a democratic society for fulfilling the duties of citizenship.

A *disciplinary* component was driven by the new teaching program advocated by James Harvey Robinson. Robinson, who began with a von Rankean emphasis upon objective, scientific history grounded in archival research, eventually came to believe that the historian's responsibility is to sort and interpret the innumerable facts of the past in order to explain the present and promote human progress. In Robinson's hands, this "New History" emphasized class discussion and criticism of primary sources (over and against textbooks), historical continuity (whereby transitional periods took on more importance than the isolated crises of history), comprehensive treatment incorporating the methods and findings of the related social sciences, and a primary emphasis upon studying the past with a view toward enlightening the present and improving the future (Hendricks 1946).

Although specific elements of the Contemporary Civ course changed over the years—the course "was literally born revising itself" (Buchler 1954, 57)—its basic educational rationale remained constant. This basic rationale was to enable students to consider "the insistent problems of the present" by means of identifying both their roots in the past and their practical ramifications in contemporary life and discourse: problems such as nationalism, war and peace, public opinion in democracies, production of wealth, distribution of income, and distribution of educational opportunities.

Although over the decades Columbia's "Civ" symbol has rallied allegiance to the cause of general education, the use of that symbol as an orienting motif has varied. Indeed, at the University of Chicago, the term was never used, as it was at Columbia, to mediate an entrée into contemporary civic issues. What is more, assumptions about what is educational about a civilization course have shifted dramatically at Chicago. The shifts are gradual, but breaking points are easy to discern. Five phases appear.

1931–42: A Humanities requirement took the form of a civilization course that represented selected high points of Western cultural development.

1948–58: A History of Western Civ requirement signified the wish to include a specifically historical perspective within the integrated four-year program of general education.

1958–66: A number of non-Western Civ courses were developed as a result of the University's Comparative Civilizations Project.

1966–86: Students in the Collegiate Division of the Social Sciences (and only they) were held both to the Western Civ sequence and to one of the non-Western Civ sequences.

1986–98: Western Civ became one among a dozen options to fulfill a three-quarter requirement of a course in a civilization, any civilization.[1]

Civilizational Studies at Chicago

THE HUMANITIES COURSE OF THE 1930S   As taught in American high schools and colleges from the close of the Civil War through the turn of the century, "history" consisted essentially of memorization and recitation of textbooks that dealt mainly with political and military history. Consideration of primary texts was reserved for advanced graduate students only.

Ferdinand Schevill, professor of history at the University of Chicago from 1892 to 1929, pioneered a novel genre of undergraduate history course, one that focused on the great humanistic achievements of European culture. Beginning with courses on the Italian Renaissance and Modern Europe, Schevill broadened his teaching with offerings on the History of Civilization. Like his contemporary Robinson at Columbia, Schevill had studied at Freiburg with Hermann Eduard von Holst, a scholar who emphasized the need to explore the historical record as a

---

1. In 1998, the requirement was reduced to two quarters; as expected, a few years later, the hallowed three-quarter History of Western Civilization course came to an end.

means of throwing light on contemporary moral and political issues.[2] Unlike Robinson, who focused on social issues of contemporary resonance, Schevill's historical sweep was colored mainly by humanistic preoccupations.[3]

Schevill retired in the mid-1920s to pursue this kind of historiographical work further. When it came time to implement the College's New Plan of 1931 requiring four general education survey courses, it was logical for Dean Chauncey Boucher to call Schevill out of retirement to preside over the creation of the yearlong course in Humanities. Schevill did so with gusto, although the challenge moved him to state that "the shaping of the four general education courses alone is a twenty-year job," for which "our rallying cry and slogan must be: the humanities at the college level as a job for eternity."[4]

The scope of Schevill's course was enormous, in one year surveying the history of Western Europe with respect to politics, religion, literature, philosophy, science, and fine arts, in parallel and to varying extents. In each of its ten-week-long segments (The Ancient World, The Middle Ages and the Renaissance, and The Modern World), a textbook and period source materials were studied side by side. Source materials ranged from the music of Beethoven and the paintings of Michelangelo to literary classics such as the *Iliad* and *Madame Bovary* and slides of Greek sculpture. Notes for a lecture on *The Origin of Species* suggest the spirit of this bold hybrid course: "After considering the many intimations in the thought of Europe pointing to the evolutionary concept, the lecturer will explain the biological significance of Darwin's *Origin of Species* and pass thence to its implications for religion and philosophy" (Keniston, Schevill, and Scott 1935, 263).

The University's *Announcements* described the general humanities course as using the materials of history to provide "a foundation and framework for the presentation of the literature, philosophy, religion and art of the civilizations which have contributed most conspicuously to the shaping of the contemporary outlook on life." By contact with the creations

2. Von Holst came to Chicago to become head professor of history as one of the original galaxy of academic stars recruited by President William Rainey Harper.

3. At Columbia University, the goal of presenting humanistic achievements in the West was given to a separate course that paralleled Contemporary Civ—the Humanities course initiated in 1937 and expanded into a two-year sequence in 1947.

4. Ferdinand Schevill to Chauncy S. Boucher, 14 October 1932, Dean of the College, Records, 1925–58, Box 7, Folder 2, Special Collections, Regenstein Library, University of Chicago, Chicago.

of philosophers, poets, and artists, it sought to "stimulate the senses, the emotions, and the imagination . . . while developing the student's critical judgment."[5] Presented as part of a general education suited for all students, the course had an elitist thrust: to elevate students "into an intellectual-aesthetic heritage quite removed from the mainstream of American culture" (Wilkof 1973, 20). Although it paid lip service to the presentist concerns of the New History, the energy of the course flowed into engagement with cultural masterpieces, and the point of looking at European *civilizations* was seen as that of cultural uplift.

The 1937 decision to experiment with a four-year College starting after the tenth year of high school enabled the faculty to spread the crowded humanities curriculum over a three-year period. The staff, chaired now by Arthur Scott, divided the materials chronologically, with the first year covering Western civilization from ancient Egypt to the death of Charlemagne, the second year the period from the death of Charlemagne to the French Revolution, and the third-year from the French Revolution to the present day. This plan was implemented in courses designated as Humanities A, B, and C, a sequence first offered in 1939.

Although the plan to deploy these course materials over three years allayed concerns about overloading, other misgivings persisted. Dean Aaron Brumbaugh voiced certain of these misgivings in a memo to Scott in April 1938, when he commented on the absence of unifying principles in the humanities courses and on excessive lecturing about history. Beyond this memo, two objections had been raised early on about framing a humanities course in a historical perspective. For one thing, some members of the humanities faculty, led by Ronald Crane, objected to what they regarded as a purely historicizing treatment of aesthetic materials. They worried about a reductionist outlook implied in treating humanistic expressions solely with regard to their historical context. Beyond that, they raised questions about the status of history as an intellectual discipline.[6]

5. University of Chicago, *Announcements*, 1932–33, p. 50, Special Collections, Joseph Regenstein Library, University of Chicago, Chicago.

6. Crane thought that the kind of synthesis sought in Schevill's humanities course would best be produced by journalists. As for serious academic work, he said the best histories would be written not by historians but by specialists in a discipline: economic history by economists, histories of literature by specialists in literature, and so on (Ronald Crane, "The Province of a Department of History," 1933, Box 36, Folder 13, Presidential Papers 1925–45). In response, Arthur Scott tried to defend his craft against Crane's allegations that history provides no distinctive academic expertise, inasmuch as practitioners of all disciplines do work that is clearly historical, by protesting that "professional

These concerns led to the radical transformation of the humanities sequence that was unveiled in 1942 as Humanities I, II, and III. This novel sequence, discussed in chapter 5 on Richard McKeon, devoted three full years to courses that aimed to cultivate the student's powers of appreciation, analysis, and criticism, respectively. This sequence took its place within an architectonic organization of knowledge based on the implicitly Aristotelian distinction among the theoretical, practical, and poetic sciences.[7] Within this schema, the natural science sequences cultivated powers of induction and deduction essential for securing knowledge about the natural world. The social science sequences were geared to helping students acquire powers of practical deliberation, as they worked their way through problems and arguments regarding freedom, equality, justice, and community. What the humanities sequences offered, then, was cultivation of powers needed for grasping the elements and composition of works of human art—drama, fiction, graphic art, history, music, philosophy, poetry, and rhetoric—and the diverse criteria in terms of which they might plausibly be evaluated. The capstone to this curricular edifice consisted of a course designed to provide ways of integrating the entire universe of knowledge. (This was the course initially known as Observation, Interpretation, and Integration and subsequently renamed Organizations, Methods, and Principles of the Sciences. All together, these and the re-

---

historians and departments of history are primarily or preponderantly interested in history as history and for its own sake." What is more, he added: "I remain convinced that history departments may fairly attempt the restatement of the past of mankind, and that professional historians may share in interpreting the past" (Arthur P. Scott, Notes from Professor Scott to the Committee on Departmental Objectives, 15 May 1934, Arthur P. Scott Papers, Box 1, Folder 3, Special Collections, Joseph Regenstein Library, University of Chicago, Chicago).

At Chicago the rejection of history as a discipline in its own right never reached the extreme that it did at St. John's College, whose Dean Jacob Klein justified the exclusion of history from the liberal curriculum by arguing that inasmuch as the "historical way of looking at things" is not an a priori form of human understanding but has emerged only in the last few centuries, a "universal historical approach" cannot claim any absolute validity and therefore cannot be regarded as essential in a liberal arts curriculum (Klein 1965).

7. Despite the common tendency to associate this schema with the alleged Aristotelianism of McKeon, it should be noted that the schema has deep roots in Chicago curricular thinking. Indeed, before McKeon's arrival on the scene, an official policy statement of the College Curriculum Committee, criticizing any absolute "commitment to the Aristotelian-Thomist realist view," averred that the goal of the College under the New Plan had been "to deal educationally with the whole person—with men and women as knowers and doers and appreciators" (College Curriculum Committee 1934).

quired courses in English, math, and foreign language involved the completion of fourteen comprehensive exams, which gave that curriculum the nickname of the "14-comp College.")

Although this entire banquet was understood as offering an integrated approach to grasping the fruits of Western civilization, from 1942 until 1947 the College offered no course explicitly tied to a treatment of civilization as such.

THE HISTORY OF WESTERN CIVILIZATION COURSE OF 1948

The tight, coherent organization of knowledge embodied in the 1942 curriculum excluded certain special academic interests, which came bubbling to the fore as the decade wore on. They included an interest in requiring more science for premedical and pre-science students and an interest in advanced foreign language training for potential humanistic scholars. Of all these excluded interests, that regarding history proved to exert the greatest force.

Not long after the 1942 baccalaureate curriculum was set, some faculty members began to worry that, with its emphasis on the systematic disciplines and its restriction of the integrating experience to philosophical perspectives, a major intellectual approach was being neglected—that which proceeds by examining the particularities of events and locates all achievements in a temporal perspective. Professional historians and many others at the University of Chicago worried that the planners of the Faust curriculum had not only extracted humanistic texts from their historical contexts but also seemed to deny history any status as an intellectual discipline. To be sure, the Social Sciences I course combined a survey of U.S. history with an examination of documents representing key problems and deliberations of the American experience, documents published in a pathbreaking two-volume set called *The People Shall Judge*. What is more, the Humanities II class spent its first seven weeks reading historical works by Herodotus, Gibbon, Tawney, and others, with an eye to helping students learn how to discern "the historian's aims; the kinds of data which he regards as relevant to his aims; the kinds of causes by means of which he explains the relationship of events; the sources of his evidence; and the philosophical assumptions, if any, which have determined his view of the nature of historical action" (Ward [1950] 1992, 110). And even when it came to the study of a universal discipline such as rhetoric, the course provided a historical account of theories about the art of rhetoric (109).

Nevertheless, several members of the College faculty insisted on a more prominent place for history in the undergraduate curriculum. They included such historians as J. Fred Rippy, who wanted to make sure that potential history majors received a solid undergraduate introduction to the profession, and others, including sociologist Edward Shils and biologist Ralph Gerard, who felt that historical work formed an essential part of liberal learning. These two dispositions—the preprofessional interest and an alternative educational philosophy—informed a gathering coalition that came to press for an explicitly historical presence within the Chicago curriculum.

After protracted deliberations, this coalition pushed through a bid to establish a course known ever since as the History of Western Civilization. In December 1946, the faculty authorized the organization of such a course on an experimental basis, and by 1949, the resulting course had become a requirement for the bachelor's degree. As Neil Wilkof's perspicacious account of these developments makes clear, the faculty authorized this course without any focused agreement on its concrete objectives (Wilkof 1973, 98 ff.). A variety of aims were formulated, each pointing in a different curricular direction. Was a requirement in history there to provide facts for foundational work in later work in the social sciences and humanities, as Bert Hoselitz had argued? In that case, the work should appear early in the student's course of study. Was it to provide understanding of the historian's distinctive way of looking at the world? Then why would not any set of historical materials do? Was it to provide a linkage of present-day experience with earlier formative episodes? Then it should present a panoramic view of Western civilization. Was it to serve as an alternative mode of integrating the components of the four-year curriculum? Then special attention had to be paid to how those lines of integration might be drawn. The last two of these objectives were embraced by the College Faculty Committee on Policy and Personnel, whose adopted proposal was to institute a history course designed "to acquaint the student with the history of Western Civilization from the River Civilizations to 1938 [and] to provide an historical integration of the College curriculum." [8]

8. These two general objectives were in turn divided into the following goals for the Western Civ course:

To locate major events and personalities in time and space;
To give the students a sense of the continuity of Western civilization through an understanding of the manner in which one age influences another and particularly the extent to which their own civilization has drawn on the past;
To present certain personalities, periods, institutions and movements with such completeness that the student may understand the complexity and richness that lie behind the panorama presented in the historical textbooks used in the course;

As some faculty noted at the time, these two aims were in tension if not incompatible. The former represented a wish to provide a panoramic overview of Western civilization, the kind of course by then so popular across the country that it seemed obligatory for Chicago to include it. The new course did so by including a chronological spread of topics, from the Greek polis, republican and imperial Rome, the rise of Christianity, and medieval towns to the Renaissance, Reformation, absolutism and the French Revolution, the Industrial Revolution in England, and the Communist takeover of Russia. Linkages among these discrete topics were forged through weekly lectures and a handbook.[9] This format corresponded to what was generally acknowledged as the orginary aim of the new course: "to insure that each student 'know some History.'"[10]

The integrative directive, however, posed novel problems that pushed the coherence of the 14-comp curriculum to the breaking point. The underlying contradictions came to the fore during a review of the course during winter quarter 1948. The integrative character of the course was to be assured by including faculty who were also teaching one of the other required courses. (William McNeill, an architect of the course, had himself taught both Humanities II and Social Sciences III.) It was further linked by including units that offered historicizing treatments of themes from the rest of the course, such as perspective in painting or cosmic views of time and space. Nevertheless, the way the course was to be conceptualized posed major difficulties.

The generative aim of the course, according to founding instructor Sylvia Thrupp, had been to cultivate a "historical sense," to sensitize students to processes of historical change, contextual particulars, and temporal flow. The official College record of deliberations reports that "the

---

> To invite the student's critical judgment of particular formulations of history, and illustrate the way in which other disciplines make use of history; and
>
> To place in their historical context the authors, materials, and ideas with which the students have become acquainted in other College courses.

This language about the five subsidiary goals of the course from the November 1946 modified Report of the History Committee appears four years later in McNeill's account of the current objectives of the course (Ward [1950] 1992, 232).

9. Composed by William H. McNeill, the Western Civ handbook has gone through successive revised editions and modified titles—for example, *History Handbook of Western Civilization* (McNeill 1958)—up to the present.

10. Minutes, Policy Committee, 25 April 1947, Dean of the College Records, 1925–58, Special Collections, Joseph Regenstein Library, University of Chicago, Chicago.

integrative function of History was introduced later,"[11] even if it had been uppermost in the minds of some. The question of how to construe this integrative function and conjoin it with the function of cultivating a historical sense provoked one of the richer curricular debates in the history of the College. The committee, chaired nimbly by Dean Ward, met weekly for two months and considered a wide range of arguments and positions. All concerned came to agree that it was important to fill lacunae in the student's stock of knowledge of past events and that focusing on the critical assessment of historical knowledge would dilute this purpose, which accordingly should be amplified in the Humanities II course. The key differences were articulated by Gottschalk and McKeon. Gottschalk sought to uphold history's "substantive" task by having the course present a panoramic view of the history of the West and therewith achieve integration by linking and contextualizing things known to the student from other courses. McKeon wanted the course to pursue the history of treatment of special problems and therewith achieve integration by ordering historically the materials of diverse disciplines. In the end, the two positions were conjoined through an awkward compromise: out of ten units of the course, seven would deal with problems of "general history" and three were reserved for McKeon's kind of disciplinary history. The latter consisted of units on the history of conceptions of time and space and on the development of perspectives in painting, providing some linkages with the courses in the natural sciences and the humanities, and an introductory unit on conceptions of history. The remaining discussions about the course had to do with the desired quantity of primary source materials, the desirability of staffing the course with an equal number of historians and nonhistorians, and the desirability of securing instructors who would teach the course through the full year.

In sum: if the Western Civ course was spelled *integrative,* it was pronounced "historical." If, moreover, the Western Civ course bore some superficial resemblance to Schevill's humanities course of the 1930s, its emphasis had clearly shifted from the third to the first term of the title. However else the fruits of *civilization* were presented in the other required Gen Ed courses, the course that included the term in its name had been instituted without any consideration of the nature of civilization and was conspicuously devised to embody what was repeatedly hailed as a *historical* perspective. In McNeill's authoritative words, the point of the History of Western Civilization requirement was "to find a satisfactory place

11. Ibid.

for the study of history in general education" (Ward [1950] 1992, 255).[12] With the final takeover of the course by the History Department in the 1950s, there could never again be any doubt whose course it was and what kind of course it was to be.[13]

THE REDFIELD-SINGER CIVILIZATION PROJECT   Even as the Western Civ requirement became official in 1948, some faculty were sensing that a course restricted to the civilization of the West had begun to seem a bit parochial. In the following decade, while Western Civ remained the sole civilization requirement in the College's Gen Ed program, intellectual stirrings elsewhere in the University stimulated the creation of some extraordinary new courses on civilizations outside the Western world.

Like the Contemporary Civ course at Columbia, these courses became prominent points of reference for proponents of general education in their time. And as with the Columbia course, wartime needs provided a nontrivial part of the stimulus for their creation. If the need to indoctrinate a disparate population about the foundations of democratic ideals inspired the Columbia War Issues course that inspired Contemporary Civ, so the wartime need to learn about foreign areas stimulated the studies that engendered courses on non-Western cultures following World War II. Although a few lone academics had aspired to promote non-Western studies before the war, the isolationist 1920s and the depressed 1930s did not provide a supportive environment. It would be difficult to exaggerate the impact World War II had in transforming this situation, both through meeting strategic intelligence needs during the war and in supporting the international role of the United States in the postwar period.

12. As an active participant in those events, McNeill gives a generally reliable account of the Hutchins years, including certain details that may reflect his own personal involvements. For the record, it may be noted that (1) his gloss that "what is striking about the [1942] curriculum is the total absence of history" (113) is contradicted by the inclusion of historical materials as noted earlier; and (2) his repeated assertion that McKeon and his followers denied historicity is belied by McKeon's habit of introducing nearly every subject he wrote about—from human rights and liberal education to rhetoric and metaphysics—with a historical account of their changing vicissitudes over time.

13. John Boyer, himself a member of the History Department and a later chair of the Western Civ course, has noted, "Following Hutchins's departure from the University in 1951 and the slow, but inevitable political collapse of their neo-Aristotelian rivals, the professional historians were able to declare victory and eventually take full possession of 'their' course, which led Daniel Bell in his book *The Reforming of General Education* to observe that, ironically, one of the longest surviving courses from the epoch of the Hutchins College has been the one most divorced from that curriculum's original intellectual aims" (Boyer 1999, 94).

At the University of Chicago, McKeon's decanal counterpart in the Division of the Social Sciences, Robert Redfield (dean, 1934–46), played a key role in this transformation. Like McKeon, Redfield had helped set up the wartime foreign areas training programs at Chicago; yet he quickly realized their limitations as vehicles for understanding alien cultures. At a conference in 1944, he cautioned against the temptation to reuse in postwar academic contexts the foreign area programs set up for wartime training purposes.[14] He contrasted area programs useful for educational purposes with those useful both for narrow vocational purposes and for assisting military objectives. A general education, he advised, "is marked by the ability to think well and write well about significant general ideas in the principal fields of human knowledge. . . . The object of the college is to make intelligent citizens, or to train the mind for intelligent action. . . . It must provide that aspect of higher education which is appropriate to every reasonably intelligent and adequately prepared young person" (R. Redfield 1944, 7).

Accordingly, instead of recycling wartime area studies as a basis for postwar educational programs, Redfield advocated the design of new courses about foreign areas on grounds that they might offer a fresh approach to general education, one that would introduce students to disciplines of the humanities and the social sciences and that would help them transcend the biases of their native culture. This pedagogical goal was developed further in a 1947 paper, "The Study of Culture in General Education," which held that a general education should include an acquaintance in some depth with an integrated alien culture and its language, an educational goal of particular value for Americans because they never had a well-integrated culture of their own (R. Redfield [1947] 1963, 114).[15] For this purpose, Redfield argued, the humanistic study of texts should be conjoined with the study of empirical work on human communities and should be carried out in some depth—ideally, from the first through the

14. In his characteristically gripping prose, Redfield wrote, "The sword we find in our hand today may be sharp and bright—for war—but before we plough with it let us be sure that we are indeed using it to turn the furrow and that we have indeed beaten it into a better ploughshare than the one we left rusting in the barn. . . . I suggest that we discuss how we are to organize area programs in peacetime only after we are sure why we are to do so. The ends of universities are not the same as the ends of the wartime area programs. The ends of a university are education and research. The ends of the wartime area programs are training and more training" (R. Redfield 1944, 1, 3).

15. Boyer (1999) interprets this intervention by Redfield and its sequelae as manifesting the often fruitful interaction between educational agendas and research programs at the University.

fourteen years of school—since "two years seems to me a short time in which, at second hand, to come to know a culture" (114).[16]

This educational concern joined with two other preoccupations to make the great civilizations the centerpiece of Redfield's research agenda in the following decade. One was his disposition to direct social anthropology away from the study of simple societies as relatively discrete natural systems toward a methodology that linked them with national and civilizational systems understood in some historical depth. In addition, his pursuit of integrated scholarly study of the great civilizations was fueled by a wish to promote the cause of world peace through international understanding, a motive triggered by the atomic explosions that ended World War II.[17] Redfield sought to advance international understanding by bringing what he called the "Great Traditions" of non-Western civilizations into greater comparability at the level of systematic thought and scholarly research, in the hope of "modifying in some degree the separateness with which the study of Western civilization has been carried on, and of supplementing, through a more central vision, the efforts made in UNESCO and elsewhere to develop a world community of ideas" (Singer 1976, 198). The "great conversation" between nations and civilizations required substantial knowledge of differences and similarities among various civilizations and of the common humanity underlying them—knowledge that would need to be developed, systematized, and disseminated. He defined the scholarly task as one of cultivating a new comparative approach that would bridge the humanities and the social sciences and therewith develop concepts and methods for characterizing and comparing civilizations.

Assisted by his junior colleague Milton Singer and grants from the Ford Foundation, in 1951 Redfield launched the Comparative Civilizations Project. This project supported an ongoing seminar on Comparisons of Cultures, a concerted program of scholarly research on non-Western civilizations that brought scholars from numerous disciplines together, and a related series of publications. Aspiring to produce a corpus of materials on Asian and African cultures that would meet the highest scholarly standards, the project encouraged a number of social scientists to join colleagues from

16. Redfield's strong proposal for including the holistic study of cultures in a Gen Ed program helped redirect Social Sciences II into a course on patterns of personality and culture when it was being reorganized in the late 1940s by David Riesman and his colleagues.

17. The bomb, an outcome of research on nuclear fission pioneered at the University of Chicago in 1943, moved Redfield to join Hutchins, Adler, McKeon, and others in 1946 in forming the Committee to Frame a World Constitution.

the humanities to form various committees and departments concerned with non-Western area studies. In contrast to foreign area studies programs elsewhere in the 1950s that were tied to government grants, the Redfield-Singer project aimed not at producing useful expertise but at influencing the way humans think about one another. To accomplish this, it stressed the need to think of other cultures under the rubric of "civilization," not as geographic or political entities (Davis 1985, 39). They aimed not to erect a single unified science of civilizations but "to construct a set of coordinates by which to order and evaluate existing studies, develop some new and valid methods for characterizing and comparing civilizations, and build a framework of concepts and hypotheses to guide future research" (Singer 1976, 201).

The Civilization Project got going at a time of great troubles in the University. The departure of Hutchins in 1951 and intolerably low enrollment figures in the College precipitated a determined and disruptive attack on the autonomy of the College and the general education curriculum perfected under Deans Faust and Ward. Neighborhood deterioration was one cause of the diminished enrollment and led many faculty luminaries to relocate (and even led the administration to consider moving the University itself to another part of the country). President Lawrence Kimpton sought to address all these problems by building bridges. He overcame the University's long-standing indifference to its immediate environment by building bridges with the neighborhood. He endorsed the Civilizations Project as a means of building a number of bridges: between a leading university of the Western world and regions beyond the Euro-American sphere; between the humanities and the social sciences; and, finally, between the College and the graduate divisions. In 1954, committees were set up to investigate the possibility of joint programs between the College and each of the four arts and sciences divisions.

The committee for a joint College–Social Science BA program included Singer and McNeill, who recommended that the College create a number of yearlong courses on non-Western civilizations and persuaded the committee that such courses could be an important part of a liberal education. The committee's report to the College faculty defended this point by arguing that courses on non-Western civilizations "would, we believe, not only familiarize the student with a civilized tradition other than his own, and thus permit him to glimpse the world and his own civilization as others see them, but might also enable him to understand his own cultural heritage by comparing it with another." To start with, the committee recommended the creation of three new courses — on Far Eastern, Indian, and Islamic civilizations. These courses were to be modeled on the Western Civilization sequence, aiming for "strategic selection" and thematic unity rather than "comprehensive coverage" of the civilizations as historical entities, and they would rely heavily on the discussion of primary texts (Davis 1985, 46–47).

Although this proposal aroused some controversy, the deans of the College (Robert Streeter) and of the Social Sciences Division (Chauncy Harris) strongly supported it, and Streeter secured a crucial grant from the Carnegie Foundation that helped provide materials and staffing for the courses. The courses, first offered in 1956–57, distinguished themselves from foreign area courses being introduced elsewhere by following Redfield's assumption that India, Islam, and East Asia were best studied as civilizations, that is, as organic unities of large scale characterized by distinctive cultures and forms of social organization. This assumption challenged the creators and teachers of those courses to portray each civilization as a coherent entity in ways that nevertheless did some justice to their internal complexities. Thus, in the course Civilization of India, students learned that the dominant norms of Hindu culture were *dharma* (social propriety), *artha* (economic and political success), and *kama* (sexual love), yet that other hallowed norms in that same culture involved "a complete negation or rejection" of those dominant norms, in the words of one of their readings (Edgerton [1942] 1957, 398). Students of Islamic Civ read texts by Arab scientists as well as Sufi mystics, and they delved into analyses by specialists in history, literature, theology, and the social sciences. The challenge of representing civilizational complexities could be met only by engaging scholars from numerous disciplines. As time went on, the internal complexity of the courses came to be balanced in some cases by incorporating a diversity of holistic interpretations of the civilization in question.[18]

In 1958, the College changed once again its requirements for the baccalaureate degree. At that time, the Gen Ed curriculum was reduced from fourteen to ten yearlong sequences, of which eight were required. Western Civ survived the cut. The non-Western Civ courses were acknowledged as electives and proved successful. They offered an opportunity for colleagues from various departments and divisions to collaborate on a common teaching enterprise. They illustrated the benefits to the College from involving faculty who previously were limited to teaching graduate

18. Adding this further dimension of complexity marked the reorganization of the Indian Civilization course by McKim Marriott in the mid-1960s (Davis 1985, 50).

programs. They attracted a large number of enthusiastic students.[19] The success of these courses and subsequent civilization courses on other regions provided a wealth of curricular components that would be eagerly appropriated in the curricular reorganization of the mid-1960s.

THE SOCIAL SCIENCES COLLEGIATE DIVISIONAL REQUIRE-
MENT OF 1966   The reorganization of the College under Provost Edward Levi into five collegiate divisions made mandatory the restructuring of the Gen Ed requirements. The language that mandated this new structure stipulated that all students matriculating in the College should be held to "a year in some common," and that additional Gen Ed requirements would vary by division. Dean Booth and some of his colleagues responded to that challenge by devising a "vertical curriculum." It entailed utilizing six quarter courses as a double sequence in the first year, designed to challenge and provoke students into critical self-reflection; the remaining six courses were parceled out as two-quarter sequences for each of the remaining three years, dealing with aesthetic judgment, practical judgment, and integrative work, respectively. When that proposal was shot down even before it came to the floor of the College Council, what remained was a reversion to the simple plan of the 1930s: one three-quarter sequence in each of the four academic divisions of the University.

This situation left each collegiate division free to manufacture its own second year's work in general education, what became known as the "second quartet." The Social Sciences Collegiate Division chose to invest its four courses with a positive intensity: rather than a little math and a little foreign language, it recommended two years of work in *either* math *or* foreign language. What is more, it took advantage of the rich array of offerings in the non-Western Civ area by asking all its students to complete a year's work both in the History of Western Civ and in a non-Western Civ sequence—a formal realization of the suggestion first broached by the Social Science–College BA committee a dozen years earlier. That requirement, in turn, put pressure on faculty to keep staffing old and adding new non-Western Civ courses. The courses in East Asian, South Asian, and Islamic Civ were supplemented by courses in Russian Civ, Latin American Civ, and African Civ. As the College grew (and to accommodate the diversity of interests of History Department faculty), enrollment pressure on the Western Civ course forced the faculty to come up with other

19. The latter included the future composer Philip Glass, who has traced the inspiration for his landmark opera *Satyagraha* to his work in the Indian Civilization course.

courses that could be taken as alternatives for fulfilling the Western Civ requirement. These courses included American Civ; Science, Culture, and Society in Western Civ; and Religion in Western Civ.

Although no one seemed to notice it at the time, the new curriculum introduced a double shift in status of the Western Civ course that decisively altered its educational significance. For one thing, the deliberate placement of the course, and its companion non-Western Civ requirement, at a point in the curriculum preceding a concentration in the social sciences forever changed its function from that of pretending to provide a capstone integration to that of providing an empirical foundation for focused theoretical and comparative work of some sort. Its placement alongside a non-Western Civ course, moreover, signaled a wish to have students reflect on Western Civ in a comparative perspective. The meaning of the History of Western Civilization thus shifted from the 1948 emphasis on conveying a sense for historical change within a *temporal* dimension to an emphasis on the *particularistic* character of the *Western* experience and how that compared with "non-Western" experiences.

THE COLLEGE CIVILIZATION REQUIREMENT OF 1986   Two decades after the curricular changes of the mid-1960s, the College faculty undertook a yearlong review of its teaching programs. The report most relevant to the civilizations requirement was that of the Task Force on Historical and Cultural Studies. Chaired by Bernard S. Cohn, a founding participant in the Indian Civilization course of 1957, its other members came from various fields: anthropology, art history, East Asian studies, European history, molecular biology, philosophy, Russian history, and United States history. Cohn's task force argued, in tones iterating the earlier historians' revolt that led to the Western Civ course, that students in the College typically learn formal analysis, reasoning, and criticism in abstracto; they examine literary texts and problems "in terms of the everlasting aspects of genre, formal excellence, and the timeless schemes of criticism. . . . They often study intellectual positions as if human thought had little to do with time or its cultural genesis." Moreover, they claimed, "even the best educated freshmen enter the University of Chicago with a definite conceptual bias for the world as seen by their own subculture and by their own times." Accordingly, in order to make students aware of their assumptions and biases, "we contend that all undergraduates should be exposed to the study of people who live in cultures other than their own and at times other than their own." Without arguing the case that the existing Western and non-Western Civilization courses actually accomplished this perspective-sensitizing function, they noted that under the arrangements of the 1966 curriculum—which required students in the social sciences to take Western and non-Western Civ courses but enabled students in other collegiate divisions to bypass such requirements—some 35 percent of students were graduating from the College without taking courses in *either* Western or non-Western civilization. In sum, the task force stated, "we are convinced that an historical and cultural perspective is an essential component of a liberal arts education and one to which *all* of our students should be exposed" (Levine 1984, 83–85).

The report did not insist on a specific way of remediating that deficiency. It sketched suggestions for doing so, interlarded with concerns about the chronic staffing crisis in teaching Western Civilization, the value of having non-Western Civ courses taught by staffs rather than by a single faculty person per quarter, and the difficulty of "asking faculty who are generally already overburdened and overcommitted" to design new core courses that could acquaint students with "the historical and cultural point of view" (Levine 1984, 87). Ensuing curricular deliberations about the problem identified by the task force led to the requirement described at the beginning of this chapter.

The 1986 Civ requirement, then, proceeded from a report that offered only a single reason for requiring students to take a course on some people who live in a culture or a time other than their own: the need to help them overcome the biases of their native subculture. Gone was the Redfield-Singer language about the importance of taking time to know the Other empathically and therewith to arrive at an expanded conception of humanity. Instead, the task force report dealt solely with the challenge of knowing the Self more critically, by forcing the student "to confront the peculiarities of his own conception of the world by confronting the peculiarities of other such conceptions" (Levine 1984, 84). Furthermore, the report quietly abandoned altogether earlier assumptions about civilization—that "civilized" nations had produced something of special human significance, that Western civilization had produced something especially important, or that knowledge of Western Civ should be balanced by the introduction to a non-Western Civ. It simply proffered the radical presumption that the study of *any* culture or period in some depth would do the job of making students aware of their biases by exposing them to a different cultural context, alien in space and/or in time.

Beyond that, the requirement to study a "civilization" appeared without any specification of what the term actually referred to. The door was left open for continuing faculty deliberations about that question, deliberations that stimulated some rich curricular thought but reached no clear point of consensual resolution.[20] This situation did not improve with the curriculum changes of 1998, which conjoined a civilization requirement—reduced to two one-quarter courses—with a similarly reduced humanities requirement. Both components were justified by language regarding the value of "learning how to appreciate and analyze texts intellectually, historically, and aesthetically . . . [and to study them] within a specific cultural and chronological frame" (University of Chicago 2001, 2). The resulting curriculum offered more elective freedom and sparked a major new development associated with the deanship of John Boyer—opportunities for study abroad that conjoined intensive foreign language study with a civilization course in a number of venues, from Paris, Barcelona, and Vienna to Tokyo, New Delhi, and Durban—a development quite in harmony with Robert Redfield's vision for such courses.

However, the practical need to move further toward a distribution requirement precluded a serious effort to consider anew the rationale or guidelines of the general civilization requirement. It is true that the 1998 curricular reforms precipitated a good deal of rethinking and reflection about the idea of civilization *within* individual staffs, where the design of such courses must be anchored and implemented. In the words of one participant, "The process that led to the creation of the new History of European Civilization sequence is a good case in point. The new course was born after 1998 out of countless meetings of the Europeanists over two years, meeting and debating what we thought 'Europe' was and how we might best teach 'Europe's' history and culture to first- and second-year students in the College. The U.S. historians have also gone through a major rethinking of how they approach the teaching of American Civilization."[21] But the new situation, reflecting an undergraduate enrollment substantially larger than the College of 1948, made it difficult to discourse about the civilization requirement as such. The old rhetoric remained in the catalog—to provide "in-depth examination of the development and accomplishments of one of the world's great civilizations through direct encounters with some of its most significant documents and monuments"—but there were no transparent grounds for opposition when the College administration subsequently approved a sequence initially titled Race, Slavery, and Colonization as an option for fulfilling the civilization re-

20. The deliberations included a three-day conference organized by John Boyer and Julius Kirshner in June 1987 and a number of committee meetings on the Civ courses in subsequent years.

21. John Boyer, personal communication with author, December 2005.

quirement. By that point, the idea of formulating a coherent Collegewide rationale for the study of civilizations seemed out of reach.

So, What Is Educational about the Study of Civilizations?

The educational meaning of the term *civilization* has thus varied a great deal, and courses bearing it in their title have served an array of educational purposes.

At Columbia University, the faculty followed the sense of the term, more common among German writers, that associated civilization with advanced technology and complex societal arrangements. Contemporary Civilization thus offered a vehicle for conveying ideas needed for today's citizens to cope with an array of presenting economic, social, and political issues.

At the University of Chicago, the faculty in Schevill's Humanities course employed the term in its Anglo-French sense: civilization as a repository of outstanding human creative expressions. However much lip service Schevill's course gave to preparing students for civic life, the central thrust of that course was to promote cultural uplift through engagement with masterpieces of classical antiquity and Western Europe.

If the civilizing mission of the Schevill course was to uplift unwashed Americans by exposing them to monuments of Western culture, the *History* of Western Civilization course sought to ground products of ostensibly universal excellence in the particularities of time and space. In this incarnation, a civilization course served to provide a frame for locating historical specificity and to introduce (what its proponents call "the") historical perspective.

The expansion of vistas occasioned by World War II led to new uses of civilizational studies for the goals of international understanding. For a visionary like Robert Redfield, the scholarly study of non-Western civilizations offered a royal road to the accurate and empathetic representation of the jolting differences that clothed an underlying common humanity. This vision informed the early non-Western Civ courses that his Comparative Civilizations Project engendered.

For students in the Social Sciences Collegiate Division from 1966 on, the coupling of a non-Western Civ requirement with Western Civ imparted to the latter a pointed new meaning. For now it stood to provide a way to appreciate the distinctiveness of their home culture, and the center of gravity shifted from the first to the middle term, *Western*.

As the humanitarian ethos of the post–World War II years turned into the debunking ethos of the postliberationist years in the 1980s, faculty energies turned inward once again. The point of the Civ requirement came to be to see one's own biases. What is more, for many members of Chicago's multiethnic student body, the Civ requirement came to serve as a means for reinforcing their subcultural identities, at a time when students increasingly came to associate in particularistic ethnic enclaves. Indeed, the debunking process could extend to transforming the rationale entirely into a study of oppression and subaltern creativity tout court.

Three reasons support an effort to consider the rationale for the Civ requirement afresh. First, the lack of a clear rationale for requiring students to "take any Civ course" affords administrators no intellectual mandate for staffing the courses, faculty no guidelines for constructing them, and students no criteria for evaluating their experience in them. Second, developments both in scholarship on civilization and in the civilized world in recent decades bring interesting new material to this table. Third, throughout these developments, one finds little discourse about the concept of civilization itself, and some faculty have longed to add that to the curricular discourse about the Civ requirement.

In considering grounds for having students engage in the study of a civilization as such, the work of Robert Redfield offered a fruitful resource at Chicago.[22] Redfield invited us to consider different ways in which we might think about civilizations, a mental process he distinguished both from gaining facts about a civilization and from becoming acquainted with one. He drew particular attention to two constructs relevant for thinking about them: civilizations as societal structures and as cultural structures. Paralleling work in the 1950s by Talcott Parsons and Alfred Kroeber to stabilize a distinction between social systems and cultural systems (Parsons and Kroeber 1958), Redfield differentiated between societies and cultures.[23] At the microscopic level, this meant a distinction between systems of statuses or roles and systems of ideas; at the macroscopic level, it meant a distinction between systems of communities and systems of traditions. Essential for grasping the character of that subclass of societies or cultures we call civilizations is the demand to understand them in "historic depth," as "historic structures."

Redfield's challenge to scholars to evolve ways of thinking suitable to the

---

22. One of these statements introduced the very first non-Western Civ course offered at the University of Chicago in 1956. Revised versions of these pieces were to have opened a projected book on civilization, which his untimely death in 1958 precluded; they were published posthumously in the first volume of his collected papers (M. P. Redfield 1962, 364–414).

23. The prominence of this distinction is one of several aspects of Redfield's work on civilizations that shows continuity with his work on Yucatan in the 1930s (Singer 1976).

scholarly representation of civilizations was taken up by a network of scholars owing something to another Chicago connection. In the late 1940s, the distinguished medieval historian Benjamin Nelson sojourned at the University, where he taught in the Social Sciences and Western Civ courses.[24] Thanks to that experience, he encountered the work of Max Weber, which changed his life. In later years, Nelson would define his mature work as an effort to go beyond Weber in creating a "depth-historical" representation of world civilizations.[25] This work led him to the leading comparative civilizational scholars of the time, Pitirim A. Sorokin and Arnold J. Toynbee, indeed to associate with them in a small Europe-centered network devoted to civilizational studies. In the 1960s, Nelson worked to revivify that network through what became known at the International Society for the Comparative Study of Civilizations (ISCSC). Over the years, the ISCSC has grown into an organization with some four hundred members in more than two dozen countries, an annual conference, and a quarterly journal. In the work of this organization, Redfield's call for the critical development of constructs with which to think about civilizations has been responded to with éclat.

At the 1957 Chicago conference convened to discuss the problems of an undergraduate course on the civilization of India, Redfield alluded to what may be taken as a specific educational challenge linked to any credible course on a civilization. "To think about a civilization," he advised, "I need thoughts larger than the sum of the particular facts, through which we may hold together what would otherwise fly apart into innumerable and unrelatable elements. . . . Can the mind take hold of so large, complex, and changing a thing as a civilization?" (R. Redfield 1957, 6, 10). In proceeding to provide mental constructs that enable us to think about civilizations, Redfield in effect outlined an agenda and format for courses on civilizations suitable for general education purposes. They should convey something of the panoramic sweep of sociocultural systems extended in time and space. They should conjoin examination of particular episodes and texts with large concepts that represent something of the overall iden-

24. Something of the impact of his three years at Chicago can be gleaned from a letter Nelson wrote a few months after arriving there: "In Chicago, nothing but the fundamental questions are raised. Indeed, they are raised with such insistence and frequency, that occasional flights into solitude become imperative, if only for the pasturing of the soul. . . . The campus bristles with opinionated men who are ready at a moment's notice to fly through the interstellar spaces" (Huff 1981, xii).

25. A memorial volume of essays in Nelson's honor thus bears the title *Civilizations: East and West* (Walter 1985).

tity and form of the civilization. And they should involve the disciplinary contributions of both humanists and social scientists. These ambitions do not describe the usual mental practices of present-day students, whose culture reinforces a myopic preoccupation with moments and fragments of immediate experience, nor of the typical course taught by the usual academic specialist.[26] But they might contribute to a defensible rationale for mounting a Civ requirement.

Another line of thought that Redfield pursued may broach another kind of rationale and curricular guideline. This line of thought reflects his studied concern for delimiting civilizations from other human entities. Noting that many anthropologists have used the terms *civilization* and *culture* interchangeably, Redfield pointedly reserved the singular form of the term to designate a condition of human living that emerged only as a late period in the long human history and the plural form to designate a subclass of societies or cultures. After reviewing the criteria of civilization proposed by V. Gordon Childe and others, criteria including cities, writing, role diversification, and specialized intellectual culture, Redfield— rather than fix on a single criterion or set of criteria as markers of this subclass—proffered the formulation "that any society or culture is civilized to the extent and in the respects that it has [these] characteristics" (M. Redfield 1962, 405).

Calling attention to the genesis of civilization and civilizations directs our attention to a formidable literature, which courses on civilization, including those currently taught at Chicago, tend to ignore. This literature includes the work of archaeologists and anthropologists, such as Childe, Wittvogel, and others, who problematized the origins of civilization in Euroasiatic and American prehistory. It includes the recently recovered work of Norbert Elias, whose major work concerns what he has famously described as "the civilizing process." It also includes those critics of the

26. At the University of Chicago, only special administrative encouragement has enabled the continuous offering of such courses, and even there, they have been beset by chronic difficulties, not least by the need to assign administrative responsibility for these courses either to the Humanities or to the Social Sciences Division. On this perplexing issue, the exasperated sigh of Charles Judd has come home to roost: "The College curriculum departs from the ideal curriculum for general education because it is determined in its organization by the fact that the University has four divisions—an organization which was set up to serve the purposes of specialization of advanced students and the purposes of research. That the divisional organization should reach down and determine general education and control the courses given in the period of general education is a calamity" (Judd to Brumbaugh, 1 June 1937, Dean of the College Records, 1925–58, Box 19, Folder 7, Special Collections, Joseph Regenstein Library, University of Chicago, Chicago).

civilized condition, from Rousseau and Nietzsche to Durkheim and Freud, and indeed to Redfield as well, who have identified pathological or vicious outcomes as endemic to the civilizing process.

On the other hand, this literature stands to inject a startling shift in consciousness if it is seen to include the pivotal lectures that Redfield published as *The Primitive World and Its Transformations* (1953). These talks forthrightly revived the view that standards of truth and goodness have indeed advanced beyond those sustainable by precivilized people. In this view Redfield was influenced by the soaring interpretations of Alfred North Whitehead in *Adventures of Ideas* (1933), which describes the civilized state of humankind as marked by the five great ideas of Beauty, Truth, Art, Adventure, and Peace and sees the civilizing process as one involving the long-term realization of great ideas. In a searching analysis of the vicissitudes of Redfield's thought, Clifford Wilcox formulates Redfield's view of this shift away from the "automatic morality" of folk societies: "Civilization, by contrast, represented a conscious attempt by humankind to articulate a moral order, and it is this intentionally constructed order, Redfield believed, that represented the culmination of human ethical striving" (Wilcox 2004, 129). Redfield further associated this shift with a challenge to the philosophical self-understanding of the social sciences, holding that it is by virtue of being a product of civilization that the social scientist has a range of experience within which to do his understanding-valuing and the scientific disciplines with which to describe his valuations and hold them up to critical scrutiny (1953, 165).

The notion that *civilization* refers to an advanced stage of human development flies in the face of present-day egalitarian assumptions that all cultures are of equivalent value and the relativist doctrine that no defensible criteria of human achievement can be posited. To give the student resources with which to withstand the entropic drift toward relativism and correct this dreary nihilism, we might do well to provide materials on ways that civilized societies differ from precivilized societies, review arguments on the genesis of ancient civilizations, and confront a sample of the great monuments of civilized achievement from a selection of the world civilizations.

Redfield broached yet another idea on the construction of thought about civilization. Concluding an encyclopedia article on the subject (published posthumously in 1960), he spoke for the first time of "world civilization." This idea contrasts with the historic civilizations, each of which derived from local cultures that expanded and matured in relative isolation over long periods of time. Whereas each of the historic civilizations amounted to "a tradition, a reach back into history, a set of institutions and convictions resting on the authority of long-shared experience," the new world civilization "is another kind of thing. It breaks down the old local traditions; it arises not so much from tradition as from new things — science, technology, the participation of the masses in education, standardized entertainment, public life, and organized consumption. The world becomes one interdependent region increasingly characterized by a world-wide way of life that tends to obliterate what is local and traditional" (M. Redfield 1962, 414).

In ensuing decades, the question of world civilization was taken up forthrightly by scholars of three kinds: civilizationists, world historians, and globalization theorists. In the course of pursuing extended conversations regarding foundational questions—What counts as a civilization? How should civilizations be classified? How do they arise and develop? Why might they be said to terminate?—a number of ISCSC affiliates went on in the 1980s to explore the case for representing a world civilization. One of their key figures, David Wilkinson, argued forthrightly that "there presently exists one and only one civilization, appropriately styled 'Global Civilization,' after its most obvious differentia, the engulfment of the entire planet by a single network. . . . A civilizational network, once one of several coexistent such networks, has enlarged by touching, engulfing and absorbing all others" (Wilkinson 1981, 340). More recently, Shmuel Eisenstadt (2003) has launched a major new program for comparing world civilizations, and Johann Arnason has synthesized a great deal of that effort in *Civilizations in Dispute* (2003).

A comparable conclusion had been reached by an erstwhile professor of Western Civilization, William McNeill. After producing his grand overview text for Western Civ in 1948 and in later recensions, McNeill went on to enfold the other known civilizations into a single story. It was entitled (with pointed allusion to Oswald Spengler's *Decline of the West*) *The Rise of the West: A History of the Human Community* (1963). The book challenged the Spengler-Toynbee view that firmly bounded civilizations had pursued separate careers by demonstrating that the world's cultures had experienced important connections throughout history. In later years at Chicago, McNeill pioneered a well-received course in world history. Countering the determined specialisms of most professional historians, McNeill taught that the world had a single history and that its history could and should be told as part of a general education appropriate for our time. A large number of fellow historians in other institutions came to the same position: circa 1990 they established the World History Association, which supports regular conferences and a *Journal of World History*, in an early issue of which Andre Gunder Frank of the University of Amsterdam issued an elegant "Plea for World System History" (Frank 1991).

Finally, the processes of globalization became quite prominent in sociological discourse in the 1990s, such that the work of such earlier globalization theorists as Roland Robertson came to receive a new hearing.[27] Thanks to this work, notions of globality presented in vague and innocuous terms can no longer be entertained credibly. These scholars provide incisive formulations regarding specific dimensions of the global economy, political structure, social ecology, and cultural system. The cumulative work of these three groups of scholars provides a stimulating base for beginning to think about ways to include some form of learning about the world community as part of a new Gen Ed curriculum.

Martha Nussbaum (1997) has notably recovered a classic defense of one component of such thinking in the writings of the Stoic philosophers. The Stoics not only developed the idea of the world citizen, *kosmou polites*, they made it a centerpiece of their educational program. Summarizing older Greek Stoic views, she tells us, Seneca writes that "each of us is a member of two communities: one that is truly great and truly common . . . in which we look neither to this corner nor to that, but measure the boundaries of our nation by the sun; the other, the one to which we have been assigned by birth" (58). And cultivation of habits of appreciating our common humanity has a threefold benefit: (1) thinking about humanity as it is realized in the entire world advances self-knowledge; (2) freeing our imaginations from the constraints of narrow partisanship through an ecumenical perspective enhances our abilities to solve problems effectively; and (3) the perspective of world citizenship "recognizes in people what is especially fundamental about them, most worthy of reverence and acknowledgment, namely their aspirations to justice and goodness and their capacities for reasoning in this connection" (60).

Besides the humanitarian appeal of such classic formulations, we can say quite forwardly: *If the task of general education is to help students get oriented to the world of their lives as well as to develop universally human potentials, we could do no better than to find ways to acquaint them with the complexities of the one world in which they must live.* Inventing a serious course on the modern world, globally considered, would serve both to cultivate the humanity of our students and to promote their ability to func-

<hr />

27. For a valuable overview of this literature, see the special issue of *Theory, Culture and Society* 7, nos. 2–3 (June 1990), on global culture.

tion in the world at one and the same time. And yet, one can make the case that the notion of civilization must be central to any such effort. For what is happening in our time is not only the global extension of modernity but the maturation of a single world civilization which at the same time is coming to terms with the legacies of the diverse historic civilizations. Whether or not one follows Arnason in presenting this dynamic in terms of alternative positions—viewing modernity "as a self-contained and complete civilization, a self-projection of one civilization imposing its patterns and principles on others, or as a set of infrastructural innovations that can be adapted to diverse civilizational concepts" (2003, 34)—the ability even to grasp this issue with some clarity and depth might well serve as a climactic point in the case for civilizational studies.

I conclude by noting one further aspect of the literature on civilizations and find once again a point of departure in Redfield's prescient work. This point concerns the flagrant ambiguity of the term *civilization*. Because the start-up intellectual capital for the enterprise of civilizational studies came from so many diverse donors, those who sought to pursue systematic work in this domain needed to sift and sort a number of meanings which the concept had acquired. Redfield himself reviewed some half-dozen meanings of the term before settling on the one he preferred—and even then, he noted the necessity of distinguishing between "civilization" and "a civilization."

More recent scholarship has clarified the question of the place of ambiguous terms such as *civilization* in intellectual discourse. Two major figures of the University of Chicago tradition, Edward Levi and Richard McKeon, have thrown light on this matter by challenging the contemporary dogma that concepts must be univocal to be meaningful. Noting that "[it] is only folklore which holds that a statute if clearly written can be completely unambiguous and applied as intended to a specific case," Levi has pointed out that if a rule had to be clear before it could be imposed, society would be impossible, and that the process of legal reasoning proceeds by accepting the ambiguities of words (1948, 6, 1). McKeon has generalized this point to the entirety of philosophical discourse, revealing the different ways in which ambiguity can be productive, and cautioning that "we proceed as if we were faced with a choice between the univocal and the ambiguous, and we come to the discovery . . . that the univocal has its foundations and consequences in ambiguities" (McKeon 1964c, 243). In a similar vein, the literary theorist W. B. Gallie (1964) has expounded the notion of "essentially contested concepts"—concepts that are so complex, linked with changing contexts, and used defensively by their proponents that their meaning must be permanently a matter of dispute. Levine (1985b) builds on these arguments to propose an algorithm whereby inexorable ambiguities are embraced alongside processes of disambiguation. An erstwhile junior colleague of McKeon's at Chicago, Walter Watson (1985), has usefully proposed the notion of "reciprocal priority" as one means of dealing with such intractable differences, a practice in which proponents of different interpretations engage in a dialogue in which they take turns in speaking and listening to one another's interpretations. Returning one last time to the helpful formulations of Robert Redfield, we might note that his own distinctive reflections envisioned the process of education as a dialogue, with reciprocal priority as its cornerstone: education is "conversation about the meaning of life, as each person sees some part of it, on behalf of everyone" (R. Redfield 1963, 72).

III

Reinventing Liberal Education in Our Time

The task of aligning with the formidable traditions of liberal learning in the West and recasting them in ways suited to the twenty-first century calls for intellectual engagement of an order no less difficult and challenging than the most demanding forms of scholarly research. The remaining chapters set forth one way of proceeding with that task.

I begin by reviewing the universe of principles that can legitimately be invoked to animate a reinvented liberal curriculum. I then review the experience of the University of Chicago as over generations it has sought to fashion liberal curricula in accord with each of these principles serially. This review concludes by drawing on the developments described in part 2 and affirming the principle of Powers of the Mind as a plausible basis for a contemporary renewal of programs of liberal learning.

The result is a schema of eight Powers of the Mind, divided initially between those that correspond to inhaling—those capacities to take in the world of objects—and those that correspond to exhaling—the processing and return to the world of expressions mediated through an evolving self.

That curricular framework leads in turn to an analysis of various types of teaching and the pedagogical forms in which they are executed. The book concludes by analyzing some of my own teaching efforts over the past few decades that embody these educational ideas.

8

New Goals for the Liberal Curriculum

Steps to reform liberal education over the past century were driven by imaginative responses to big social changes. Some of those reforms simply expanded available inventories of adaptive resources. These new curricula were devised to service vocational specialties, promote civic patriotism, and inculcate more demanding forms of self-discipline.

Other reform efforts harked back to old ideals rooted in the classical notion of paideia. Their sponsors intended to deal with the troubling consequences of modern conditions for the development of free human beings and citizens, conditions such as hyperspecialization, privatization, mediocrity, and intellectual anarchy. These reforms aimed to promote well-rounded personal growth; critical, reflexive thinking; adherence to high intellectual standards; ability to grasp the relatedness of different fields; and heightened levels of individuality. Together, they constituted the general education movement.

Contested Principles for the Liberal Curriculum

The pressures that energized the general education movement did not spawn concrete curricula automatically. Such curricula presumed an articulation of principles that expressed what educators had in mind when they invented educational forms to promote *generality*.

A schema useful for sorting out these conceptions classifies them according to the type of particularism or specialization they are designed to counter. When they emphasize *the character of the learner,* they promote generality in the sense of regarding the whole person rather than developing some special part alone. When they emphasize *the universe of things to be known,* they promote generality in the sense of applying to all subject matters rather than to some special field. When they emphasize *the common heritage of humanity,* they promote generality in the sense of the knowledge that should be acquired by all humans rather than what is suited to particular walks of life or parochial interests. When they emphasize *the disciplines of knowing and creating,* they promote generality in the sense of embracing all fundamental skills rather than restricting attention to some particular set of skills.[1]

Each of these curricular principles can be conjoined with any of what I have called the impulses behind general education. Each of them has been tried in more than one institution.

THE CHARACTER OF THE LEARNER   Many philosophies of education, past and present, pursue the goal of creating a special kind of person. Accounts of the earliest modes of liberal learning, those of ancient China, describe the goal of liberal education in this way: to form a man suited to govern by virtue of possessing wisdom, benevolence, loyalty, harmony, martial abilities, aesthetic skills, and knowledge of ritual proprieties. A repertoire of Western philosophies, *The Educated Man,* includes essays on some fifteen such conceptions. These include what the book's editors call the Orator, the Scholastic, the Classical Humanist, the Natural Man, the Gentleman, the Reflective Man, the Existential Man, and the Scientific Humanist (Nash, Kazamias, and Perkinson 1965).

Some contemporary general education curricula have been so designed. These programs seek to cultivate a certain type of person, whether for the sake of improving society, producing more fully developed human beings, elevating culture, or securing intellectual coherence. George Allan's

---

1. This schema is cognate with that proffered by Richard McKeon four decades ago, when he described the liberal arts as "general" in four senses: "They are general in the sense of applying to all subject matters and therefore in the sense of providing an approach to any particular subject matter placed in a context of other parts of information or knowledge . . . in the sense of embracing all fundamental skills that can be acquired in education and therefore in the sense of providing a basis for any particular skill . . . in the sense of bearing on the formation of the whole man and therefore in the sense of providing a model or ruling principle for any particular excellence fitted into achievements of a good life . . .[and] in the sense of being the arts of all men and therefore in the sense of providing guidance for each particular man and each particular association of men responsive to the cultures and objectives of other men and of mankind" (McKeon 1964a, 171–72).

discourse on colleges as places in which the determined pursuit of goals can be corrupting in fact promotes a goal of this sort: to cultivate students who are capable of free exploration and intrinsically valuable play (Allan 1999). Allan's scenario projects a curriculum whose essential features include a variegated experience of the multiple possibilities for living in order to celebrate human life with all its challenges and provide students with opportunities to reshape their worldviews.

Some person-centered curricula have been built around stages of development: for example, the goal of the freshman year is to produce sophomores—students who recognize their customary thoughtways as culturally shaped and have attained some sense of the limits of their understanding; the goal of the senior year is to produce someone who has made some defensible commitments and can speak and write with a modicum of authority in a defined area.

William DeWitt Hyde offered an early justification of programs designed to produce a certain kind of person. Hyde defined the purpose of collegiate education as "the opening of the mind to the great departments of human interest; the opening of the heart to the great spiritual motives of unselfishness and social service; the opening of the will to opportunity for wise and righteous self-control." To achieve this purpose, he recommended curricula organized in sequential fashion, with each subject presented in at least three consecutive courses extending over a year each: one elementary course; one or more courses that are broad, general, interesting, and practical; and one that is focused and intensive, offering the student an opportunity to take initiative and exhibit originality (Hyde 1904, 476).

Arthur Morgan actually instituted a program guided by this principle at Antioch College in 1921, not through three-year academic sequences but by alternating academic studies on campus with periods of work in industry or business. Although finances were a consideration behind this collegiate venture—Morgan had hoped to enable both students and college to become self-supporting—the plan was defended on educational grounds as an effort to develop the whole person. Morgan sought "to prepare men to live whole lives instead of the fragmentary lives they commonly lived" (Henderson and Hall 1946, 3). To this end, he defined the powers of the whole person as "physical health; training for work; experience in work; an appreciation of social, religious, economic, and aesthetic values . . . ; a sense of proportion; a knowledge of history, literature, and science; and a life purpose and philosophy" (3). Vocational experience and liberal education were to work in tandem to develop and integrate these powers.

While Antioch's program was keyed to developing well-rounded per-sonalities, the Swarthmore honors program forged by Frank Aydelotte at the same time was designed to elevate cultural standards. Aydelotte aspired to bring better students up to higher levels of initiative and independence and train them for leadership. His plan enabled students to devise indi-vidualized programs of intensive independent study. Students in the pro-gram selected eight (later six) subjects on which they would be evaluated by oral and written examinations administered by outside examiners at the end of the senior year.

THE WORLD TO BE KNOWN   If *general* in the first sense signifies a focus on how to promote the formation of the whole person, *general* in a second sense means applying to all subject matters and thereby orienting learners to the universe of things to be known. A curriculum of this sort would be constructed in terms of providing acquaintance with the major kinds of phenomena in the universe. In early modern Europe, such an ap-proach appeared in the program of the renowned Moravian educator Comenius, whose notion of "Pansophia," or universal knowledge, pointed to mastery of the essential truths of all scholarly fields. Comenius held that pupils must "be taught to become wise by studying the heavens, the earth, oaks, and beeches, but not by studying books; that is to say, they must learn to know and investigate the things themselves, and not the observa-tions that other people have made about the things" (Rusk 1965, 97). This principle was reproduced in Comte's curriculum, a coordinated intro-duction to the positive sciences of specified categories of objects: abstract relational patterns, celestial bodies, masses, molecules, organisms, society, and human morality.

Courses that follow this principle have often been designated as survey or orientation courses, which overcome the parochialism of specialized subject matters by offering students a wide range of facts from numerous fields. Some advocates of this approach propose to use history to provide an overarching perspective for organizing a complete curriculum. Such was the idea of A. C. True who, in "The Relation of the College Curricu-lum to Human Life and Work" (1915), proposed to take history out of the hands of a single department and give it to large groups of scholars who would contribute all manner of information relating to historical periods broadly conceived.

One of the most influential of such general courses was the Contempo-rary Civilization course at Columbia, designed in 1919 to enable students to consider insistent problems of the present by means of identifying both their roots in the past and their practical ramifications in contemporary life and discourse. The course covered a broad array of problems, such as nationalism, war and peace, public opinion in democracies, production of wealth, distribution of income, and distribution of educational opportunities. That course was subsequently supplemented by a yearlong humanities sequence; courses on art and music; courses on cultures and civilizations of Asia, Africa, and Latin America; and a three-course requirement in the natural sciences. Columbia has described its core curriculum as an oasis of order and purpose, and it stands as an exemplar of what can be accomplished using this curricular principle.

A recent expression of this principle appears in Martha Nussbaum's *Cultivating Humanity* (1997). Although Nussbaum would espouse an elective-based curriculum when she intervened in the University of Chicago's curricular wars just a year later (as noted in the foreword), in this influential book her curricular prescriptions include eloquent arguments for requirements in an array of subjects (albeit, notably, not in mathematics, natural science, or social science). As a curriculum superior to "an amorphous elective diversity requirement" (71), she proposes, for example, that all American students should be required to take, alongside some central course in American history and the major sources of its culture (144), courses in depth on some non-Western culture (chap. 4), foreign languages (70), nonverbal arts (171), the interdisciplinary study of sexuality (256), and, as a "non-negotiable part of the undergraduate curriculum," a study in the major world religions (145).

A COMMON HERITAGE   *General* in a third sense refers to a corpus of learning common to all educated persons in a particular cultural tradition. Conceptions of this sort appeal to the principle of mastery of, or at least immersion in, certain supremely valued works. This view represents a huge expansion of the educational objectives in civilizations oriented to study of the hallowed texts — the analects of Confucius, Bhagavad Gita, the Torah, the Qur'an.

This principle found weak expression in another best-selling book that appeared at the same time as Bloom's, E. D. Hirsch's *Cultural Literacy: What Every American Needs to Know* (1987). The literacy canon in question included a universe of items from a cappella and DNA to quarks and zeitgeist. Hirsch advocated this principle as an essential corrective to curricula based on the primacy of cultivating skills.

A more demanding embodiment of this principle surfaced in liberal curricula organized around Great Books or World Literature. This idea harks back to Matthew Arnold's notion of "the best that has been thought and said in the world" and derives from Sir John Lubbock's (1896) list of "one hundred best books" and John Erskine's pioneering General Honours course at Columbia which featured a list of books he called "classics" or "masterpieces." At St. John's College in 1937, President Stringfellow Barr and Dean Scott Buchanan initiated a prescribed, four-year curriculum that all students were required to master. Barr, Buchanan, and the next dean, philosopher Jacob Klein, developed a Great Books curriculum, which stemmed from their conviction that a throughgoing education of that sort puts learners in direct contact with the achievements of the greatest minds of their civilization. They began with a list of one hundred books that address fundamental, perennial human questions. The principle of commonality extended to the faculty, too, who were expected to learn enough to teach the entire curriculum, including languages and laboratory work. The readings moved in chronological order—from ancient Greek authors and their pioneering ideas about the liberal arts in the first year and Roman, medieval, and Renaissance texts in the second to seventeenth- and eighteenth-century books written in modern languages and, finally, works from the last two centuries.

KINDS OF DISCIPLINES *General* in a fourth sense refers to the notion of embracing all fundamental skills and thereby providing a basis for any particular skill. The archetype for this curricular principle appears in Aristotle's *Nicomachean Ethics,* which enumerates powers (*dynameis*) whose actualization results in a set of intellectual virtues. This notion was represented formally in the medieval curriculum of the seven liberal arts. The trivium—the arts of dialectic, grammar, and rhetoric—taught the operations of the mind itself, the arts of proper reasoning and expression. The quadrivium—mathematics, geometry, astronomy, and music—cultivated disciplines for comprehending the natural world. Many educators of the nineteenth century, heeding Yale president Jeremiah Day's celebrated metaphor of the mind as a muscle that needed "daily and vigorous exercise," followed his call to expand the powers of the mind through the classical disciplines. They defended the study of Latin by asserting its unique potential for promoting mental discipline. Although Dewey abandoned what he considered abstract studies such as Greek and Latin in favor of a curriculum based on direct experiences, he retained the curricular principle of fundamental skills by regarding the formation of strong intellectual habits as the basis of a defensible curriculum.

A historic expression of this principle appeared in a 1934 talk by Henry M. Wriston, president of Lawrence College (later of Brown University). Opening the first major educational conference to take the topic of general education for its central theme, Wriston lampooned the notion that general education could best be acquired through mastery of some quantity of facts. Instead, he advocated an education whose universal validity was found in the identification and experience of broad modes of thought, or "mental methods," which he termed "disciplines." Wriston's own philosophy identified four basic disciplines: (1) the discipline of precision, (2) the discipline of appreciation, (3) the discipline of hypothesis, and (4) the discipline of reflective synthesis (Wriston 1934). Following in Wriston's footsteps at Lawrence in 1945, President Nathan Pusey initiated a program of freshman seminars to introduce students to fundamental skills.

Reed College was one early institution to focus on basic intellectual disciplines. Reed's faculty manipulated the elective system in such a way as to provide a broad range of skills through immersion in whatever subject a student chose. They shored up the elective courses with a rigorous atmosphere and by requiring all students to pass a single, comprehensive examination in the junior year and to write a senior thesis. Reed emphasized the verbal skills of students in particular, requiring them to participate in intensive freshman seminars and pass an oral thesis exam as seniors. Beginning in the 1920s, senior seminars provided for an integration of skills as students wrote the thesis and prepared for the oral exam.

Choosing a Path

THE UNIVERSITY OF CHICAGO   Among institutions that experimented with new approaches to liberal learning in the twentieth century, the University of Chicago stood out for sustaining a multigenerational matrix of generative ideas about the reinvention of liberal learning. Its special contribution, as indicated in the prologue to the present volume, stemmed from three factors. One was the exceptional leadership of a number of presidents and college deans, among whom the visions and rhetoric of two presidents, William Rainey Harper and Robert Maynard Hutchins, were crucial. A second factor was the sustained vitality of traditions of intense faculty concern with liberal education. The third consisted of distinctive institutional arrangements, including a group of faculty especially charged with responsibility for undergraduate teaching;

TABLE 4 Notions of general education, 1900–1950

Curricular principle	Supporting educators	Experimental institution	Manifestation at Chicago
Character of learner	W. DeWitt Hyde (1904) Arthur Morgan Frank Aydelotte George Allan (1999)	Antioch, 1920s Swarthmore, 1920s	Harper's junior colleges, 1892–1920
Knowable world	A. C. True (1915) Martha Nussbaum (1997)	Columbia, 1919	1920s survey courses
Knowledge (common heritage)	S. Barr, S. Buchanan, J. Klein E. D. Hirsch (1987)	St. John's, 1937	1930s Great Books plan
Disciplines of knowing	Henry Wriston (1934)	Lawrence, 1945 Reed, 1920s	1940s Faust-Ward College (aka "Second Hutchins College")

college deans empowered with their own budgets and powers of appointment; and the mechanism of the staff-taught course, where faculty from diverse fields come together to devise and teach collaboratively courses organized around broad themes of a nonprofessional nature.

Peculiar to Chicago's involvement with liberal learning is that each of the four principles just enumerated has been adopted at various points. The first Chicago plan focused on the principle of the character of the learner. It separated the first two undergraduate years as an "academic college," whose mission was to shape young minds in such a way that their bearers could properly be admitted into the rigorous work of university-level specialties. Harper quite innocently saw the point of liberal learning at that level to be the cultivation of Academic Man.

During the 1920s, when fresh winds of general education were blowing across the land, Chicago faculty engaged with a new curricular principle. In this second mode, they sought to orient students to their world by offering a grand synthesis of human knowledge—first on the natural universe, then on human society and on the arts (see chapter 3).

In the 1930s, yet another curricular principle came to the fore, when some faculty attempted, albeit without success, to organize an undergraduate curriculum around a common corpus of texts that represented a significant portion of the human heritage: the Great Books of the Western World.

What finally became adopted during the Hutchins presidency, and arguably marks Chicago's most distinctive contribution to the general education movement, was the idea of a curriculum formed to cultivate a *determinate range of intellectual skills*. One can trace forerunners of this idea in Harper's own depiction of junior college work, which he sometimes described as an effort to cultivate "systematic habits" and "control of intellectual powers" (Harper 1905, 272–73). The ideas of Dewey were particularly pertinent for such a goal, inasmuch as he inspired experimentation with ways to cultivate those powers directly. A faculty report of 1924 picked up this rhetoric and enumerated three types of power necessary for proper adjustment to modern society: powers of independent thinking, aesthetic appreciation, and moral judgment. Their ideas became embodied in subsequent curricular structures that sought to cultivate the capacities for appreciation, interpretation, and criticism of works of art; for searching deliberation on matters of public policy; for grasping the methods of scientific inquiry; and for understanding world civilizations. Table 4 exhibits this parade of curricular ideas.

The language would reverberate further in the definition of an educated person offered by Hutchins and then be reconfigured through the
work of Richard McKeon and Joseph Schwab on liberal curricula and
pedagogy. McKeon showed how to construct elaborate curricula on the
principle of cultivating identified powers. Schwab showed how that
could be done even in the intractable case of the natural sciences. Beyond
that, he helped show how those powers could be cultivated through innovative forms of pedagogy and assessed through imaginative examinations. Redfield expanded on the theme by emphasizing the powers involved in coming to understand the architectonics of a world civilization.
My own experience (as will be described in chapter 12) showed that on
their own, individual faculty members could extend this type of teaching
into a variety of domains and through a variety of forms.

FROM SEVEN ARTS TO EIGHT POWERS   The reforming of liberal
education presents one of the most complex intellectual and social challenges of modern life. It requires more attention than what an occasional
conference or well-appointed colloquium affords. Among other things,
it requires institutionalization of such concerns in sustained efforts nourished by local traditions—a rare and precious feat. The University of
Chicago is one place where that actually happened.

In the course of working out those concerns, the University moved
progressively from curricular principles focused on the character of the
learner to the knowable world, then to knowledge, and finally to an emphasis on disciplines and powers of the mind. In proposing a course of dialogue among educators for the twenty-first century, I draw now on ideas
from the Chicago experience discussed earlier in this chapter and in part
2. In so doing, I assume that following a principle of powers does not
exclude considerations of the three other principles; rather, it sets up a
framework within which those considerations can find their place.

In seminal papers of the 1960s, Richard McKeon showed that interpretations and uses of the liberal arts have changed continuously over the
past 2,500 years. He went on, as noted, to fault contemporary responses
for simply redistributing old disciplines in new packages and for failing to
take the present world situation into account. The liberal and humanizing
arts must be constituted anew as they had been reconstituted in the past
to meet new problems. McKeon pressed for changes that offered responses
to such circumstances as increased numbers of disciplines, choices, and
people.

Since the Renaissance, most of what have been thought of as disciplines are differentiated by subject matter. In this vein, most disciplines have come to be organized either on the basis of a certain subject matter (French literature, zoology, chemistry, education, African history) or a subject matter linked with a certain methodology (economics, astronomy, glottochronology, archaeology). Given that, to reinvent a liberal curriculum oriented to the cultivation of disciplines as powers requires us to proceed afresh by looking for what McKeon calls "universal skills required to do particular tasks" (1964b, 43). To put it bluntly, inasmuch as a curriculum based on the principle of powers cannot be achieved by a distribution of required courses in existing disciplines, *adhering to that goal forces us to invent new disciplines,* in the older sense of arts that pertain to all or a wide range of subject matters (such as grammar, dialectic, and rhetoric). If we could recast older arts in the form of universal skills appropriate to contemporary civilization and the modern world, what might a new system of disciplines look like?

Curricula designed to cultivate powers proceed ideally from a working consensus about what powers there be and which are most worth cultivating. Short of binding pronouncements from an authority, that consensus can emerge only from conversations among those who are preparing, or are at least prepared, to teach such a curriculum. To facilitate such conversations, I offer a working paradigm.

Compiling a list of powers of the mind is just as defensible, and just as arbitrary, as listing a set of human instincts. Like any such schema, it offers a tool to work with. Boundaries among the powers must not be thought to delineate separate entities. The boundaries dividing them are naturally permeable. Each power interpenetrates each of the others.

The taxonomy that follows (and is illustrated in figure 3) enumerates eight kinds of powers. I divide them between powers of prehending — those that work primarily to capture the properties of objects — and powers of expression — those that work primarily to articulate a subjective center (with all due apologies to those upset by yet another reproduction of a supposedly obsolete self-object dualism). I ground this distinction in the most fundamental of all human life processes: breathing.

As we inhale, we take in take into our sensory-motor systems elements that are external to our bodies. Internally, those elements are processed and then, as we exhale, returned to the external world. More generally, all life and growth takes the form of an alternation between taking in and putting out. In the area of culture, Benedetto Croce has famously portrayed this process as one of intuition and externalization.

To the first quartet belong those powers that evolve from natural abili-

FIGURE 3 Eight powers of the mind: a working paradigm

Powers of Prehension
   1. Audiovisual powers
   2. Kinesthetic powers
   3. Understanding verbal texts
      a. Interpretation
      b. Analysis
      c. Application
   4. Understanding worlds
      a. Natural worlds
      b. Cultural worlds

Powers of Expression
   5. Forming a reflexive liberal self
   6. Inventing statements, problems, and actions
      a. Composing statements
      b. Finding and resolving problems
   7. Integrating knowledge
      a. Assessing evidence and argument
      b. Constructing encyclopedic knowledge
      c. Commissioning deep structures of knowledge
      d. Finding connected paths of inquiry
   8. Communication
      a. Self-expression in context
      b. Enlarging the scope of dialogue

ties to make sensory and mental contact with external objects—seeing, hearing, feeling, making sense of things. These powers offer entrée into the worlds we live in. They equip us to function in our natural and human environments and to enjoy the beauty of natural and cultural forms. Properly cultivated, they can enable persons to withstand some of the noxious features of the modern order, including the reduction of knowledge to discrete bits conveyed through electronic media and the exploitation of those media to convey information and understandings that cannot stand up to intelligent critical scrutiny. This quartet represents the kinds of objectives pursued by coherent programs of general education like that of the Hutchins College described in chapter 3. I name them as (1) audiovisual powers, (2) kinesthetic powers, (3) powers of comprehending verbal texts, and (4) powers of understanding worlds.

To the second quartet belong those powers manifest in the workings of human agency. They process the elements that have been taken in, converting them to means of regeneration and continued growth and mediating their return, transformed, into the world. I call them the powers of (5) creating a self, (6) composing statements and resolving problems, (7) integrating knowledge, and (8) sharing meanings with others. These powers relate to the expressions of subjects. They capacitate ways to articulate one's place in these worlds and to initiate changes in them. These powers equip persons to deal constructively with complex knowledge, globalized cultures, semantic mayhem, and normative confusion. This quartet represents the kinds of educational programs linked with Cicero's system of rhetorical skills, Dewey's notion of creative learning, and McKeon's proposals for architectonic sophistication. They issue in curricula that emphasize electivity and individuated development, on the one hand, and communicative skills, on the other.

9

Goals for the Liberal Curriculum I: Powers of Prehension

Disciplined observation requires a trained ability to use organs of prehension, a capacity to use the mind to interpret the sensations that those organs prehend, and a cultivated awareness and control over the observer's prejudices. Using available organs involves familiarity with the range of pertinent observational methodologies and the ability to concentrate focus in utilizing them. Using the mind involves learning how to analyze and relate the elements of objects and to grasp their significance. Overcoming prejudices requires the cultivation of openness toward the unknown or unfamiliar. These prejudices derive from cultural bias, parochial limitations, and psychological blocks. To pursue the metaphor of breathing in this context, we could say that inhaling optimally involves acquaintance with a variety of breathing techniques and some awareness of internal constrictions that inhibit access to deep, fluid, energizing respiration. As illustrated in figure 3 in chapter 8, powers of observation include the first two of my eight powers of the mind: audiovisual powers and kinesthetic powers.

Audiovisual Powers

Although the traditional liberal curriculum has been couched exclusively in terms of readings, I begin this list by attending to the nonverbal powers. This approach is partly to counteract the logocentric excesses of modern culture and to bridge the harmful chasm between the mind and the sensuous powers. For adult humans, the world of objects is prehended primarily through the organs of sight and hearing. "Seeing just what is there" sounds easier than it is. The eye must be trained, both to identify different kinds of matter and to recognize different kinds of form. The eye can be trained to see such visible patterns as the use of differing elements and their placement relative to one another and to see innumerable predicates of visible objects, including contrasts of dark and light, textured or smooth, complex or simple, focused or scattered, and the like. The pertinent skills here also include the capacity to observe both resemblances and differences—in particular, resemblances among ostensibly very different objects and differences among ostensibly identical objects.

These skills can be applied liberally in the everyday world. Doing so requires acute awareness of subtle details in the environment, details that often go unnoticed but which carry symbolic meaning or even historical significance. Landscape historian John Stilgoe (1998) teaches classes in which students are encouraged to explore such aspects as the height and direction of power lines in the street, the shape of manhole covers, and product packaging and placement in supermarkets. Such exercises enhance awareness of the built environment, the kind of awareness that is inhibited by the preoccupation with words and numbers within much ordinary schooling.

The powers of beholding can be deepened through training in such subjects as drawing, painting, architecture, geometry, astronomy, biology, and microscopy as well as through focused attention to art, nature, and objects of the everyday world. Beyond the pragmatic uses of sight, different uses appear in the domains of theoretical and aesthetic objects. According to recent research, these modes of perceiving involve processes physiologically distinct from those used in pragmatic, visuomotor seeing, and the latter yields perceptual representations that are apparently more fine-grained and informationally richer than the conceptual contents of thought (Jacob and Jeannerod 2003).

In the aesthetic domain, the ability to apprehend form takes on a much more significant role. Art historian Joshua Taylor calls to our attention the difference between subject matter and "expressive content" in works of visual art, highlighting the importance of "the combined effect of subject matter and visual form" (1981, 43–44). Artists evoke feelings and meanings through subtle nuances of depth, curvature, repetition, and overlap of lines; isolation, compactness, and value of forms; contrasts of horizontal and vertical planes; and texture. Manipulation of the color environment involves the use of variety or uniformity of color; blending of hues; value or lightness of color; warmth or coolness of tone; and the domination, saturation, or equilibrium achieved among colors. Also playing into the expressive content of a work are its symmetry; use of perspective; presence of evocative symbols; softness, clarity, shape, proportionality, and relative positioning of forms; the shape and scale of the work of art itself; and how all of these elements combine into an overall composition. Certainly, one power of the liberal mind must be to understand the varieties of visual art as comprising dialects of a distinctive language and to translate this understanding into verbal expression.

The same points hold true, mutatis mutandis, for perception through the aural faculty. The universe of audibles shows numerous parallels with the universe of visibles. Pitch, timbre, rhythm, harmony, and monophonic and polyphonic melodic structures comprise the elements whose recognition requires nontrivial training. The human ear experiences exquisite displays of patterned periodicities of sound waves as simple tones and harmonies. All musical harmonies are based on the relationship among overtones, yet the overtones of a single note are not entirely obvious to the ear, and the overtones of the overtones are less obvious still. When we sing tones compounded from these overtones, "we are making audible and sensible a real but inaudible world locked inside the fundamental tone" (Mathieu 1997, 12, 40–41). Beyond learning the elements of music, the trained ear learns to recognize the enormous variety of forms that constitute musical compositions. In addition, listeners can be empowered to understand intellectual discourse about music and to think about the relationship between music and other spheres such as mathematics, visual arts, and even morality.

Similar learning can be directed toward phonemes and grammatical elements in language. Both sets of symbols can be rendered either orally or in written form. Though symbols technically may be seen or heard, they are perceived somehow through a mental capacity to interpret more than sensory details alone (Greek: *nous*). Grammar, in music and in language, is the discipline that enables one to identify formal and semantic structures. Thus, when we see a transitive verb in a language we know, we become alert for the actor and the object. Modifiers lead us to what is modified: adjectives to nouns, adverbs to verbs. When we hear an alarm, we become alert to a nearby danger. A sentence, a paragraph, a book, and a symphony each have an intelligible beginning, middle, and end, and despite the enormous variety of beginnings and ends, we become proficient at distinguishing them and become able to enter and leave these worlds of feelings and meanings.

Whether oral, graphic, or written symbols are used, comprehension of what another human being is expressing poses a distinctive set of challenges. Beyond the usual limits on audiovisual capacities imposed by parochial experience and cultural habits, these challenges also involve the discipline of controlling our reactivity to the statements of others. A special discipline is needed here to control the intrusion of one's preferences and prejudgments so that one stays open to what the other is expressing. The response to hearing what others say or write is often misunderstanding, not equable understanding.[1] In *The Power of Extraordinary Listening* (2000), Richard Moon offers a number of insights and exercises that deal with the way natural reactive processes default into self-protective behavior that corrupts the process of listening. Moon is fond of the dictum he attributes to Plutarch: "Proper listening is the foundation of proper living" (2).

In today's world, numerous instruments amplify human audiovisual powers. They range from microscopes and spectroscopes and X-ray photographs to radar, helioscopes, radio telescopes, sonar devices, recording technology, and oscilloscopes. Also, upgraded language learning techniques and electronic translation programs increase the accessibility to communications in other tongues. At the same time that today's educated person has access in principle to an extravagantly expanded set of perceptual tools, our natural sources of sensation become compromised by the sweep of inputs that today's mass media disseminate. Facts reach us predigested and out of context when not prefabricated.

This domain also involves learning that although each tool is subject to problems of misuse and distortion, no particular observational medium provides truer or more valid findings than another. Since scientific disciplines and artistic genres and styles differ with respect to the distances from which they view things, it is important to learn not only what distances are associated with each but also how the universe of visibles is constituted. As Georg Simmel observed, a view gained at any distance whatever has its own justification; each distance has its own correct picture and its own margin for error (Levine 1971, xxxiv).

Since the optical and aural systems are parts of the body, moreover, the

1. The psychoanalytic tradition has long identified the obstacles to empathetic reception of another's communications as well as stipulating that the analyst's own technique should consist primarily of an attitude of evenly hovering attention. For various discourses on how messages from others are misunderstood, edited, disavowed, and the like, see Ichheiser 1949, Moraitis 1981, and Levine 1985b.

interaction between the organs of sight and hearing with their physiological substrata will always be salient. When we speak of being touched by
music, or moved by a natural landscape, how alert are we to the impinge-
ment of tonal periodicities or visual harmonies on our neuromuscular
systems? The liberally educated person of the future will know that right
attunement of the body affects perceptual capacities and will find ways of
returning to the body's center to recover clarity of vision and attentive
listening.

Kinesthetic Powers

To include a section on responses of the body in a discourse on powers of
the mind might not seem so odd to those master educators of classical antiquity who invented the liberal arts. The Hellenic system for creating a
higher type of human being conjoined instruction in bodily arts with intellectual arts. Commenting on this conjunction of physical and mental
disciplines, Isocrates observed, "These are twin arts—parallel and complementary—by which their masters prepare the mind to become more
intelligent and the body to become more serviceable, not separating
sharply the two kinds of education, but using similar methods of instruction, exercise, and other forms of discipline" (2000, 180–82).

The very culture that brought us the language to talk about inherent
powers (*dynameis*) used one term (*arete*) to designate both excellence of
bodily powers, such as strength and vigor, and excellence of mental powers, such as sharpness and insight. Ancient Greeks regarded athletic competition as well as philosophical speculation as divine activities.

A comparable chord was struck in ancient China. During the latter
sixth century BCE, Confucius described the ideal person to be produced
by the Chinese version of paideia: a man who possesses wisdom, courage,
and magnanimity, and who is accomplished in courtesy, ceremony, and
music. Training in both literary and martial subjects was thought essential
for producing such a broadly cultivated person.[2]

In the Western canon of liberal learning, physical training declined and
eventually disappeared, yielding to attitudes that disdained the corporeal.

2. "A liberal education included five kinds of ritual, five kinds of music, five ways of
archery, five ways of directing a chariot, six kinds of writing, and nine operations of mathematics. . . . The training was moral, physical, and intellectual in character. . . . The ideal
of education of the time of the Chou seems to have been the harmonious and symmetrical
development of the body and mind, and may be said to represent a combination of Spar-
tan and Athenian ideals of education, which called for a training at once intellectual and
moral, as well as physical and military" (Kuo 1914, 18).

Although training in martial arts dropped from China's curriculum also, the Confucian-Taoist ideal of gaining an enlightened mind, in the sense of coming to grasp the remarkable harmonies of nature, left the door open to kindred pursuits. Other Asian traditions invented disciplined bodily practices as paths to such enlightenment and invoked them to cultivate a higher humane spirit for some 2,500 years. Ranging from yoga and meditation to tai chi and aikido, these practices have now emerged from the secrecy of monasteries and esoteric cults into secular public domains.

During the twentieth century, Western educators began to recover a psychosomatic dimension of liberal learning, as originary bodymind healers—from Sigmund Freud and Wilhelm Reich to F. Mathias Alexander, Elsa Gindler, Ida Rolf, and Moshe Feldenkrais—investigated dimensions of bodymind unity and ways in which bodily changes and mental functioning affect one another. John Dewey championed the incorporation of such experiences into educational programs. Dewey's inclination to make lived, embodied experience the focal point of learning was substantially advanced by his work with Alexander, with whom he began to take "lessons" in 1916. This work formed a turning point, not only in relief from psychophysiological problems that had plagued him since youth, but also in the maturation of his philosophical thought.[3]

Central to Alexander's discoveries was a version of what may be called *bodymindfulness*—for him, using attention to bodily sensations as a means for altering the way in which parts of the body function. Through subtly guided movements of the upper body, postural distortions are relieved, and *conscious control* of how one uses the body is achieved. The technique works not through directly willing a certain change but by means of increasing awareness, inhibiting dysfunctional responses, and allowing proper physical expressions to emerge.[4]

---

3. Dewey would later acknowledge that his theories of using the mind to control bodily action derived crucial support from Alexander's work. This would be clear to any reader of *Human Nature and Conduct* at all familiar with the Alexander Technique. Dewey's illustration therein of the difficulty of changing posture just by willing requires explicit reference to Alexander, as does his relentless critique of "the current separation of body and mind" ([1922] 1988, 49).

4. Somatic educator Thomas Hanna has written that "what Dewey learned and extolled in the Alexander Technique was how it solved a physiological problem by experimentally interrupting a habitual pattern and then sensing its several components in order to enrich one's awareness of what one is unconsciously doing. What was habitually unconscious was made conscious by means of new sensory information. This allowed new motor control to occur. Dewey saw Alexander as the pioneer of a radically new venture in physiological self-education—a procedure which achieved a better integration of the reflexive and voluntary elements in one's response patterns" (1990–91).

In Dewey's perspective, supreme value inheres in aesthetic satisfactions from nondiscursive, immediately lived experience. In work that builds on this Deweyan assumption and draws on Merleau-Ponty, Wittgenstein, and Foucault as well, Richard Shusterman analyzes nondiscursive, embodied experience as a legitimate object of analysis, a site for self-improvement, and an essential tool for inquiry.[5] To that end, he wants to practice philosophy, more than as discourse and writing, as "a discipline of embodied life" wherein the search for truth and wisdom "would not be pursued only through texts but also through somatic exploration and experiment" (Shusterman 1997, 176).

By now, a number of educators have explored modalities of learning through attention to embodied experience. These modalities include Thomas Hanna's concept of "somatic education," Wendy Palmer's program of Conscious Embodiment, and Paul Linden's modality of Being in Movement. Linden teaches, for example, how to become aware of the body processes that undergird personal intentions and thereby to realize how different ways of holding one's body can produce feelings of power and love. Linden's discipline elucidates the somatic basis of an array of seemingly different problems — interpersonal and international conflict, ethnic or gender prejudice, drug abuse, family violence and child abuse, and environmental degradation. (See Hanna 1990–91; Palmer 2000; Linden 1988–89.)

To reinvent liberal teaching along these lines will require a search for techniques and new curricular structures to bring bodily functioning and its attendant feelings into greater consciousness. For one thing, such a program will need to investigate how bodily processes affect the mind. Mental issues — concentration, openness to new ideas, critical reading, dealing with contradictions, and the like — have determinate bodily counterparts that can be noticed and explored. Dewey's own testimony bears witness to some of the educational possibilities here, for he emphasized how much his somatic learning through the Alexander technique helped him hold a philosophical position calmly once he had taken it or to change it if new evidence came up warranting a change, and he contrasted this

5. The key texts include "Dewey on Experience: Foundation or Reconstruction?" (1994); *Practicing Philosophy: Pragmatism and the Philosophical Life* (1997, chaps. 1, 6); *Performing Live* (2000a, chaps. 7, 8); and *Pragmatist Aesthetics: Living Beauty, Rethinking Art* (2000b). In *The Body in the Mind,* another philosopher, Mark Johnson (1987), explores ways in which bodily experiences form the basis for image schemata, such as those for balance, scale, paths, and cycles, which are then extended through metaphors to express abstract meanings and rational connections.

disposition with the rigidity of other academic thinkers who adopt a position early in their career and then use their intellects to defend it indefinitely (Jones 1976, 97). Ken Dychtwald's *Bodymind* (1986) surveys a number of practices that illuminate how physical tensions, ingrained muscular patterns, and organic vulnerabilities affect one's scope of vision, level of defensiveness, capacity for differentiated understanding, creative problem solving, and the like.

The converse inquiries would concern how mental processes affect bodily functions. For example, since energy follows attention, attending to various parts of the body can direct energy in ways that produce feelings of relaxation, strength, stability, or harmony. And then, combining these two interactive paths, bodymindfulness curricula could address what have hitherto been treated as purely intellectual problems. Thus, one might learn, in the face of an opaque passage in which one is stumped and stuck, that diverting attention to one's bodily reactions to the difficulty — frustration, anxiety, anger, self-recrimination, and the like — might mobilize energies that could lead to a more effective resolution.

The bodymind modalities referred to in this chapter were created to promote higher levels of personal and social well-being. From them and from future explorations, one can identify numerous routes by which various bodymind practices can promote personal well-being, right action, and enhanced social participation.[6]

The introduction of such practices into liberal curricula need not await the formation of new disciplines. Numerous reputable bodymind disciplines already have in place practitioners who have undergone extensive training and passed stringent accreditation tests. At a minimum, they include at least the following: Alexander lessons, Feldenkrais somatic education, guided meditation, yoga, tai chi, and aikido. A year of work in any of these disciplines under a qualified and properly certified teacher will sensitize students to the interactions between mind and body and empower them to realize how awareness of their connections can improve well-being and understanding. Such work could serve for now in lieu of the more ambitious programs just described. If the general idea is taken seriously, qualified educators will devise novel curricula and pedagogies. In the continuing reinvention of liberal teaching, the area of bodymind disciplines offers an exciting frontier.

6. For a schematic listing of ways in which somatic education can address the traditional philosophical aims of knowledge, self-knowledge, right action, and discourse on the good life, see Shusterman 2000b, 267–71.

Understanding Verbal Texts

A fine line separates processes of observation from processes of interpretation. Even so, it is worthwhile to focus separately on skills involved in making sense of coherent sets of aural, oral, graphic, and written symbols — all of which can be construed as texts of some sort.

Interpreting written texts forms the bread and butter of what passes for teaching the liberal arts.[7] Just what constitutes the set of powers involved here has been a subject of extended and continuing debate. At the very least, one presumes that students will learn to identify the aims, methods, and rhetoric of texts of increasing difficulty.

Benjamin Bloom and his colleagues investigated a set of such intellectual abilities and skills with heuristic resources that emerged in good part from the educational experiments at the University of Chicago in the 1930s and 1940s. The heart of their "taxonomy of educational objectives" (B. Bloom et al. 1956) concerned skills involved in the interpretive grasp of texts. These skills included the ability to interpret the meaning of a passage or text, the ability to analyze material into constituent parts and track the way those parts are related, and the ability to extrapolate and apply the ideas of a text to other appropriate contexts and subject matters.

Understanding verbal texts involves the third of my eight powers of the mind: powers of comprehension. To grasp the meaning of an object requires interpretation on two levels. We seek to know, first, what something means in itself: what is a quadratic equation, what is a triptych, what is meant by natural selection.[8] At this level, students *translate* text into a coherent message, which involves observing symbols and associating them with understandable concepts or ideas. Through translation, a student reconfigures an abstract notion into a concrete, familiar term or condenses an extended communication into a brief message. This preliminary level of interpretation is crucial because it inevitably links behaviors associated with knowledge attainment to the more sophisticated processes of application and analysis.

---

7. Some of my own exercises of this sort will be presented in chapter 12.

8. The Bloom taxonomy builds from the notion that knowledge attainment is the simplest form of learning. This assumption is appropriate given a somewhat flat definition of observation that hinges on the ability to perceive spoken or written communications. Knowing that interpretation is more complex than mere observation, the committee belabored the concept of "comprehension" (a concept which covers only a part of what is deemed *interpretation* here) more than any other. Here we encounter terrain familiar to higher education professionals, where the first level of interpretation begins.

One can transform a message's symbols and groups of symbols into concrete terms, or one can further streamline them into more concise symbols. Once these pieces have been reformulated in the desired terms, the relationships among these terms may be considered. Further analysis of the message can reveal organizational principles or other resonances that assist in uncovering these relationships. Thus one not only should be able to interpret the parts of a message but also should be able to account for how the parts work together.

For example, $x + y = y + x$ should be recognized as more than a trick for manipulating addends; it expresses the principle that quantitative sums can be added in any order. When this communication is considered carefully, one realizes that qualitative elements cannot be added so freely. The order of addition of qualitative elements can affect the resulting sum, precisely because relationships among the addends, like political alliances for example, can form before all the elements are added in.

The ability to apply appropriately what one observes in a text to other situations signals that one has a firm footing on the first level of interpretation. Being able to solve a set of math problems, for example, suggests that one has interpreted correctly the laws of arithmetic to which one has been exposed. The ability to extrapolate past communications into generalizations that can be applied to other contexts and subject matters is akin to the ability to predict conditions at some point in the future, given the specifications of a current trend toward that condition—a cornerstone of modern science.

The second level of interpretation is more sophisticated in that it fuses perception, translation, and application. Those who are practiced in the art of interpretation know that a text is an inadequate tool through which to convey all thoughts and ideas. Communicators often rely upon implications and innuendoes and expect perceivers to mine deeper, higher-order meanings from their passages. Attunement to the tone of a message and knowledge of the conditions under which it was written may alert the reader to the fact that a text is shaped by a certain perspective, which may originate in the unique experiences or motivations of the communicator. The ability to anticipate a speaker's train of thought, as it is intimated in both the substance and form of a communication, is the product of advanced interpretive ability.

To interpret a form completely, we need to know what contextual meanings it harbors. Once one has discerned, for example, the form of a triptych, one needs to know what the triptych signifies—aesthetically, spiritually, historically, and the like. The process of seeing involves the observer's unique associations, memories, and speculation. The perceptual process is mediated through "the mind's eye," which "enables us to see an aspect of the world we cannot see with our eyes" (Finn 2000, 11). In this process we bring together the abilities to recognize and understand manifest symbols as well as latent context, and to relate separate parts of a piece to each other to obtain a sense of its whole.

The complex of visual powers involved in observation and interpretation includes not only making sense of what stands before the observer but also the ability to locate facts pertinent to an inquiry. Knowing whether a scientist's research is funded by a private corporation or shaped heavily by his or her record of attempting to "prove" a pet theory may help us understand the structure of the scientist's hypotheses and perhaps the wording of his or her conclusions. Today's panoply of electronic media provides methodologies that must be included in this category of empowerment. These media deliver the coup de grâce to the old-time notion of teaching as transmission of bodies of factual information. They open the door to fresh questions about the credibility of different types of evidentiary claims and the grounds for distinguishing between shadows of objects and the objects themselves.

Understanding Worlds

A set of observed particulars can be extended in at least three directions. One is through the logic of generalization. Once an empirical generalization has been hypothesized or confirmed, powers of abstract reasoning can be applied to amplify the scope and implications of such formulations. Second, observations can be organized to encompass problems of varying size and scope. Generalizations here take the form of propositions regarding properties of various forms or kinds of situations.

Finally, generalizations can be extended to delimit worlds of different kinds. The power to understand the central structural features of any world — the fourth of my eight powers of the mind, as illustrated in figure 3 in chapter 8 — requires imagination and intellectual creativity of exceptional scope. One could define a number of worlds that presume a demand for understanding of this sort, including the various worlds of human action and the worlds of culture. Here we shall attend to two worlds of the broadest compass, that of the natural universe and that of civilizations.

NATURAL WORLDS   All discrete visibles and audibles belong to enormous universes that have some sort of structural coherence. It behooves the liberally educated person to acquire a nontrivial familiarity with major ways of thinking about these universes. For the natural world, this means gaining some purchase on how scientists understand phenomena from the smallest fields of energy through the most encompassing fields and the kinds of similarities and differences that pertain to these levels.

Natural scientists at the University of Chicago have tried various formats through which to introduce this kind of understanding, by organizing sequences of courses taught by faculty from a wide range of disciplines. One course sequence uses concepts of structure and function—equally applicable to chemistry as to Miesian architecture—to look at the natural world from the scale of elementary particles (physics) through molecules (chemistry) to cells, organisms, and ecosystems (biology). At each level, students learn to connect structure to function and to see how each level in the hierarchy provides building blocks for the levels above it. At the same time, it enables them to examine whether or not the laws at each level are reducible to those at other levels. Another course sequence organizes itself in a temporal framework, studying phases of cosmic biochemical, planetary, floral, and faunal evolution. This approach teaches students ways to conceptualize the origins of the universe and solar system, the elements and circumstances of life, and causes of extinction. More recently, a third one offers a six-quarter sequence in environmental sciences, focusing on the relationship between human society and its natural environments. Students are here introduced to ways to determine the composition of the atmosphere, to analyze the effects of global industrialization and agricultural development, to understand how scientists produce forecasts of global warming and other climate models, to grasp the use of linear programming in the comparison of dietary choices and their consequences, to employ statistical research methods in an ecological setting, and to explore the paradigmatic question "What is life?" *Powers of Ten,* a public television presentation also offered in book form (Morrison 1982), presents the natural world as consisting of nested, spatial fields of varying proportions. Whatever the format, the liberal powers cultivated here involve the capacity to grasp the central ways of representing and explaining any given natural situation by setting it in transcending ontological contexts.

CULTURAL WORLDS   Although all the elements of human action can be regarded as products of "natural" causation in some sense, the domains that involve human symbolism and creativity introduce a radical break. Of all the constructs deployed to represent such domains, that of civilization represents the domain most regularly associated with the notion of liberal learning. This is so whether one regards the term *civilization* as referring to societies and cultures extended in time and space, when the liberal empowerment relates to capacities to stretch the imaginative mind; when it is taken to designate a complex of cultural creativity and monumental formations, in which case its liberating function is to elevate students toward "the best which has been thought and said in the world"; or when it connotes a distinctive, major kind of adaptation to the world, in which case the empowerment concerns abilities to understand oneself and others. One could even make a case for treating it as linked primarily to evolution of specialized tools, written language, architecture, and cities, as archaeologists want to do.

At any rate, as I intimated in chapter 7, orienting the modern liberal curriculum toward understanding the worlds of civilization would work well through cultivating the following powers of the mind:

- in considering the diverse meanings of the term *civilization,* a capacity to work productively with the ambiguities of an important essentially contested concept;
- in considering both the genesis of civilization and some of its most monumental achievements, a capacity to articulate and apply rationally defensible standards of value;
- in considering a particular civilization extended over large tracts of time and space, a capacity to use the mind expansively by relating particulars to concepts of high levels of abstraction; and
- in considering the single civilization of the contemporary world, a capacity to link current events to a global context and to realize the goal of education for humanity that the Stoics so eloquently envisioned and that our one small planet now desperately requires.

Although my goal or task in these pages is not to draft concrete blueprints for actual curricula, I shall at this point retrieve such a blueprint for an optimal civilizations curriculum which I conceived more than two decades ago. This curriculum both deals with how to think about the worlds of civilization and affords entrée into major lineaments of some of those worlds. It follows the curricular engineer's usual schematic devices and fits within the framework of a sequence of six quarters or four semesters.

3 weeks: the idea of civilization. Writings by scholars who hold various conceptions of civilization, with an eye to grasping the significance of their varying takes on this essential contested concept.

4 weeks: introduction to scholarship on the genesis of civilization and the nature of the civilizing process.

3 weeks: introduction to the major civilizations of the ancient Old and New Worlds.

20 weeks: immersion in one of the world civilizations, in which humanistic texts and social scientific analyses are conjoined, and panoramic structures are linked with particular events and texts.

20 weeks: immersion in a contrasting world civilization.

10–15 weeks: modern world civilization: the past two centuries.

Placing a unit of conversation about the meaning of civilization in such a course instantiates its subject matter. To paraphrase the 1892 dictum of the University of Chicago's annual register: no student is qualified to be a college graduate who is unfamiliar with the most notable achievement of the world's civilizations—the ability to follow and participate in civilized dialogue.

10

Goals for the Liberal Curriculum II: Powers of Expression

Contemporary approaches to education often stop with the kinds of powers delineated thus far; they concentrate on means of learning about the worlds of objects. The most advanced taxonomy of powers to evolve from the Chicago explorations, that of Benjamin Bloom and his colleagues (B. Bloom et al. 1956), greatly sophisticated the cognitive domain, treating the mind more like a computer than a mere filing cabinet, but it did not change the emphasis on the prehension of worlds of objects. Moreover, although the Bloom group effectively differentiated among cognitive, affective, and psychomotor domains of learning, they treated the cognitive and affective domains each by itself—in separate volumes, after all—and the psychomotor domain not at all. A recent critique of this work observes, "The Bloom taxonomy misses precisely that notion of a whole person, and a sense of how one relates to the larger environment, which would lend purpose to the student's several skills and abilities. To reach the apex of intellectual powers, one must experience oneself as a whole person, and encounter the world with all of one's powers together and, at the same time, responsively" (Cornwell 2004, 3).

To take that challenge seriously means going to places where contemporary educators have generally feared to tread. It means bringing the whole person, not just the whole mind, explicitly back into the curricular problematic.[1] It means acknowledging the bodily basis of experience, not just as the site of a continuous stream of perceptions, as the previous chapter described, but as an integral stratum of a sense of expressive selfhood. As a power of the mind, it means to engage a continuous interchange between the mind as prehending and then directing the body and between the mind as thus energized by, and then expressive of, the bodily self. This engagement manifests a double interchange akin to an iteration of inhaling and exhaling. One senses and expresses one's center as one senses and exhales from the diaphragm.

Forming a Self

Forming a reflective liberal self is the fifth of my eight powers of the mind. To broach this unfamiliar approach to liberal learning, one could scarcely do better than to recall the educational philosophy of John Dewey. Dewey viewed humane learning as a thoughtfully ordered sequence of experiences designed to empower people to live better lives through self-understanding, critical self-reflection, and self-direction. In this spirit, he espoused programs that promote the integration of mental and bodily energies. They promote self-knowledge by teaching how bodily and mental functions affect each other. They promote self-reflection by enhancing the ability to diagnose difficulties in one's functioning in any area of experience. They promote self-direction by enabling persons to direct their actions with greater awareness and greater power. Building on that notion, how might we draw the lineaments of a liberating education that embodies concern for developing the self?

Although most scholars agree that selves come into being through processes of social interaction, there remains a lot of debate about what it is that is thereby attained. The question of selfhood propels us into a thicket of dense disputations. We need not resolve that question in order to engage in discourse on the kind of self to be pursued through liberal learning. As before, we have much to gain by pursuing this notion through comparisons with types of selfhood in other, nonliberal cultures.

THE CONVENTIONAL SELF　A distinguished lineage of social thinkers—Adam Smith, G. W. F. Hegel, and William James foremost among them—have shown that the opinion one has of oneself derives

---

1. Liberal educators of the classical rhetorical tradition long sought to cultivate a unified command over bodily expression, style, and persuasive logics (Corbett 1971).

initially and consequently from perceiving how others appear to regard us. In the book for which he was best known during his lifetime, *The Theory of Moral Sentiments,* Smith classically provided the core formula for all conceptions of the self that attend to its essentially social character: "We endeavour to examine our own conduct as we imagine any other fair and impartial spectator would examine it. . . . [I]t is here that [one] first views the propriety and impropriety of his own passions, the beauty and deformity of his own mind" (Smith [1759] 1976, 110). Smith describes society as a "looking-glass," which persons use to comprehend and judge themselves. The self, in this formulation, is what the individual sees and assesses when taking the role of spectator.

George Herbert Mead drove this notion home by identifying certain of the experiential elements that enable it. Mead (1934) observed that ability to make use of verbal symbols constituted an essential prerequisite for self-formation and that grasping the meanings of symbols used by others toward one constituted the essential work of self-formation. Interactive processes of this sort form the grounds of human selves in all societies. The "impartial spectator" or "generalized other" who contributes the materials for this work gives every person the notion of just what it means to be a person in that culture and what constellation of social roles they are to play. To be a human is to be a Kuku Yalanji, a Tikopia, or a Baluchi; and to do what a mother, brother, villager, or hunter, as defined in one of those cultures, does.

The first step in the progression toward a liberal self takes place when prophetic innovators begin to encourage people to stop living in unreflecting habit and usage. This process, mentioned earlier, initiates the axial turning which informs all of the world civilizations.

THE CIVILIZED SELF AND THE INDIVIDUATED SELF   A special process of cultivating selves sets in when charismatic innovators generate a body of beliefs and practices that transcend the customary. In all these cases, the call is to turn from customary ways toward an objective order defined by revelatory visions and texts. Rather than comprising the normative model that all members of a culture can attain, the attainment of a higher order of selfhood is limited to an elite who undergo the special training designed to implement the axial vision.

Hindu tradition created the model of a *pure* self (*atman*). The process of cultivation consisted of a complex of demanding disciplines: meditation and yoga, leading to union (*ga*) with the Absolute; fulfillment of *dharma,* one's personal set of communal duties, in an upright and joyous manner; and *bhakti,* steadfast devotion to a deity, manifested through singing hymns, reciting mantras, dancing, going on pilgrimages, and observing temple rituals. Only those born to an elite stratum, the Brahmans, and who also undergo some program of arduous self-discipline prescribed by a guru, are eligible to attain this higher, salvific level of selfhood.

The Taoist ideal of selfhood was open to anyone but required disciplines to produce moderation in desires and emotions, and a special order of wisdom about life. Yogic exercises and meditations were practiced to produce humility, cleanliness, and emotional calm, and special techniques were practiced to ensure a long life, a major goal of Taoism. Alignment with the Way of the universe—the intuited pattern of cosmic rhythms—enabled those with special cultivation to surpass ordinary limits and achieve transcendence.

The Hebraic tradition came to focus on the study of sacred texts as the prime basis for attaining superior selfhood. In this tradition, the notion of an elite is subdued; the entire population comes to be described as a "kingdom of priests and a holy people." Even so, the study of its great books, especially *the* Book, becomes exalted to the extent that one who devotes his life to Torah is held in the highest esteem.

In a second type of civilizing work, the goal is not to discipline learners to adhere to objectively valid orders but to help learners cultivate themselves as a *special kind of person.* In classical times, we noted in chapter 1, this idea appeared in two notable sites. In China, it took the form of the Confucian gentleman, a person trained to exhibit consummate etiquette, polished artistic skills (especially in composing poetry and drawing), and accomplishment in the arts of war. In Hellenic Greece, it was manifest in the cultivation of a gentry elite, produced through rigorous training in both athletics and intellectual arts. In the modern West, it developed from the notion of knightly conduct and courtly etiquette into the post-Renaissance ideal of the gentleman.

Against all such orders of producing a civilized person through conformity to some sort of cultural ideal, there developed in the modern West a historically unique ideal, that of forming a self precisely not to be measured against any such ideal but through discovery and expression of a unique, distinctive person. The construction of this model can be traced through the self-interested citizen of Locke, the self-cultivating person of Humboldt, the existentially searching individual of Kierkegaard, the nonconformist authentic hero of Emerson, and the self-affirming individual of Nietzsche. This kind of individualism, Georg Simmel has shown, differs from all others in the past by virtue of its emphasis on unique individuality in contrast to culturally affirmed excellence (Simmel 1971, chaps. 15–17).

THE REFLECTIVE LIBERAL SELF   As the nineteenth century wore on, the notion of a uniquely individuated self became subtly transfigured. The emphasis shifted from the *content* of being utterly distinct to the *process* of reflective self-formation. Such a notion had its point of departure in philosophers of the distinctive ego, such as Emerson, whose doctrine of character formation included a serious moment of dissension from conventional norms on the basis of personal reflection. The process was further celebrated in Nietzsche's panegyric to heroic self-formation. It found powerful resonance in such places as Weber's discourses on value judgments and Simmel's conception of the individual law (*das individuelle Gesetz*), which stipulated that each individual has an obligation to make serious life choices and then reflect on them as part of a continuing process of self-development.

This sort of notion formed the heart and soul of Dewey's approach to education. Dewey did not care if the student was like or unlike others, "civilized" or not, a specialist or a generalist. His emphasis was on cultivating the ability of persons to raise questions, pursue inquiries, and think for themselves. Dewey found the capacity for independent thought to be especially essential in times of change, when established forms no longer seemed adequate for meeting human needs. When habits get disrupted by novel circumstances, the only constructive alternative to an eruption of impulsivity or to a frightened return to customary ways can be found in the practice of taking stock of the situation and subjecting it to intelligent reflection and creative reconstruction.

Dewey's follower W. I. Thomas retained this concern for personal reflexivity. Thomas championed what he called the "creative" person over against the hidebound "philistine" traditionalist and also the reactive "bohemian" rejectionist. For Thomas, humans are driven by desires both for stability and for new experience, wishes embodied in the philistine's love of social order, on the one hand, and the individual's demand for new experience, on the other. The creative person, he argued, reconciles society's demand for a maximum of stability with the individual's demand for a maximum of new experience by redefining situations and creating new norms of a superior social value (Thomas 1966, 171–81).

A generation later, David Riesman reproduced Thomas's typology in his influential schema of the adjusted, anomic, and autonomous forms of social character (Riesman and Associates 1950, 19). Riesman's ideal was what he called the autonomous self, a person capable of holding his or her own ground while exploring fresh territory with an inquiring and liberal mind. His emphasis on autonomy signaled a rejection of the tendency to polarize cultural attitudes by contrasting conventional beliefs and norms with emancipated, nonconformist, and oppositional attitudes. In educational terms, this position found its way into the Chicago tradition of pedagogy that aimed to cultivate independent thought, especially through the "teaching by discussion" approach of which Riesman was a prime exemplar.

What I am calling the reflective liberal self confronts the world by embodying a point of view with which to investigate the given objects of the prehended world and to express considered as well as authentic responses to them. It expresses not just an independent standpoint but emanates from a center that itself is continuously evolving. Both thinking and acting presuppose a certain amount of understanding but never absolute and total foreknowledge. The twin impediments to a reflective liberal self are the rush to closure and fixity, owing to insecurity about continuous change, and the flight from commitment to what a given situation evidently calls for.

I propose four marks of a self so constituted: individuality, autonomy, creativity, and authenticity. *Individuality* signifies the attainment and consolidation of features that distinguish one person from another. *Autonomy* signifies that such work derives from active choice. *Creativity* signifies the invention of responses that emanate from the individual's dispositions in the face of inadequate existing conditions. *Authenticity* signifies that these dispositions in fact reflect the individual's core values.

How might one set up an educational program explicitly designed to foster this set of powers? For individuality, one could present learners with an array of objects from which they would be encouraged to make selections. To enhance autonomy, one would encourage them to reflect on the sources of their selections—whether through imitating others, reproducing socially established preferences, or from themselves. For creativity, one might confront them with situations for which existing objects do not suffice and invite them to invent new kinds of responses. For authenticity, one could ask the learner to assess those responses by considering the extent to which they express the person's core values.

Inventing Statements, Problems, and Actions

Whereas the power of self-formation involves responding to a wide variety of objects in order to advance an evolving organization of a person's interests, tastes, and values, a different set of skills pertains to expressions by the self so formed. As illustrated in figure 3 in chapter 8, inventing statements, problems, and actions is the sixth of my eight powers of the mind.

COMPOSING STATEMENTS   We arrive first at what in earlier times was taught as a core—for some, like Isocrates and Cicero (as noted in chapter 1), *the* core—of liberal learning: the arts of rhetoric. Known commonly as invention, the first of these arts pertains to composing statements through symbolic media of varying sorts. When the classic masters of rhetoric spoke of invention, they had in mind the ability to summon appropriate and persuasive statements to substantiate claims.[2]

In providing some encouragement to invention, Aristotle distinguished between the persuasive force of untutored statements and that of *technoi pisteis,* or "artistic means of persuasion," which involves sophisticated abilities that are the fruit of discipline. These *technoi pisteis* include, for instance, the ability to know when it is appropriate, in the course of an argument, to define and compare subject matter, to specify its place in relation to other subjects (such as in a cause-and-effect relationship), and to note its limitations. External aids to invention include testimony from authoritative sources.

Cicero argued that inventive prowess is among the fruits of years of a liberal education that forces one to formulate statements concerning a wide variety of subjects and situations. Today, the avalanche of easily accessible facts discourages the cultivation of compositional skills derived from personal experience. Students are now drilled in the use of inventive aids, such as search engines, encyclopedias, and research indexes, and get good at reproducing materials on demand. What needs much more attention today is the ability to discriminate and select knowingly among the various kinds of sources and to use those selections to express one's evolving, complex self through appropriately complex symbols.

A second order of skills pertains to the genre and style in which statements are formulated. Truly liberal learning can include familiarity with expressive genres ranging from articles, abstracts of monographs, executive summaries, and outlines to reviews of poems, songs, plays, and photographic essays. It also includes knowledge about the media and venues of expression, to speak or to write, to publish in a journal or a magazine, to present at a conference or to post on the Web. It might also be time

2. See Aristotle's *Rhetoric* or Cicero's *De Inventione* for extensive meditations on the discovery, or invention, of arguments.

to reconsider the sense of memory, so much emphasized by classical rhetoricians, as a vehicle for recovering genres appropriate to a particular subject or situation and for specific or general audiences.

One need not comment at length on the general decline of writing skills in contemporary society. Problems—to name just a few—include poor vocabulary, inappropriate diction, overuse of figures of speech, and muddled paragraph composition: what are generally called problems of style. Rhetoricians have distinguished among three general styles geared to the subject of both oral and written composition: subdued (as in providing explanations); moderate (as in expressions of moral judgment); and grand (as in emotional calls to action). A well-disciplined heart produces a well-disciplined composition.[3]

Whether and at what point one should raise one's voice, or pace about the room while speaking, or raise an eyebrow at a criticism from a member of the audience are all features of communication that fall within the rhetorical domain known as delivery. Without an understanding of these subtleties, speakers risk being ineffective at communicating key points, appearing disinterested, failing to hold attention—in short, putting their audiences to sleep. Delivery is best learned not by reading but by practicing speech. Even though a large portion of communication involves speaking, very little attention is paid to teaching students how to do it well. Delivery was once a core feature of the American education system, as taught in elocution classes, but it is attended to now, if at all, only in such venues as debate forums and Model United Nations conferences.

FINDING AND RESOLVING PROBLEMS　　Perhaps the area of most dramatic difference between the liberally educated person and others concerns the ways in which problems are discovered, defined, and resolved. The conventional mind perceives problems when there is a conflict, defines the problem as limited to the symptoms of the conflict, and uses familiar, ready-to-hand methods for resolving it. The "civilized mind" identifies problems as failures to attain the high standards of its cultural heritage and solves them by an infusion of specialized cultural lore. The specialized mind identifies and defines problems through the lens of a particular set of notions acquired through training in a particular discipline and proceeds to address those problems with the tools that discipline has transmitted.

The powers of mind that liberally educated persons have acquired

---

3. On the relationship between grammar and rhetoric, see Corbett 1971, 416–18.

enable them to look beyond the surface of immediately given conflicts. Those powers further enable them to draw on a variety of civilized and specialized notions, in order to see which ones lead to more meaningful assessments and prefigure optimal outcomes. In an age of unprecedented specialization and cultural pluralism, this may well be the most difficult of all of the goals of liberal learning to approach.

In my teaching experience, the task of finding and formulating a problem has long posed the most difficult challenge faced by students. When not simply investigating a problem assigned by an instructor or principal investigator, they usually take the point of departure for inquiry from familiarity with either a body of data or a set of methodological skills. The most baffling question I put to students tends to be: What is your problem, and what is significant about it? Offering students a protected space in which to deal with such questions patently belongs to the repertoire of teaching responsibilities.

Students need to know how to discriminate among the kinds of inquiry involved, whether it is theoretical, technical, or practical. If theoretical, they need to know how and under what conditions a cognitive problem emerges and is justified. Comparing a number of exemplars of this sort can be a fruitful way to learn how cognitive problems get identified. If technical, they need to know how to identify and sift through a range of available techniques. If practical, a question becomes an object of the art of invention in a distinctive sense. Here what is invented is not simply the answer to an intellectual puzzle but a course of action designed to deal with a concrete problem about what to do in a given situation. The heart of acting well was depicted by Aristotle as the ability to choose a course of conduct in which one acts in a timely and appropriate manner that suits the occasion and is undertaken for valid reasons.

The ability to formulate problems can scarcely be fostered under systems of education in which students are never required to define and solve problems of their own. Curricular formats for this purpose can be imagined readily. In order to assist students to discriminate among radically different kinds of problems, however, it is imperative that they learn to distinguish different kinds of problems—for example, problems of pure knowing from problems of practice and problems of making. They also need to recognize problems of varying orders of magnitude— to distinguish finite problems that are solvable in principle with accessible tools and those enormously complex problems for which there is no such thing as a "solution" and which involve the collaboration of specialists from a variety of fields. To be able to make such distinctions requires capacities of another sort, those having to do with the integration of knowledge.[4]

Integrating Knowledge

Integrating knowledge is the seventh of my eight powers of the mind. This refers to integrating observations and interpretations with evaluative criteria, grasping ways in which the universe of knowledge can be systematized, finding and relating the deeper cognitive structures that map the universe, and finding connections among diverse paths of inquiry.

ASSESSING EVIDENCE AND ARGUMENT   Critical assessment of observations and texts goes on all the time in our lives. Even those who believe that all opinions are equally valid rely implicitly on standards and criteria. Liberally educated persons, classically and more than ever today, stand in need of resources that equip them to articulate and defend the grounds of their judgments and to apply those criteria judiciously and appropriately.

One difference between routine assessment and that based on sound liberal learning lies in the self-consciousness of the latter regarding those grounds and awareness of a repertoire of resources that could be applied. The third-year course in the humanities sequence of the Faust-Ward curriculum at the University of Chicago focused precisely on such skills and resources. It introduced students to a select group of aesthetic critical positions and then invited them to apply these positions to a given work of art. I am unaware of any curriculum in the natural or social sciences that does the same thing. My essay "The Forms and Functions of Social Knowledge" (1986) presented a paradigm of such criteria for assessing work in the social sciences, but any of these criteria would be applicable in the natural sciences as well. One set of such criteria concerned the functions or objectives of an inquiry—what they are, how they are defended, and how well they are defended. Toward creating a paradigm of functions (Levine 1986, 280–81), I once proposed the following outline:

    A. Cultural functions
       1. Grounding a worldview
       2. Grounding normative criteria

---

4. Schwab provided an especially penetrating and creative analysis of practical inquiry (see chapter 6).

3. Providing aesthetic symbolism
4. Providing empirical understanding
   a. of universals and variants
   b. of self-experience and others
B. Social systemic functions
   1. Technical knowledge
   2. Counsel to rulers/insurgents
   3. Shared beliefs/enhanced communication
   4. Clarifying collective values and enhancing their transmission
C. Personality and behavioral system functions
   1. Increasing consciousness about self and self-situation
   2. Increasing clarity about one's values
   3. Enhanced cognitive competence

A second group of criteria concerned the appropriateness of the cognitive forms employed for the purpose of pursuing that inquiry. Are the forms employed because of the author's investment in, if not addiction to, a particular way of looking at things or because such ways are fashionable or politically advantageous? Are they employed exclusively when they might better be complemented by another kind of approach? What is the line of connection, and how transparent and how strong, supple, or transparent is it?

Regarding the intrinsic or internal quality of those forms—their degrees of excellence, economy, human relevance, and potential damage—the paradigm (Levine 1986, 278) posited three categories of criteria:

1. Criteria of validity
   a. Accuracy
   b. Logical consistency
   c. Clarity
   d. Completeness of scope
2. Criteria of significance
   a. Heuristic value
   b. Appropriateness to content of inquiry
   c. Appropriateness to purpose of inquiry
   d. Quality of relevant purposes and values
3. Criteria of quality of execution
   a. Extent to which forms are properly or elegantly realized
   b. Extent to which forms remain linked to defensible purposes

Imagine how exciting, and empowering, it would be for a group of students to apply a set of such criteria to texts of various kinds, not to mention to generate their own inventory of such resources!

CONSTRUCTING ENCYCLOPEDIC KNOWLEDGE   A hallmark of liberal learning has always been the broadening of outlook and expansion of the scope of knowledge about the world. At one time, it might have been possible for the most cultivated person to acquire a basic grasp of all that was known about the world in some systematic way. On the eve of the modern era, the aspiration to systematize all that knowledge in a single set of volumes incited the effort to fashion an all-embracing course of general education, or *encyclopedia*. As Diderot famously described the generation-long campaign to create such a product, "The purpose of an encyclopedia is to collect the knowledge dispersed on the surface of the earth, and to unfold its general system" (Diderot [1755] 1961, 92). In their early forms, encyclopedias fulfilled three functions: to provide some kind of intellectual order for the universe of knowledge; to set paths and topics of inquiry for scholars; and to provide students with an accessible comprehensive store of information.

In our time, only the last of these functions remains, and it is this function that we commonly associate with the encyclopedic enterprise. Encyclopedias of all sorts—from the global *Britannica* and *World Book* to specialty works like the encyclopedias of *Mineralogy, Mongol History,* and *Medical Devices and Instrumentation*—afford ready access to the most arcane bits of knowledge. We have come to use the epithet "encyclopedic" to describe those whose vast stores of knowledge make them truly well educated.

But would we consider them liberally educated? Does possession of a wide range of facts in itself entail a power to integrate facts into a comprehensive perspective of understanding? Is there really much of a difference in kind between people who know such wide reaches of fact and one who has memorized half the contents of a telephone book? Such learning affords no real opening up of the spirit.

To be sure, the liberally educated person knows how to make prudent use of the world's stocks of knowledge, all the more so in these days when computer storages require a certain level of electronic adroitness. It is important to be able to connect, say, what happened in Neolithic agriculture to what happened in the religious and artistic worlds of that epoch and to be able to determine which facts are most salient. Here, however, the learner remains at the mercy of a world of knowing that grows outside of him or her and is relevant to his or her purposes only in a limited utilitarian sense.

It is when one deals with questions of how a whole world of knowledge is to be ordered that one begins to feel empowered and creative vis-à-vis the known and knowable universe. This empowerment relates, on the one hand, to a critical awareness of how published organizations of knowledge can be organized—whether, for example, by date, themes, illustrious figures, or simply alphabetically. On the other hand, it relates to an even broader conception of philosophical ordering, such as how one holds facts in relation to probabilities or opinions in ascertaining what one actually knows.

COMMISSIONING DEEP STRUCTURES OF KNOWLEDGE   In our time, we take for granted the fact that everyone must become proficient in a certain epistemic domain; we specialize for our professions. The beginnings of liberality in this extremely specialized setting come when the specialist reaches out or thinks to see how that domain connects with others. We determine what is pertinent to our larger goals by assumptions regarding the ways in which various fields can be interconnected. Doing so requires a cognitive map of the universe, which in turn proceeds from underlying assumptions about that universe.

Surely, one of the strong ways of doing so is found in the course that Richard McKeon and colleagues devised at the University of Chicago, initially called Observation, Interpretation, and Integration (OII) and later Organizations, Methods, and Principles of the Sciences. That course compared various responses to such questions as the meaning of theoretical knowledge, the forms it might take, and what purposes it serves; a range of warranted methodological approaches and kinds of rationales employed on their behalf; diverse assumptions about what the knowable world consists of; and the types and meanings of practical knowledge and how they relate to the theoretical.[5] Learning experiences of this sort can do wonders to liberate learners from accepting conventional packaging of knowledge as inevitable and universally pertinent.

FINDING CONNECTED PATHS OF INQUIRY   Given the amount of resources that go into disciplined investigation in our society and the opportunities for people to acquire them, the question of how and where to commit those resources takes on unprecedented significance. Indeed, this

5. For a later version of that course, see chapter 12.

question looms large in public deliberation about the allocation of vast sums in the budgets of federal and state agencies and of diverse foundations. It is difficult to know how to make such decisions without at least a rough sense of priorities based on what is already known and what is worth knowing next, itself predicated on assumptions about the knowledge most worth having.

Such considerations also need to attend to questions regarding connections among established fields that may not be transparent to someone pursuing or evaluating any particular research proposal. A line of investigation that seems to mark a major breakthrough in one field may simply reproduce what has already long since been accomplished in some other field. What is more, awareness of a broader context of knowledge may reorient an inquiry in some more fruitful direction. It should not be hard to find dramatic examples of wasted resources, missed opportunities, and deeply misguided projects to provoke a student's awareness of such issues.

Before the special interests of students become hardened into structures that exclude and often devalue the work of other specialists, they can taste the possibility and potential of a more inclusive, collaborative even, type of inquiry. This point raises the more general issue of the promise and difficulties of communication, a concern that arguably forms the apex of a program of liberal learning designed to develop powers of the mind.[6]

Communicating

The last of my eight powers of the mind is the power of communication. This includes two highly significant skills, the ability to create expressions that are attuned to the pertinent audience and the ability to engage in mutually transformative dialogue.

SELF-EXPRESSION IN CONTEXT   The first order of powers of personal expression concerns the work of forming a self and drawing on that form to invent statements and discover problems. The second order concerns expanding that effort to take into account wider or more inclusive domains. Along the way, the self must acknowledge the pertinence of other selves.

To begin with, the communicating self needs to take into account the needs and background of the hearer. This process entails making educated guesses about what the audience already knows or thinks it knows

---

6. For a searching investigation of ways that specialists differing on such dimensions might be educated to communicate more adequately, see Kissel forthcoming.

about the topic in question. It involves no less some educated sense of what their probable emotional reactions are likely to be, in order to maximize both the reception of the message and the likelihood that the hearers will proceed to act in a manner desired by the speaker. These concerns formed a significant part of the teachings of classical rhetoric.

Beyond that, the speaker needs to have some understanding of the legitimate limits that the hearers may themselves place on the acceptability of what the speaker is propounding. This power leads quickly to a sense of humility, in the sense of displaying enough respect for the hearer to refrain from a wholly instrumental attitude. One thing this power evinces is an acceptance of fundamental ambiguities in the meaning of concepts. One of the more challenging goals of liberal learning may be to acquire the capacity to articulate clearly the meaning of a core concept while at the same time respecting the hearer's potential and right to use it in a different sense.

Failure to develop some of this reflexive liberality accounts for the ubiquitous pathologies of everyday interaction: the hammer who sees each problem as a nail, the pianist who plays against the strings rather than with them, the health enthusiast who inflicts each favorite remedy on all comers. Martial arts practice can stop with kata whereby the practitioner employs a perfected technique in all situations; or else, as in aikido, it can recognize that rigidity of form betokens weakness and foolhardiness, since situations, protagonists, and interlocutors vary among themselves and over time.

ENLARGING THE SCOPE OF DIALOGUE   In the schema I have been proposing, the climax of liberal learning appears in the experience of genuine dialogue. In acquiring the ability and taste for dialogue, the learner becomes capable not merely of respecting the characteristics of the hearer in order to advance his or her own purposes. The learner also rises to a point of acknowledging that the hearer offers a constant challenge for mutuality and growth. This condition is inherently stressful and difficult to realize. Yet it follows finally from the core conception of the reflexive liberal self, which demands that the growing, learning self consider constant input from others as part of a normal life of the bodymind.

At this point, learning proceeds to encompass a power that has hitherto been almost totally unexamined in the liberal curriculum. That is to develop a working awareness of the forms, functions, and dynamics of dialogic interaction. This domain offers a challenging frontier for educators open to reinventing the liberal curriculum.

For one thing, there is the dialogue of presenting some facts and learning from someone else that some of those facts are disputed. There is the dialogue of recognizing the right of others to contest the meaning of one's favored concepts. There is the dialogue of being challenged to look at familiar and commonly accepted facts from a wholly contrasting perspective. And there is the dialogue of acknowledging the legitimacy and impact of another's use of radically contrasting principles.[7]

As one gains experience in the use of dialogic powers, the whole point and purpose of liberal learning become transfigured subtly. The reflexive liberal self exists no longer as the sole subject of the entire enterprise. If full development of that self becomes linked inexorably to the quality of interaction between two subjects, then the point of liberal learning has to expand to include the quality of respectful interchange between two growing centers. If the quality of respectful interchange is to be sustained, then liberal learning will to some degree have to be grounded in the values and norms of an encompassing community.[8]

7. In the remaining chapters of this book, I shall say more about this domain, both in reflecting on its cultivation through different forms of pedagogy and in reviewing how I have come to try to promote this power in courses developed at Chicago over several decades.

8. Projected onto a theological plane, this idea becomes equivalent to the notion of an evolving universe based on continuous interaction with an evolving deity.

11

New Ways of Framing Pedagogy

However elegant a curriculum, it does not teach itself. Yet what "teaching" amounts to remains more underanalyzed than the notion of liberal education. Unlike the latter term, *teaching* rarely attracts critical attention. Assuming that everyone knows what it means to teach, and what teaching means is something simple and straightforward, liberal arts administrators tend to see their task as finding enough teaching bodies to fill the classrooms.

In arguments as apt today as half a century ago, Robert Maynard Hutchins and Joseph Schwab stressed that what goes into being a good teacher differs radically from what makes a research specialist good. That point, however, forms only the beginning of a discourse. Ambiguous to the core, the concept of teaching covers an array of modalities, none of which by itself suits all existing educational objectives. New instructional technologies, being employed extensively long before they come under critical scrutiny, now complicate the matter further.

To broach this disarmingly complex question, I distinguish several modalities of the teaching-learning process according to the particular ends that they serve (see table 5). I do so on the assumption that instructors teach more effectively and students learn more successfully by getting clear about just what type of teaching-learning process is intended. These modalities are then illustrated by applying them to teaching some of the powers identified in previous chapters. Following that, I discuss four

TABLE 5 Means and ends in teaching and learning

End	Material	Instructor's task	Student's task	Outcome
What to answer	Information	Transmit	Apprehend, remember	Knowledge
How to perform	Skills	Demonstrate	Train	Artfulness
How to act well	Virtues	Model	Imitate, practice, internalize	Character
How to reflect	Personal challenges	Educate	Select, integrate	Authentic formed self
How to live	Insight into a way	Teach	Understand	Wisdom

forms of instruction available for these teaching-learning processes: didactic, referral, dialogue, and assignment (see table 6).

Modalities of Teaching and Learning

One kind of teaching consists in the transmission of *information* about the world. The periodic table, the structure of haiku, the sonata form, the parameters of population change, the members of a language family—such are among the innumerable kinds of things that teachers impart and students retain. The goal is to give students knowledge so that they will know what to answer when questions of fact and context come up. Good teaching requires that the instructor be knowledgeable and possess effective ways of packaging and delivering the information. Being a good student means being alert to such presentations and to ways of organizing and retaining that information.

This modality encompasses all that is customarily understood when one makes reference to the learning process. The question of the knowledge most worth having becomes rendered as a question of identifying the most valuable kinds of subject matter. Herbert Spencer (1861) answered that question by designating the natural sciences because the understanding of the world they provide leads to improved adaptation. Others point to knowledge of one's culture, or of other cultures, or of existential conditions in the modern world.

TABLE 6 Forms of teaching

	Form of Instruction			
Desired Outcome	Didactic	Referral	Dialogue	Assignment
Knowledge	Lecture	Study of publications	Ask about experiences; guide inner and external observation	Answer questions about facts
Artfulness	Show techniques; monitor learner	Referral to manuals, experts	Practice how to converse	Show how to do something
Character	Elucidate right ways to act	Exemplary figures	Model inquiry and expression	Perform in accord with standards
Authentic formed self	Show self as learner	Exemplary texts	Interpret, compare, evaluate, argue, integrate	Articulate personal significance of something learned
Wisdom	Profess an ideal	Assigned scriptures	Lead conversant to experience the way	Show the way

A little reflection, however, shows that the end of learning cannot be restricted to the mastery of facts, however broad, however privileged. For we also expect someone who has finished a course of education to be able to *do* some things he or she could not do, or do so well, beforehand. A second type of learning addresses this expectation. It involves the acquisition of *skills*.

When students learn how to conduct lab experiments, interpret poems, play music, analyze aggregate data, or compare language families, they develop capacities they can use on their own to utilize facts or create new ones. The goal of such learning is an ability to perform some kind of activity. Good teaching requires that the instructor be competent and experienced enough to demonstrate the skills in question in a robust and nuanced manner. It also requires some organization of the learning process to fit varying levels of development. The student's role involves willingness to train and keep on training, an active process of trying and "failing" and trying again. When successful, this kind of learning results in the attainment of one or more arts.

Once an art is learned, it can be practiced on a number of levels. There are temptations to rush to conclusions at the expense of methodical work, to cut corners, to simulate, to plagiarize, and to settle for a mediocre rather than an excellent outcome. Performing something well then becomes construed as action in accord with certain *virtues*. In this context, one can learn to be scrupulous in taking measurements in the lab, fair in the interpretation of poems, attentive to the performance of music, fastidious in the representation of data, and sensitive in dealing with language. Then too, respect for the people and objects of one's world embodies virtues that constrain the use of skills for narrow or destructive purposes. For this kind of learning, the teacher stands as a model, and the student's job is to imitate the model, practice the pertinent virtues, and internalize the ideal standards. The outcome will be some forms of virtue, components of what has been called "character."

To this point, the modalities of teaching and learning have been couched in terms of their relevance to engagement with external objects. None of these modalities, however, quite taps the semantic root of "education," which connotes rather a drawing out from and engagement with the self. This mode plays a central role in Rousseau's *Émile* and, above all, in the German idea of *Bildung* (personal cultivation) exemplified by Johann Wolfgang von Goethe, Johann Gottfried von Herder, Alexander von Humboldt, and, in the United States, Ralph Waldo Emerson. This educational vision was articulated in Georg Simmel's notion of subjective culture and implemented in his proposals for educational reform (Levine 1991c). It directs attention to the developmental needs of a subject who evolves through engagement with and reflection on *personal challenges*.

In this dimension, one treats engagement with elements, poetry, music, statistics, or language as ingredients that help form a maturing self. The goal is to fortify students' resources for finding distinctive personal paths and expressing themselves authentically. Good teaching requires instructors to be sensitive to the differences among individual students and to possess a repertoire of resources suited to minister to each. The good student here strives to be open, courageous, and reflective, so that the outcome of this type of learning is a well-constituted personality.

There is, finally, a type of teaching and learning associated with persons who have historically been glossed as Teachers, such figures as Moses, Socrates, Confucius, Pantanjali, Buddha, Jesus, Muhammad. This is the notion celebrated in Kierkegaard's discourses on the Teacher. In our own time, the notion is widely represented by the Sanskrit loanword *guru*. The founder of aikido, Morihei Ueshiba, became generally known as O Sensei, literally Great Teacher.

Introducing this type into our repertoire of resources for liberal learning does not signify that instructors should strive to reproduce the teachings of these extraordinary teachers. I mean only to use them as exemplars to suggest kinds of teaching and learning that can take place anywhere when the teacher allows or encourages a student to connect some present experience to the broadest cosmos of meanings, which could be described as a moment of epiphanic *insight* into a *Way*. It is perhaps the moment Simmel celebrated when noting how one could take any surface detail of experience and use it as a channel for plumbing the ultimate depths of being and meaning (Simmel [1907] 1978, 55).

In this mode, the student's task is one of being open to transcendent understanding, of engaging an episode of powerful and empowering integration. This kind of teaching can follow a number of routes. One occurs when the teacher promulgates visions and mandates in order to connect the individual with the broader universe. In another, teachers simply present themselves as models for general emulation.[1] A third involves a kind of Socratic leading of the student's reflectivity toward including self-concerns in increasingly broad contexts. The outcome of such learning is sometimes thought of as wisdom, as an evolving foundation of understanding about the good life.

---

1. This distinction follows Max Weber's typology of prophets as "emissary" and "exemplary" (1978, 447–49).

From "Teaching" to Teaching Powers

The teaching modalities just outlined can all be employed on behalf of any of the curricular principles outlined in chapter 8: the character of the learner, the universe of things to be known, the heritage of human productions, or the powers of knowing and creating. Given the approach taken in this book, I want to explore how one might revitalize liberal education on the basis of lessons from the Chicago experience—by reinventing a curriculum organized around the cultivation of powers.

POWERS OF PREHENDING OBJECTS   To cultivate any of the powers requires a minimum of factual knowledge. Becoming acquainted with auditory, visual, or literary texts requires *information* regarding such obvious, if commonly overlooked, matters as date of publication, issues of translation, obscure references, and, to a greater or lesser extent depending on the pedagogical point at hand, facts pertinent to locating such artifacts in their historical contexts. In acquainting students with Weber's *Protestant Ethic* essay, one needs to attend, for example, to the important point that the author's foreword was written sixteen years after the original essay, or to the fact that the word *Beruf*, like "vocation," embodies double meanings of a verb signifying "to call."

Prehending any text also involves a number of *skills*, some obvious, some often overlooked. They include the abilities

to create a compact, meaningful schema of the text, such as an outline or an index of key elements and ideas;

to discern and assess the author's agenda(s) and underlying assumptions;

to analyze the form of the author's presentation;

to determine what would happen to the author's argument if one or another assumption were relaxed; and

to compare some of the author's propositions or models with those of others or with those in other texts by the same author.

The role of teachers who embody *virtues* deserves to be acknowledged as a source of empowerment. With this point in mind, teachers may be encouraged to provide ideal models in their own best moments and to honor heroic figures whom the students may be led to emulate. The virtues to be acquired include habits of precision in personal apprehension, humility before the objects themselves, care in hearing the statements of others, and integrity in all aspects of the prehension of objects.

A different set of powers comes into play when one attends to learning modalities involved in actualizing a reflective self. In contrast to a curriculum designed to promote the character of the learner, where discrete and determinate personal challenges form building blocks that structure the entire learning experience, in a curriculum organized to cultivate discrete powers of knowing and creating, such challenges nourish particular powers. For example, the teaching and learning of aikido can be organized as a method to produce a particular kind of human being or to cultivate such discrete powers as self-confidence, patience, or openness. When objects are prehended as *personal challenges,* they become elements that teachers and learners can select as aids to self-criticism and self-formation.

Is there a determinate power or set of powers that comes from teaching and learning a Way, a vision of the good life? One approach to this question might emphasize the power to experience epiphanies sparked by the synthesis of virtues of prehending objects together with externalizations of a reflective self. The power of prehending a Way involves a synthesis of virtues of relating to the worlds of objects and the powers that constitute a reflective self. To be in or on the Way means being informed by and transforming the world.

POWERS OF EXPRESSING SUBJECTS   Transmitting information, developing skills, inculcating virtues, reflecting on challenges, and glimpsing a Way also relate, in differing degrees, to advancing the second set of powers. These are powers that pertain to articulating one's place in the worlds of objects and initiating changes in them. More concretely today, these powers equip persons to deal constructively with the complexities of intermixed cultures, divergent functions, and normative confusion. This quartet represents the kinds of educational programs linked with Dewey's notion of creative learning and with curricula that emphasize electivity and individuated development.

The formation of a self requires information about one's autobiography, one's social and cultural genealogy and heritage, and the existential circumstances that configure one's options. For many students, acquiring such information might entail learning parental home languages or aesthetic traditions. Skills of observation and interpretation infuse the growth of the self. Issues of authenticity depend on virtues of carrying out such processes with honor, integrity, and openness. The power of self-formation draws continuously on the processing of personal challenges, including those painful ones brought by life's inevitable misfortunes. The capstone of self-formation appears when subjects glimpse their ultimate connections with the grounds and summits of being.

With a little thought, one can articulate ways in which the five teaching-learning modalities apply as well to cultivating the powers of inventing words and deeds, of weaving one's personal synthesis of knowledge, and of engaging in fruitful communication with others. All of these powers benefit from information about life situations that have elicited certain creative responses in others and about exemplars of efforts to solve problems and integrate fields. All entail the learning of discursive skills — translation, analytics, diagnostics, and prescriptions. They incorporate the teaching of virtue, including openness to difference, generosity of understanding, imagination, foresight, and control over one's passions in decision making. They mature through experiences that prod the person to engage in reflection and further integration, which in turn adumbrate a life of prudence, wisdom, and creativity.

A Repertoire of Teaching Forms

The word *teaching* commonly evokes the image of someone standing at a lectern or sitting at a desk, directing streams of information toward relatively empty minds. It is easy to take offense at this image, especially when it is taken to imply that that is all there is to "teaching." As we have just seen, the full range of teaching tasks includes demonstrating, educating, modeling, and professing, as well as transmitting. What is more, the full battery of pedagogical *methods* includes means other than lecturing. Teaching and learning also take place by referring students to learning resources, such as libraries and computers; engaging them in focused conversation; and designing pertinent assignments. Even so, the teacher who leads from the front can accomplish a great deal. How much gets accomplished depends on both the style and the content of what is conveyed. Since little is gained if the teacher simply repeats material available to the students through outside sources, the lecture should focus on clarifying, supplementing, and correcting material students have been asked to cover, and it should do so in ways that will magnetize the students' attention.

Monologic teaching can also serve each of the other teaching tasks. It is perhaps the most effective method of all for demonstrating skills. Learning specific techniques, such as laboratory procedures, statistical manipulations, or using a foreign language, is achieved most effectively through seeing or hearing them done by a master practitioner first and then having the master supervise the learner's practice.

In addition, ways of thinking can be represented didactically as when, for example, the teacher lectures about interpretation, comparison, evaluation, argument, or integration, or by modeling, when the teacher uses his or her own conduct to exemplify those intellectual powers. Finally, the teacher can direct students monologically to understand and embrace pertinent ideals about learning and living.

However effective monologic teaching at its best, other forms offer ways to perform certain teaching tasks more effectively or uniquely. One involves the teacher's referring students to outside resources. Familiar from the ubiquitous recourse to reading assignments, this method of teaching can be upgraded by devising more differentiated paradigms of work. For retrieving information, the teacher can empower the student with assignments that require independent recourse to sources including data banks, encyclopedias, search engines, library stacks, and people with knowledge or special experiences. For developing skills, the student can be directed to read technical manuals, watch expert practitioners, and develop habits through regular training with others. For cultivating intellectual powers, students can be directed to texts specifically chosen to exhibit the skills at work. They can also be directed to exemplary figures who model such work. And they can be pointed to scriptures that profess ways of living a good life and enable students to encounter Great Souls.

The least commonly exploited pedagogical mode is that of conversation. This is the modality for which a campus setting is most essential. If one can access libraries and Web sites on one's own, and even audit great lecturers on video, one still cannot experience the powerful surge of learning that takes place through personal interaction with other students and master teachers.

Even at the pedestrian level of securing *information,* conversation can be important. One can ask students in a class to relate their experiences in other countries, for example, or in speaking different languages. One can elicit conversation about why it is important to secure a certain body of facts and about the most effective ways of determining them. Many performative *skills* are enhanced through coaching by members of an audience. If someone is struggling to execute a blackboard picture of a model, a literary translation, or a dramatic technique, it is often helpful to have others in the group take part in coaching or offering suggestions to the performer.

Arguably, the most effective way to cultivate basic *intellectual powers* is to have an experienced teacher draw out a student's responses to a number of analytic questions. For example, the teacher might ask, "What is the author assuming about human nature in this case?" "If you make a different assumption about human nature, how does that affect the rest of the author's argument?" "Could you apply this mode of comparing plants to the comparison of vertebrates?" "What is the relation of what is said in the introduction to what is said in the conclusion?"

Conversation is also useful for reinforcing all of the *norms* that are embodied in the use of the powers. When participants face one another, they are likely to be more keenly aware of their need for clarity, integrity, openness, proficiency, and the like, and they are also positioned to receive the sanctions attendant on their practice or abandonment of such qualities. Finally, the process of communication is the key ingredient in forming a community, and communal legitimization and even sacralization of the good life through successful discourse can provide a powerful experience.

The point of all this analysis is to evoke a well-differentiated set of pedagogical tools. Let us look, for example, at how one might apply the options outlined in table 5 to the cultivation of the powers of self-formation and of communication. Thus, in the area of forming selves, the instructor could transmit information about such processes, explore a range of pertinent arguments, and model from her own experience moments in which options were faced, values were assessed, and choices were made. The instructor might further direct students to the lives of significant figures whose autobiographies document the process of self-formation. Or in teaching through conversation, the instructor might—in a setting where trust and openness have been established—ask students to discuss issues of their own self-formation, past, present, or future.[2]

In the area of communicating, the instructor could lecture about instances of successful and unsuccessful communication and what the causes and consequences of those instances seem to have been. He or she could demonstrate some simple skills of listening and public speaking, raise questions about the factors that enter into the communication process, and analyze studies of various rhetorical forms. The instructor could use his or her own person to model the attentiveness, openness, and nondefensiveness that are essential to good communication. Alternatively, the instructor could refer students to stories of great orators, handbooks of rhetoric, exemplary texts, or cases of tragically failed communication.

The dialogic method conspicuously recommends itself for teaching the power of communication. Self-reflection on the processes of communication in a group, facilitated now through techniques of video and audio taping, can provide a cache of evidence useful for subsequent analy-

2. The idea to have students reflect on their intellectual autobiographies at the end of the senior year was broached in the Report of the Task Force on the Senior Year (University of Chicago College Center for Curricular Thought 1984a).

sis. Participants could get instant feedback regarding their skills in listening and speaking (see chapter 9). Since everyone has lifelong experience in communicating, issues regarding the elements of good and bad communication can readily be examined in class discussion. If and when the group achieves this level of trust and openness, its members may even glimpse a moment of what it means to partake of a good human life—which, as Martin Buber among others has argued, takes place only in the process of dialogue.

Approaches to Testing

In compiling their taxonomy of educational objectives, Benjamin S. Bloom and his associates (B. Bloom et al. 1956) held the problem of testing constantly in mind. They valued precise identification of teaching objectives as a means to link curriculum, pedagogy, and assessment closely. New programs of liberal learning suffer from vagueness and incompleteness when they are not integrated transparently with appropriate modes of testing experience and assessment of skills achieved. Even programs that place weight on effective teaching often neglect to examine pertinent instruments of testing.

The value of a considered system of testing is fourfold. It requires a more precise articulation of goals and outcomes than might otherwise be forthcoming. It enables teachers to focus on what kinds of learning they are actually expecting students to experience. Tests also facilitate the articulation of distinct levels of achievement in a given area. Such a focus would patently rule out any sort of "teaching for exams" when the exams in question bear no relationship to stated goals of the pertinent curriculum.

From the point of view of the learner, the additional element of anxiety involved—insofar as it can be held to an appropriate level—can make the learners more aware of their levels of greater and lesser development. It can also energize them to perform in a superior way if the test is meaningful. In fact, a properly designed testing assignment can contribute so powerfully to the experience of learning that I have chosen to include it as one of the principal forms of teaching rather than as a distinct category of events within the educational program.

Perhaps we could go even further. If testing indeed constitutes a form of teaching, there should in principle be no difference between the type of authority manifest in the testing situation and that in other kinds of teaching situations. That has rarely been case. The minute that examinations and grades come up in a course, the atmosphere changes. The relation between teacher and student shifts subtly, in a direction that arguably interferes with the optimal educational experience of the student. This shift was so apparent to Schwab, Bloom, and other architects of the Faust-Ward College, or "Second Hutchins College," that they established a Board of Examiners that was structurally independent of the faculty teaching the courses. That way, went the rhetoric, teachers would be removed from a role that made them antagonists of the students, and they could work with the students against the (nasty old) examiners.

Although that arrangement had its advantages, it did not go far enough. If challenging students with experiences wherein they are assessed can be construed as inherently educational, then why should those experiences be tinted as more alienating or threatening than any other appropriate form of pedagogy? Why not build right into the learning process the expectation that it will contain some mixture of monologue, referral, dialogue, and assessment, as appropriate to the subject and educational objective at hand?

Suppose, then, we relax the assumption that testing distorts the learning process and include it among the normal expectable tools of instruction, and proceed to review types of testing assignments with an eye to noting their respective strengths and weakness for a variety of educational purposes. It is evident that no single type of test is suitable for identifying and assessing all kinds of powers. When the desired outcome is knowledge, a familiar battery of testing instruments is at hand. These instruments have been the subject of extensive assessment themselves, or so I hope, so I shall move on to consider ways to facilitate diverse kinds of learning through other assignments. When other types of learning objectives are in play, I suspect that we have almost no codified understanding at the collegiate level, at least regarding ways to assess those outcomes.

Exploring this territory should be one of the many fascinating agenda items for educators of the next generation. They will want to consider types of assignments that can elicit efforts to demonstrate a variety of capacities, productions that could begin to fill a learning portfolio. They may find ways to articulate a set of virtues that can be assessed by type of performance. It should not be difficult to assign for that portfolio some kinds of evidence of thought regarding how some of the learning experiences have helped develop them as genuine persons. And then, who knows, they may even find ways to move students toward manifesting the larger Teachings they have tasted in the course of a liberal education.

The following chapter will include examples of some of the ways in which I have sought to weave specially designed testing experiences into the warp and woof of the liberal curriculum.

12

My Experiments in Teaching Powers

At the University of Chicago, from time to time, a combination of special institutional structures . . . , exceptional presidential leadership and rhetoric . . . ,
and traditions of intense faculty concern with education have [served] to generate excellent educational thought and practice.   P R O L O G U E

And so it is that, living within those structures, inspired by that rhetoric,
and exposed to that thought, I was led to reflect on these matters while
composing a repertoire of teaching initiatives. This is to say that although
I may at times have deliberately constructed a course in order to help students acquire certain disciplines, just as often I did so in a state of barely
conscious enactment of some dimly discerned cultural script. I propose
now to bring those diverse initiatives for forging powers of the mind to
fuller consciousness.

Searching for Disciplines

No doubt about it, foundational questions are the hardest. They are also
the most interesting—which is why seasoned scholars often love to teach
barely literate young students. In their naïveté, the latter do not hesitate to
raise compelling questions that are often unanswerable.

Pedagogues sometimes think they are getting into deeply foundational
issues when they raise the question of how to teach. That is not at all so.
Prior to asking how to teach, one must already have settled the question of

what one is to teach. And prior to deciding what to teach, one must resolve the question of *why* something should be taught. Although such questions remain perennially open to debate, sound pedagogy presumes some coming to terms with them with some level of sureness. In chapter 2, I reviewed arguments about the nature of educational goals and the appropriate means to attain them. Among key foundational principles of a liberal-general curriculum, most salient was the principle of promoting *disciplines,* in the sense of cultivated powers of the mind (rather than as fields of study defined by subject matters). Since at the University of Chicago that principle has enjoyed the most substantial development and remains one I find deeply congenial, it is the one I find myself returning to most often when I consider foundational questions of the liberal curriculum.

To focus on disciplines is to open an inquiry into their nature and scope. One thing about that issue I can assert with confidence. There is not, nor can there be, some perennially valid, single inventory of disciplines that might arguably be relevant to cultivating human beings and citizens in a liberal manner. Just as the skills needed to function in a society of hunter-gatherers differ from those needed in agricultural societies, so the liberal disciplines appropriate to an era of religious humanism differ from those appropriate to an era of high-tech internationalism. In our time, the emergence of dazzling new methodologies—biochemical analysis, new bodywork modalities, chaos theory, clairsentient somatics, comparative civilizational studies, computer programming, conversation analysis, empathic introspection, genetic engineering, high-energy experimentation, lexicostatistics, magnetic resonance imaging, rational choice analysis—makes it barely possible to imagine a single comprehensive inventory. What is more, rapidly changing societal circumstances call for new kinds of leadership skills and intellectual capacities that have barely been identified.

Reviewing the teaching projects of my career, I realize that they have been animated by a more or less continuous effort to identify and cultivate new kinds of intellectual disciplines. In the early 1970s, I sought to delineate disciplinary forms that pertained to the educational value of sociology. The results of that effort, I hope, might remain relevant to readers of this book. I argued that "sociology may be seen as one of a number of social sciences all of which employ some combination of a number of related intellectual disciplines. In other words, to understand what sociology has to offer as an educational subject we must deal with disciplinary forms that crosscut the conventional boundaries of sociology as well as some that are no longer included within sociology" (1971, 6). Using this perspective, I identified a set of basic social disciplines, organized as simple, compound, and complex. The *simple* disciplines each deal with a single basic intellectual function: observation, conceptualization, or evaluation. What I call *compound* are those that involve two of the simple disciplines. *Complex* disciplines combine multiple terms.

> *Simple:* empirical methodology, categorical theory, normative philosophy;
> *Compound:* scientific reportage, utopiology, casuistry;[1]
> *Complex:* explanation, criticism, diagnosis, prescription.
> *Empirical Methodology* is the general name for the disciplines of making controlled observations. In sociology alone it consists of a number of subdisciplines, including content analysis, descriptive statistics, fieldwork techniques, historiography, interviewing techniques, laboratory techniques, phenomenology, and projective testing.
> *Categorical Theory* is the discipline of grounding and articulating conceptual schemes.
> *Normative Philosophy* is the discipline of grounding and articulating evaluative standards.
> *Scientific Reportage* combines empirical methodology with categorical theory. It is the discipline of making controlled observations within a framework of articulated theory.
> *Utopiology* combines categorical theory with normative philosophy. It is the discipline of imaginatively realizing a set of evaluative standards in terms of an articulated model of social reality.
> *Casuistry* combines empirical methodology and normative philosophy. It is the discipline of applying normative standards to phenomena that have been observed and represented in a disciplined way.
> *Explanation* is the discipline of relating one set of observations to another set of observations in terms of an articulated model which posits some kind of causal or other meaningful relationship between the two orders of facts involved. This discipline contains a number of subdisciplines which may be termed genetic explanation, structural explanation, functional explanation, and reductive explanation. (Levine 1986)
> *Criticism* is the discipline of applying a set of evaluative standards germane to a particular model of reality to a determinate set of observations.
> *Diagnosis* is the discipline of identifying practical problems, determining relevant explanations, and generating conceptions of kinds of possible solutions.

---

1. I have added casuistry to my original list.

Prescription is the discipline of determining the best possible course of practical action by calculating the probable benefits, probable negative consequences, and opportunity costs of alternative solutions to actual problems. (Levine 1971, 6–7)

I then experimented with courses organized in the terms of this schema. One in particular stands out: a section of a common core course in spring 1971, a variant I called Reportage, Explanation, and Criticism—a title inspired by the famed course of the late 1940s created by McKeon, Schwab, et al., Observation, Interpretation, and Integration. For the disciplines of scientific reportage and explanation, I utilized three publications by Emile Durkheim: his programmatic *Rules of Sociological Method* and parts of his first two substantive monographs, *On the Division of Labor in Society* and *Suicide*. To begin with, we considered Durkheim's prescriptions for the scientific observation of social facts in *Rules* and analyzed his application of those rules both in the use of data on legal forms as indicators of social solidarity and in the use of data on suicide rates as indicators of types of suicide. We then discussed his strictures regarding two kinds of explanatory logic, distinguishing efficient causes and functional explanation, and examined his application of those logics to the analysis of social differentiation and forms of suicide.

I also used the Durkheim selections to adumbrate the disciplines of criticism, diagnosis, and prescription. In so doing I felt I was breaking new ground by attempting to formalize methodologies for those disciplines. We took writings commonly regarded as exemplars of social criticism and analyzed them with an eye to formulating criteria implicit in their assessments of social phenomena. Thus, writings by Freud, Sapir, and Marcuse were shown to exhibit variations on the issue of the relation of culture to self-development; writings by Veblen and Ortega to illustrate a functional assessment of various social strata; and writings by Riesman and Cleaver to illustrate criteria related to the quality of experience in social interaction. To give students practice in this discipline, I assigned a midterm paper with the following instructions:

1. *Identify* a "critical fact" discussed by Ortega.
2. *Analyze* the standards (normative assumptions), models (theoretical assumptions), and facts involved.
3. *Apply* this critical apparatus to some contemporary phenomenon.
4. *Evaluate* the critical apparatus from the point of view of (a) Durkheim, Sapir, or Henry; and (b) Freud or Marcuse.

In a similar vein, a few years later I offered a course for advanced graduate students in sociology organized to focus directly on the cultivation of
certain intellectual skills. With a touch of irony I called it Practicum in Sociological Theory, to make the point that there are specific trainable skills
appropriate to what I would come to call "theory work." With Joseph
Schwab's classic paper "What Do Scientists Do?" ([1960] 1978) doubtless in the back of my mind, I developed the course by asking the question, "What do social theorists do?"[2] In this practicum I identified ten intellectual skills that constitute discrete forms of theory work. These
included:

1. exegesis;
2. critique;
3. clarification and construction of concepts;
4. formulating propositions;
5. formalization;
6. codification;
7. defining, grounding, and solving problems;
8. grounding and articulating general frameworks;
9. comparing frameworks and approaches;
10. grounding the discipline.[3]

For each of these theoretical practices, we looked at texts that exemplified them, and I assigned exercises that required students to *do* them.
For example, for skill number 1, I gave students the option to "select some
sociological work which in your judgment deserves exegetical explication.
Justify your selection and present a short (3-page) explication of part or all
of the work." For number 4, I asked them to "formulate two different kinds
of propositions, one each to one page, using the concept treated in the third
paper. Use the following format. PROPOSITION: KEY CONCEPT
(how concept was construed in 3rd paper): BRIEF EXPLICATION:
ILLUSTRATION: JUSTIFICATION: NATURE OF PROPO-

2. In answering that question, the theoretical writings of Robert K. Merton were particularly helpful. I revisited Merton with these notions when I helped draft the introduction to a volume of his (Merton 1996b) and yet again in a more general analysis of Merton's
contributions to sociological theory (Levine 2006).

3. Here, as in so many other cases to be noted later in the chapter, I found myself
sooner or later producing a publication that was an outgrowth of my teaching program. In
this case, the paper in question did not appear until decades later: "Social Theory as a Vocation" (Levine 1997).

s i t i o n . " For number 6, I asked them to "work out a codification of three or more items related to anomie theory."

Although I believe the aforementioned ways of construing disciplines still hold promise for organizing thought about the liberal disciplines of the social sciences, I have gone on to emphasize a different order of discipline: identifying, comparing, and participating in various kinds of *conversations*. This approach finds its point of departure in the notion that all the disciplines I previously listed as well as other kinds of intellectual work can be construed as practices that involve different kinds of languages. To that notion, which some have glossed as a linguistic turn, I would now emphasize what has been called a dialogical turn. That is to say, I would gloss disciplines here as *determinate skills needed to appreciate and participate in various conversations.* In thus privileging the notion of conversation, I call to mind themes long resonant at Chicago. I hark back to Robert Redfield's luminous definition of education—as "conversation about the meaning of life, as each sees some part of it, on behalf of everyone" (Redfield 1963, 72), or to the words of the distinguished English philosopher Michael Oakeshott, which Robert Hutchins quoted admiringly: "Education, properly speaking, is an initiation into the skill and partnership of this [age-old] conversation, in which we learn to recognize the voices, to distinguish the proper occasions of utterance, and in which we acquire the intellectual and moral habits appropriate to conversation" (Oakeshott 1962, 199; Hutchins 1969, 126).

I propose now to examine a series of educational efforts in which the point was to promote habits that enabled students to listen more intelligently to various kinds of conversations and to participate more knowingly in such conversations.

Basic Practice

Whatever the disciplines featured in any course, there are certain elementary conversational skills I try to promote in just about every course I teach, and I usually do so by devoting at least one class to their cultivation. They include such basic skills as knowing how to grasp an author's agenda and how it may differ from other agendas a reader brings to the text; being able to apprehend and develop a curricular agenda; and being able to converse sensitively with other partners to a live conversation. These skills I shall review presently; others will emerge later on.

Many teachers, I assume, are equipped and motivated to help students read a text with full respect for what its author is trying to say, although it is my sense that this aspect of pedagogical work has been in decline. In my experience, even the most sophisticated students benefit from being constrained to confront this task directly and in a sustained manner. All too often, readers of a text (or hearers of a lecture) rush in with biases of many sorts that inhibit their ability to listen to what an author is actually saying.[4]

When I find students rushing in this way, I like to remind them that critical reading involves two stages. Before the stage of criticizing an author, there comes a stage of criticizing the reader, that is, asking oneself what predilections, ignorances, and resentments color one's response. Taught patiently (which I have trouble doing myself), this lesson alone can easily take up the better part of a class. A good way to broach this lesson is to force students to respond to the question: What is the author seeking to accomplish? With this question, one introduces the notion of an author's agenda. It is amazing how often readers (or listeners) fail to meet this simple challenge. Of course, some texts are much more explicit about their agenda than others. One reason I like to teach Adam Smith's *Wealth of Nations* is that his goal is embarrassingly transparent. After spending a fair amount of time understanding the simple, if slightly archaic, language of the first three sentences of Smith's introduction, students often are led to realize with a start that the primary agenda of his book is set forth precisely in its title: *WN* is indeed "An Inquiry into the *Nature* [sentence 1] and *Causes* [sentences 2-3] of the Wealth of Nations" (A. Smith [1776] 1976).

With that realization more or less clearly in mind, students can be led to make sense of the arguments of selections from book 1 (the first cause) and book 2 (the second cause), which enables them to develop the capacity to discern what an author is doing as well as saying. The work of grasping an author's agenda, then, involves identifying the method the author is using to accomplish a set goal, the arguments adduced in support of that method, and the pertinent conclusions. Along the way, one might engage material that is not so directly connected but in fact represents secondary or hidden agendas. This material may lead readers to appreciate what has inspired the author's ostensible or primary agenda—in Smith's case, the wish to combat mercantilist policies and to cajole idle aristocrats into diverting their resources into productive economic enterprises.

---

4. Aware of this widespread deficiency, Wayne Booth once challenged listeners at his Aims of Education address to write a summary, in 100 to 250 words, that "really reconstructs what *I* think I mean," and he offered a twenty-five-dollar reward to any who could do so successfully. Not one of those six hundred freshmen succeeded (Booth 1988, 183).

With the author's line of argument more or less firmly in hand, one can proceed to address a text with questions of one's own. At this point I bring in considerations having to do with the reason for including that text in a course in the first place. Those reasons will of course vary with the curricular point of the course. Once that point has been made, the pedagogical task is then to move back and forth between the author's agenda and the agenda of the instructor, with an eye to showing students how they could bring their own alternative agendas to bear as well.

Thus, a second basic practice follows: helping students learn how to formulate and develop independent agendas. For this purpose, I like to devote at least part of one class to an exercise in which I not only reveal the logic of the curriculum of that course but also show how and why it has been so constructed and how one might proceed to develop alternative curricula using the same text. Once again, Smith's *Wealth of Nations* provides a convenient foil for such an exercise. In a course in which I teach *WN* against Marx's *Wage Labor and Capital* and Durkheim's *Division of Labor in Society,* I sometimes ask students to imagine two other texts against which one might read *WN* and what the curricular point of such a sequence might be. Figure 4 shows a sample of such alternative curricula.

In thus playing off attention to an author's agenda with the agenda the reader brings, I seek to identify and model the ingredients of an ideal conversation. This, I take it, is dialogue in which one fully respects the views and arguments of others without losing sight of one's own criteria of significance of validity and one's own center of curiosity. Within the flow of class discussion, then, I seek to make sure that students are communicating with one another in this fashion. If Student B says something after Student A that makes me wonder whether the respondent has grasped what the first student was actually saying, I sometimes ask Student A if Student B's comment was really responsive to his or her statement. It usually turns out not to be. I ask Student A to repeat the statement and then encourage Students B and A to communicate back and forth until there is clarification of the actual substance of the discourse.

Disciplines as Ways of Getting into Conversations

The method of guided discussion seems essential to the cultivation of conversational disciplines. Keeping the flow from veering into the spontaneous back-and-forth of the "bull session" without harnessing it to a rigid frame remains a constant challenge. It helps to have some clear idea of what sorts of conversational habits one is working to promote.

FIGURE 4   A smorgasbord of Smithian curricula

A. to discern how *The Wealth of Nations* fits into Smith oeuvre:
   Smith, *The Theory of Moral Sentiments*
   Smith, *An Inquiry into the Nature and Causes of the Wealth of Nations*
   Smith, *Lectures on Justice, Police, Revenue, and Arms*

B. to examine Scottish moral philosophy:
   Hume, *An Enquiry Concerning the Principles of Morals*
   Ferguson, *Essay on the History of Civil Society*
   Smith, *The Wealth of Nations*

C. to examine fundamental issues regarding the good life:
   Aristotle, *Nicomachean Ethics*
   Smith, *The Wealth of Nations*
   Sartre, *Being and Nothingness*

D. to contrast Scottish, French, and American documents of the Enlightenment:
   Rousseau, *The Social Contract*
   Smith, *The Wealth of Nations*
   Jefferson, Declaration of Independence

E. to examine the approach of natural science in the late eighteenth century:
   Smith, *The Wealth of Nations*
   Lavoisier, *Elementary Treatise on Chemistry*
   Laplace, selections

F. to analyze germinal works in the history of economic theory:
   Smith, *The Wealth of Nations*
   Jevons, *Theory of Political Economy*
   Keynes, *General Theory of Employment, Interest, and Money*

G. to consider some basic problems, ideas, and methods of the social sciences:
   Smith, *The Wealth of Nations*
   Marx, selections, including *Wage Labor and Capital*
   Durkheim, *On the Division of Labor in Society*

Although I did not have the kind of systematic awareness I now do regarding what was going on in the following courses to be reviewed, I like to think I possessed a minimal sense of what I was about. In the terms I now employ, they seem to fall into two broad categories. One set has to do with engaging a particular conversation: how to catch its flow; how to find and articulate its justification; knowing what ranges of conversations are out there; learning ways to reconstruct a conversation. The other has to do with ways of connecting different conversations.

TYPE I. FOLLOWING A GIVEN CONVERSATION   One type of course introduces students to a complex conversation. The conversation in question can take one of two forms: diachronic or synchronic. The former traces certain issues across the years, generations even; the latter may take contributions at different points in time but treats them as voices compresent in an ongoing dialogue.

The diachronic form became the basis for a course I helped devise in the late 1960s for entering graduate students in the Department of Sociology. Until that time, the experience of entering graduate students was atomized. They had no common learning experience, no other structured social interaction, nor any opportunity to become acquainted with members of the department faculty other than those whose courses they happened to choose. We decided to institute a two-quarter required course, Sociological Inquiry, Sociology 301–302, to be co-taught in half quarters by four members of the department, each of whom would present a segment that related to his respective area of interest. It was my suggestion to organize those segments so as to exhibit the cumulative treatment of a topic within a particular research tradition.

When I have taught that course, one of my favorite curricula has centered on the theme of the division of labor in society. Although the particular list of readings has varied, I like to include selections from Smith's *Wealth of Nations* and writings by Comte, Marx, Spencer, and Durkheim. This sequence provides a convenient complex of materials for elucidating the components of the problem and how subsequent contributions relate to their predecessors. Along the way, a paradigm of questions develops: How is the division of labor defined? What are its origins? How does it develop? What are its positive and negative consequences? We ask what specific contributions each author makes and seek to identify the generic character of those contributions—for example, whether the later contribution expands the scope of the analysis, provides a more differentiated analysis, sets the phenomenon in question in a larger theoretical perspective, refutes particular propositions, or challenges the assumptions of an author's predecessors. In this first type of course, the conversations we consider have actually occurred, at least to some extent. Regarding the theme of the division of labor, for example, both Comte and Marx respond to Smith, and Durkheim responds to all three of them and to Spencer as well.[5]

The other type of course, in which I organize an array of readings around a particular theme, requires us to construct a conversation. Thus, the Common Core Social Sciences course that I taught to underclassmen

5. A detailed analysis of Durkheim's complex dialogue with Comte appears in Levine 1995, 167–72.

for many years sought explicitly to construct a set of conversations among diverse social scientists concerning "interpretations of culture." My course became the basis for the third quarter of a staff-taught three-quarter course named Wealth, Power, and Virtue. Although specific readings changed somewhat from year to year, the objectives remained constant. They were formulated as:

1. to explore some things social scientists do when they examine the cultural dimension of human experience;
2. to explore some kinds of understanding social scientists seek when they compare different cultures; and
3. to explore ways in which they formulate judgments about cultures.

Figure 5 presents the syllabus of the course, called Social Science 103, as it was offered in spring 1996. The first segment focuses on diverse meanings of the core concept and why those differences are significant. Thus, we consider Georg Simmel's definition of culture as subjective cultivation, how he distinguishes it from a notion of objectified culture, and why that is important (because it enables him to mount a critique of modern culture as involving a hypertrophy of objects that threaten the culture of subjects). We consider a notion of culture as customs and how that differs from a notion of symbolic codes, and why Clifford Geertz finds the latter so much better (because it enables him to propound a conception of human nature involving symbolic codes as external programming of an organism in ways that challenge received notions of human evolution). More generally, what I try to do in this sort of unit is engage students in the work of dealing with what W. B. Gallie (1964) has famously described as "essentially contested concepts." This description refers to concepts whose meaning must permanently be a matter of dispute — the fate of concepts that are internally complex, linked with changing historical circumstances, bound to disputes that cannot be easily resolved, and defended energetically by their proponents.[6] To tell the truth, I consider the experience of articulating and coming to terms with the ambiguity of contested concepts so fundamental a discipline that it nearly belongs to the category of "basic practice."

6. Sometimes I use the opening paragraphs of Edward Sapir's classic "Culture, Genuine and Spurious" to illustrate the reality of such contested concepts:

There are certain terms that have a peculiar property. Ostensibly, they mark off specific concepts, concepts that lay claim to a rigorously objective validity. In practice, they label vague terrains of thought that shift or narrow or widen with the point

FIGURE 5   Social Science 103: Wealth, Power, and Virtue III (Spring 1996)

I. The Cultural Dimension of Human Experience
Simmel, "The Nature of Culture" (handout)
Geertz, "The Impact of the Concept of Culture on the Concept of Man," *The Interpretation of Cultures* (IOC), chap. 4
Geertz, "Religion as a Cultural System" (IOC), chap. 2
Weber, "Author's Introduction," *The Protestant Ethic and the Spirit of Capitalism*

II. Modalities of Comparison
 1. Comparing Cases that Bear on General Hypotheses
Weber, *Protestant Ethic*, chaps. 1–5 (omit 128–55)
Weber, "Confucianism and Puritanism"
 2. Making the (Inscrutable) Other Intelligible
Benedict, *The Chrysanthemum and the Sword*, chaps. 1–3, 5–11
Geertz, "Deep Play: Notes on the Balinese Cock-Fight" (IOC), chap. 15

III. Diagnoses of Contemporary Cultures
 1. Culture and wealth
Bell, *The Cultural Contradictions of Capitalism*, intro. & chap. 1
 2. Culture and power
Radway, *Reading the Romance*, intro. & chaps. 3–4
Barber, "Jihad vs. McWorld"
Zakaria, "Paris Is Burning"
 3. Culture and virtue
Sapir, "Culture, Genuine and Spurious"
Ortega, *The Revolt of the Masses*, 1–2, 5–8, 11–12, 14 (omit 1–106)
Lasch, *The Revolt of the Elites*, chap. 2

If the first segment mines the ambiguities of the culture concept, the second opens up the diversity of intellectual practices subsumed under the commonplace of "comparative" study. Just as scientists generally mean and do quite different things when they claim to be proceeding

of view of whoso makes use of them, embracing within their gamut of significances conceptions that not only do not harmonize but are in part contradictory.... We disagree on the value of things and the relations of things, but often enough we agree on the particular value of a label. It is only when the question arises of just where to put the label that trouble begins. These labels—perhaps we had better call them empty thrones—are enemies of mankind, yet we have no recourse but to make peace with them. We do this by seating our favorite pretenders. The rival pretenders war to the death; the thrones to which they aspire remain serenely splendid in gold.

I desire to advance the claims of a pretender to the throne called "culture." Whatever culture is, we know that it is, or is considered to be, a good thing. I propose to give my idea of what kind of a good thing culture is. (Sapir [1924] 1949, 308) "scientifically," so social scientists (and others) do quite different things when they claim to be comparing cultures. Rather than lecturing students about these different things, as Joseph Schwab insisted, it is always better to let them emerge from concrete cases (although the temptation to short-cut this learning process is always present). I have identified more than half a dozen things that social scientists do when they compare cultures. They include:

- examining variations on common human themes (e.g., organizing the transition from childhood to adulthood, dealing with illness, resolving disputes);
- gaining deeper insight into one's own culture by comparing it to another;
- making sense of the apparently bizarre or inscrutable behavior of others by interpreting it as a plausible alternative cultural pattern;
- searching other cultures for ideas for fresh options about how to solve a particular problem;
- testing a causal hypothesis by using Mill's method of difference; and
- suggesting causal relations through the analysis of concomitant variation.

In any ten-week course, it is impossible to cover more than a couple such modalities of comparison. What is important is to raise awareness of what is going on when cultures are compared and to suggest the types of potential fruitfulness of carrying out such comparisons.

In the third segment of this course, we construct a conversation about ways to diagnose culture. This exercise automatically challenges the common assumption of radical cultural relativism that there is no legitimate way in which one can defend judgments about better or worse cultures. We simply look at a variety of well-considered attempts to express such judgments and bring them into conversation with one another. Thus, we might consider Sapir's criterion of coherence as the touchstone of a genuine culture or look at critical diagnoses (e.g., Bell's *Cultural Contradictions of Capitalism*) that appear to assume such a criterion. We may listen to elitist and populist views of culture, where the values of responsibility, excellence, or equality loom larger than the value of coherence. Or we might consider a diagnosis in which certain intrinsically troublesome traits appear to permeate a culture (e.g., Jeffrey Goldfarb's *The Cynical Society*).

TYPE 2. JUSTIFYING A CONVERSATION   In Autumn 1979, I offered a brand new kind of course. I've never heard of anything quite like it. It was organized partly to protest the notion that the justification for conventional disciplines is self-evident but mainly to equip students to deal with the competing and often conflicting claims about why a given discipline is worth pursuing. I called it Ideologies of Sociology. Students seemed to love it.

What we did was problematize both terms, *ideology* and *sociology*. We began with a brief examination of some major sociological conceptions of ideology, especially in Mannheim's *Ideology and Utopia* and Geertz's "Ideology as a Cultural System," and with side glances at Bacon, Marx, Nietzsche, and Barth. The bulk of the course then reviewed a number of writings that set forth a systematic exposition of a particular conception of what sociology should be and do. They included writings that took sociology to be primarily a guide for society (Spencer, Durkheim, Dewey), as primarily a goad to heightened self-awareness (Weber, Berger), and as a variant form of art (Nisbet).

Although I have not offered that course again, I have frequently used the discussion of justifications for intellectual agendas as a kind of basic practice in a number of courses (see subsequent discussion of the course on conflict theory).

TYPE 3. IDENTIFYING A UNIVERSE OF CONVERSATIONS   It is particularly consonant with the aims of a liberal-general curriculum to introduce students to a range of conversations in a number of fields. The skills involved here include understanding the boundaries and particular features of a variety of conversations. This learning genre provides immediate entrée to the exercise of many sorts of powers, including the ability to listen, to interpret texts, to grasp cultural worlds, to test and express the self, to integrate knowledge, and to study the ways of communication.

Courses that aspire to promote such skills are no less appropriate at the graduate than the undergraduate level. Perhaps the most successful course of this sort was in fact one that I helped devise to solve the problem of inducting graduate students into a master of arts program that spanned the social sciences.

The University's Master of Arts Program in Social Sciences began in the early 1930s as a one-year program for prospective teachers of social studies at the high school and junior college levels. It attempted to secure subject matter breadth through a distributional requirement involving basic courses in five of the division's eight departments. Reorganized in 1947 (and then called the Divisional Masters Program) under Ralph Tyler and Earl Johnson, the curriculum was altered in rejection of the principle of "proportional representation" in order "to show the *inter-relations* of the social science disciplines."[7] Thus, instead of taking ordinary departmental courses, the program required batteries of courses in three broad substantive fields, most often called Society, Culture, and Personality; Political and Economic Institutions; and Science and Social Decision. After Johnson's retirement, the program limped along for some time and was revived by Sol Tax in 1971 to provide both an advanced program of liberal education and a somewhat professional degree for public service. In the late 1970s, it was expanded to provide a multipurpose home for students interested in some graduate work in the social sciences but either not aspiring or not yet qualified to enter doctoral programs in one of the departments.

From time to time, managers of the program had struggled with the task of devising an introductory course suited for students being introduced to the entire scope of the social sciences. For a half-dozen years after 1947, this introduction amounted to a patchwork three-quarter sequence called The Scope and Method of the Social Sciences, which was organized around general methodological texts and a course in statistics. Discontinued in 1955, it was revived as a one-quarter course in the late 1970s in order to provide some coherence for what had meanwhile become a highly elective program. In autumn 1979, I was asked to teach the course and took that assignment as an opportunity to create a novel curriculum, one informed by the concept of introducing a set of disciplined conversations that transcend the conventional categories of subject matter disciplines. In other words, rather than offer students a smorgasbord of introductions to such conventional, departmentally based disciplines as anthropology, history, political science, and the like (an approach which the Tyler-Johnson committee had rejected three decades before), or even a broad-gauge substantive course that exhibited inter-relations among departmentally based disciplines, I sought to present investigative *perspectives* that informed work in a plurality of departments and that could be applied to virtually any substantive problem.[8] We called the course

7. Earl Johnson, "Report on the Divisional Master's Program," n.d., Box 258, Folder 4, Sol Tax Papers, Special Collections, Joseph Regenstein Library, University of Chicago, Chicago.

8. Years later, I was to spell out the rationale for such an approach:

Since the late 1960s a number of secular developments weakened the boundaries of the several social sciences that had grown so robust in the two postwar decades. For one thing, each of those disciplines established beachheads or won converts among the practitioners of other disciplines. At present few major concepts, methods, or problems belong exclusively to a single social science discipline. Anthropologists interpret dreams to find motives; psychoanalysts scrutinize docu-

Perspectives in Social Sciences Analysis and included six such analytic perspectives: rational exchange, domination, functionalism, cultural hermeneutics, cultural analytics, and motivation. For each perspective, I presented an introductory lecture on Monday, we heard from a committed proponent of that perspective on Wednesday, and we discussed readings that exhibited the perspective in question on Friday. For each perspective, we asked: What is it? Who embodies it? Where did it come from? What is it good for? Although I taught the course just that one year, its name and essential framework have remained the same ever since, while undergoing continuous change in readings and format.[9]

TYPE 4. KNOWING DIVERSE WAYS TO RECONSTRUCT CONVERSATIONS   Beyond acquaintance with the universe of conversations in various areas and learning how to grasp what's going on in them, one attains a higher level of consciousness by exploring the problematic character of drawing boundaries around conversations.

Acquiring this kind of discipline is arduous work; doing it properly involves a great deal of time and intellectual effort. My principal effort to impart it evolved slowly over a number of years, in connection with the History of Social Theory course, which I have taught intermittently since the late 1960s. During those years, I developed a complex argument about the history of Western social theory, viewing it as a set of transgenerational

---

ments to find the causes of war; sociologists and political scientists use "economistic" modes of analysis to study decision making; economists do field work to study behavioral patterns in primitive societies; psychologists and anthropologists use survey research methods to examine processes of modernization. Terms like motivation, reinforcement, status, legitimacy, authority, exchange, unconscious, symbolism, norms, and cost-benefit analysis have come to be used with decreasing self-consciousness by people in disciplines other than those in which these terms were formed. . . . Even more significant than this movement among disciplines has been the emergence of research programs that defy any disciplinary labeling altogether. (Levine 1995, 290–91)

9. By the mid-1980s, other faculty teaching the course (subsequently managed mainly by Ralph Austen and John MacAloon) had amended the set of perspectives to include historical narrative, Marxism (vice domination), evolution-modernization, psychoanalysis (vice motivation), symbolic interaction; and structuralism (vice cultural analytics). In addition, they have come to divide the readings for each perspective into two sorts, those that represent the perspective generally and those that apply it to a particular theme, such as crime or gender. According to a longtime director of the program, "I can attest that the post-1979 core has been critical in giving MAPSS both intellectual and social coherence, something which was lacking earlier" (Austen, personal communication, 4 August 2001).

conversations within various national communities—principally, Britain, France, and Germany, but also including Italy and the United States as well as ancient Greece. The more I led students through the materials that showed the fruitfulness of this argument, the more uneasy I became that they were not being made aware of alternative ways of constructing that history. Addressing that unease, I began to list supplementary texts that defined those transgenerational conversations in other ways and later went on to assign one or two such texts as background reading. Finally, in autumn 1990, I offered a full-blown version of this corrective under the title The Sociological Tradition. That course systematically compared a number of alternative constructions—including Nisbet's *The Sociological Tradition,* Parsons's *The Structure of Social Action,* and Sorokin's *Contemporary Sociological Theories*—and classified them according to the generic type of conversation they set forth. I identified six major types of what I came to call *narrative structures:* positivist, pluralist, synthetic, humanist, contextual, and dialogical.[10] Since then, I have at times invited students and colleagues to perform the exercise of constructing different types of narratives about other kinds of topics (other cultural traditions, nations, institutions). In introducing the exercise, I sometimes ask participants to problematize "history" with reference to their own lives, asking them to construct autobiographical sketches of their own biographies that vary according to the present interest (student; Chicagoan; religionist; family member; etc.) on which they choose to focus.

Disciplines as Ways of Connecting Conversations

Courses designed to show how to connect different conversations can take many forms. The four types we will examine here connect different conversations by comparing one conversation with another; by comparing a number of related conversations through analysis of historically related conversations and their linkages to a common problem; by connecting conversations internal to a student's personal experience; and by exploring conversations about the universe of conversations that exist.

TYPE 5. COMPARING ONE CONVERSATION WITH ANOTHER
Most students, as undergraduate majors or graduate specialists, find themselves at some point committed to engagement with a *discipline* in

10. This material was developed into part 1 of *Visions of the Sociological Tradition* (Levine 1995).

the conventionally defined sense of the term. As part of the process of being inducted into such a field, they encounter the principal conversations among its professional practitioners. This process empowers students by familiarizing them with a finite set of conceptual and methodological tools and imparting a structured way of looking a the world. At the same time, it runs the risk—in some fields, at least—of leading them to think that their new way of looking at the world is privileged, omnipotent, in some sense absolute.

To reduce this risk, it has seemed worthwhile to find ways to give students the sense of owning something of value that is nevertheless not an all-encompassing worldview, such that they would not be overwhelmed by its disciplinary point of view. Thus, a further step of liberation is called for, one that shows how one can fully respect the boundaries and achievements of a particular field and yet consider its limitations and distinctive potentials when compared with another field. One could, for example, get this kind of a purchase on sociology by comparing it systematically with such fields as history, anthropology, or economics. In one instance, I chose psychoanalysis, in a course called Psychoanalysis and Sociology, which I offered for committed undergraduate sociology majors and some graduate students a few times between 1973 and 1979—a period when I had been collaborating with clinical colleagues in workshops at the Chicago Institute for Psychoanalysis. In describing the course, I wrote that it "takes the form of an inquiry into the kinds of issues that may be raised and insights gained when one undertakes a systematic comparison of two related disciplines. It presumes at least an elementary acquaintance with the two disciplines being considered." [11]

In carrying out the comparison of these two conversations, I began with a historical overview—The Careers of the Two Disciplines—and then looked at the observational methodologies peculiar to the two. Most of the course then was devoted to considering conceptual frameworks of the two fields, in ways that made them easily comparable. That is, we took the organization of classical psychoanalytic theory in terms of the dynamic, economic, structural, and genetic perspectives, and then we considered some of the more recent metapsychological perspectives. We then examined sociological theory in terms of its own repertoire of perspectives, which included structural, function, genetic, dynamic, and

11. For students with very limited familiarity with one of these fields, I recommended Charles Brenner's *An Elementary Textbook of Psychoanalysis* or Lewis Coser's *Masters of Sociological Method* as background reading.

economic perspectives. And again we looked at some newer trends in sociological metatheory. Finally, we considered certain areas of integration
between the two fields, including integrations by Parsons at the level of
general theory, by Slater and Bion at the level of group dynamics, and by
Jackson and Framo with respect to family dynamics and therapies. The
course concluded by looking at interpenetrations of the two fields in
analyses of modern society and culture, such as Mitscherlich's *Society
without the Father* and Rieff's *The Triumph of the Therapeutic*.[12]

TYPE 6. COMPARING A NUMBER OF RELATED CONVERSA-
TIONS   In a related type of course, I have compared conversations of
varying sorts that have actually been in conspicuous contact with one another as they have considered a common set of problems or texts. Thus,
in courses concerning a particular civilization or culture area, it is common to employ analyses from a variety of disciplinary fields. My own early
background in Ethiopian studies led me to create a course, Ethiopian Society and Culture, which came to be presented as an opportunity to look
at how different disciplines complemented one another in throwing light
on that subject. Thus, in considering the ancient, Aksumite period, we
looked at the respective contributions of such diverse fields as archaeology, church history, epigraphy, glottochronology, and numismatics. In
considering the major developments of the past six centuries, we looked
at distinctive contributions of anthropology and musicology as well as
political and religious history. In this work, we attended as well to what
the works on Ethiopia said about the disciplines in question as well as vice
versa.

Turning again to the course I have offered most frequently over my career, History of Social Theory, it is fun to track its development over the
years into a course comparing transgenerational conversations. It began
in the late 1960s as a conventional course on sociological classics — simply
exposing students seriatim to selected works by Durkheim, Simmel, and
Weber. Before long, I was looking at antecedents of those authors in earlier writers such as Comte, for the former; and Dilthey and Tönnies, for
the latter. Gradually, the historical purview extended to the early nineteenth century, and then to the eighteenth century; and also expanded
geographically to include some writers in the British tradition up to
Spencer. Eventually I found it essential to include Hobbes and then Aris-

12. An essay that grew out of this course was "Psychoanalysis and Sociology" (Levine
1978).

totle, as the prime figure against whom Hobbes was reacting. Finally, I expanded the course to include Marx, some Italians, and some Americans, which now required a two-quarter format.

Over the years, I developed a number of charts in order to indicate the lineages of the transgenerational conversations and a number of graphic representations to illustrate some of the thematic arguments. After teaching the course for some two dozen years, I finally committed it to writing and published it as part 2 of *Visions of the Sociological Tradition* (1995). Once the book was out, it seemed somewhat redundant to offer the course in that same format again, even though I know the students would have continued to benefit mightily by reading the primary sources that I always had them read.

Accordingly, when I taught History of Social Theory in 1999, I created a very different sort of syllabus and organizing principle. This time, the course was organized around the figure of Emile Durkheim and approached his oeuvre in four ways. To begin with, we examined a selection of his own writings by asking how one might get an overview of his oeuvre, identify his main projects, analyze them, and assess them. Then we put his work in the context of diverse narratives about the sociological tradition, narratives identified in the course on The Sociological Tradition described earlier and spelled out in part 1 of *Visions*. We did so by examining the diverse ways Durkheim was interpreted by such authors as Madge, Sorokin, Parson, Habermas, Nisbet, Gouldner, and Levine. Third, we considered Durkheim in a comparative context by contrasting his work with that of his contemporary Simmel—and read Durkheim's own critical essay about Simmel. Finally, we briefly traced some of Durkheim's intellectual progeny, including Radcliffe-Brown and Merton.

TYPE 7. CONNECTING INTERNAL, PERSONAL CONVERSA-
TIONS   It is also valuable to offer students a structured opportunity to process conversations in which they have some personal interest and to connect those with ongoing conversations beyond themselves. At a minimum, this opportunity can take the form of an individual research project such as an undergraduate might carry out to satisfy the requirement of a bachelor's paper. These projects can be done individually or as part of a class experience. Students in the sociology concentration program at the University of Chicago discuss their projects in a seminar in the autumn of their senior year and summarize their papers in the spring.

Valuable ideas for structuring such opportunities were presented in the report of the Task Force on the Senior Year from Project 1984 (see chapter 3). The report recommended that each senior participate in a senior tutorial consisting of between one and six students working with a faculty tutor. In consultation with the faculty tutor, students were to be responsible for articulating both the aspirations and the accomplishments of the tutorial in a formal way. The report advocated providing a wide range of options with instructions, including the following:

> Laboratory Tutorial: Go solve a research problem.
> Research Tutorial: Go write a book(let).
> Reading Tutorial: Go read a book.
> Writing Tutorial: Go write about a question or address it in a form you care about.
> Journal Tutorial. Go learn about a current line of research.
> Performance Tutorial: Go perform artistically.
> Internship Tutorial: Go out into the real world and come back and write about it.

In addition, the task force recommended that students be given an opportunity to reflect on relations between the discipline they have studied and the larger context and fundamental questions of their general education, and to reflect on and clarify for themselves their activities as students and human beings and the personal significance of their studies and college experiences (Levine 1984b).

The course in which I challenge students most directly to engage their own inner conversations with external ones is called Conflict Theory and Aikido, which I offered several times between 1986 and 2005. This course directs students to connect what they learn with their bodies to concepts and ideas they read and talk about in a conventional academic setting. A central requirement of the course is an average of three hours of training each week in the Japanese martial art of aikido.

The learning structure of this course is multifaceted. I describe the integration of aikido practice in the course as offering an opportunity to enhance mind-body connections, to explore Asian cultural traditions, and to learn and live more effectively. I describe the substantive material of the course as offering an opportunity to explore the understanding of social conflict from various perspectives. A full syllabus is given in the appendix.

Conflict Theory and Aikido affords multiple occasions for engaging in what I have described earlier as basic practice. We help each student evolve a personal agenda for investigating conflict and for improving the ability to listen and respond meaningfully to others in the class. We read classic writings on conflict by Simmel, Coser, Boulding, and Coleman, and in each case attend to each author's distinctive agenda in undertaking to investigate the problem of conflict. We learn quickly that conflict is an essentially contested concept, and we work not only to disambiguate it but also to understand why, for example, Simmel and Boulding have opposing views on the relationship between the concepts of conflict and competition. We also consider different ways in which agendas for inquiry into conflict can be justified.

Accordingly, at the first session, I ask students to articulate reasons for an inquiry into conflict by prodding them to answer the question: What is the most important thing you would like to learn about conflict? In one format or another, the students then look at the whole array of such reasons — invariably, they are impressively diverse — given by members of the class. With that exercise we are on our way, proceeding to examine conversations about such issues as: What is conflict? Is it good or bad? What different forms does it take? What are its causes and what are its consequences? How can it be controlled (by encouraging it if good, preventing it if bad, or resolving it if inexorable)?

In examining written texts about conflict, we examine conversations from such fields as sociology, economics, anthropology, psychology, political science, and philosophy. We also look at the practice of aikido as a kind of nonverbal text and ask what that practice contributes to our understanding of the aforementioned questions. The climax of the course consists of a final paper in which students attempt to synthesize aspects of those two sets of conversations.

TYPE 8. EXPLORING CONVERSATIONS ABOUT WHAT CONVERSATIONS EXIST   The most reflexive sort of discipline in this universe takes the form of examining what kinds of conversations have been carried out to organize the universes of conversations. For this purpose, I have taught two kinds of courses, an upper-level undergraduate course called Organizations, Methods, and Principles of the Social Sciences (OMPSS) and a graduate seminar called Forms and Functions of Social Knowledge.

The syllabus for OMPSS derived directly from the autumn quarter of the old OMP course described in chapter 10. We looked at five authors: Aristotle, Kant, Comte, Marx, and Parsons. For each author, we considered how he organized the entire universe of knowledge and then looked more closely at how he organized the human sciences. See the appendix for the syllabus of the course we followed in the years 1974 through 1978.

TABLE 7 Course offerings in teaching powers

Course Type	Course Number and Name	First and Last Dates Offered
Disciplines as Specific Arts and Skills		
oa	Social Sciences 123/sec. 05: Reportage, Explanation, and Criticism	SPR 1971
ob	Sociology 440: Practicum in Sociological Theory	AUT 1977
Disciplines as Ways of Getting into Conversations		
1a	Sociology 301: Sociological Inquiry	AUT 1979, WIN 1998
1b	Social Sciences 103: Interpretations of Culture	SPR 1986, SPR 2000
2	Sociology 207/307: Ideologies of Sociology	AUT 1979
3	Social Science 300: Perspectives in Social Science Analysis	AUT 1979
4	Sociology 319: The Sociological Tradition	AUT 1990
Disciplines as Ways of Connecting Conversations		
5	Sociology 228/336: Psychoanalysis and Sociology	WIN 1973, SUM 1979
6a	Social Sciences 228: Ethiopian Society and Culture	SPR 1973, SPR 2001
6b	Sociology 323, version I: History of Social Theory	AUT 1968, SPR 1996
6c	Sociology 323, version II: History of Social Theory	SPR 1999
7a	Senior Seminars	
7b	Sociology 258: Conflict Theory and Aikido	AUT 1986, AUT 2001
8a	Social Sciences 271: Organizations, Methods, and Principles of the Social Sciences	WIN 1974, WIN 1982
8b	Sociology 530 (now 570): Forms and Functions of Social Knowledge	WIN 1986, WIN 2002

The other type of course in this vein approached the problem by engaging the issue of the inexorable plurality of modes of organizing the universe of conversations. In my seminar The Forms and Functions of Social
Knowledge, inspired by my paper of the same name (Levine 1986), I began with a definition of the presenting problem and proceeded to explore
foundations of a pluralist perspective in the work of neo-Kantian philosophy, pragmatism, and McKeon. In the 1992 version of the course (see the
appendix), I distinguished pluralistic perspectives according to whether

they focused on the pluralism of things, thoughts, words, or deeds. After presenting the paradigm of my 1986 paper, we looked for ways to apply it in the contemporary world.

Table 7 lists some fifteen courses, mentioned in this chapter, that have emerged over my career, in my time and place, as I attempted to construct curricula around new disciplinary forms. These tried-and-tested forms could offer a basis for liberal-general curricula in diverse settings from junior colleges through research universities, in the spirit of their construction if not in the details of their contents.

The purpose of the college . . . is . . . to develop in the man systematic habits; to give him control of his intellectual powers. WILLIAM RAINEY HARPER, 1905

There is also the problem of forming or developing what may be called basic intellectual habits—basic in the sense of being fundamental to all more advanced and specialized intellectual effort whether within the University or without. . . . The development of these powers . . . would seem to me to be . . . the most important and valuable fruits of a well considered "General Education." RONALD CRANE, 1931

The commodification and marketing of higher education are unmistakable today, and we can't jolly dance along and not pay attention to them.
HUGO SONNENSCHEIN, 1998

Epilogue: The Fate of Liberal Learning

Having considered what a curriculum for liberal learning suited for the modern world might look like, and having reviewed a variety of ways in which one might think about teaching it, we face now the question of whether such an enterprise, however conceived, has a future. As conceived in this book, the enterprise of liberal learning takes time, self-searching, and communal openness. These features contrast with the ethos now sweeping the world and therewith many universities, an ethos that prizes quick fixes, instant gratifications, self-aggrandizement, and expanded gated communities based increasingly on the market model. Insofar as these two ethics stand in opposition, the hegemony of the latter will be served by educational programs that can only be described as illiberal, and which threaten to dominate the world of higher education.

There is an old sociological truth that someone will doubtless recall at this juncture: it is impossible to change the world by changing educational systems. This dictum gets by, like so many others, because it is disembodied. Put a few determined actors into the equation, and then recall Margaret Mead's counterdictum: there is no doubt that a small group of thoughtful committed persons can change the world.

Whether or not the larger forces that dominate the world can be contained sufficiently to admit penetration by the motives for liberal learning, at the very least it should be feasible to secure a number of patches of protected space dedicated to the cultivation of humane powers. In such places, perhaps, the ancient, evolving dream of producing higher levels of humanity can be revitalized. The conditions of modernity are sufficient to support, if not to guarantee, this possibility. And when it happens, I hope that some seeds from the University of Chicago experience may bear strange new wonderful kinds of fruit.

Children ought to be educated, not for the present, but for a possibly improved condition of man in the future; that is, in a manner which is adapted to the idea of humanity and the whole destiny of man.   IMMANUEL KANT

Nothing under the sun is greater than education. By educating one person and sending him into the society of his generation we make a contribution that extends to a hundred generations to come.
JIGORO KANO, FOUNDER OF JUDO

Appendix: Three Syllabi
for Teaching Powers at Chicago

AUTUMN 2001/SOCIOLOGY 258/D. LEVINE

Conflict Theory and Aikido

I. LEARNING CONVERSATIONS

9/24 1. Learning with aikido
    a. enhance mind-body connections
    b. explore Asian cultural traditions
    c. learn and live more effectively
    d. examine and control human conflict
  2. Learning about conflict
    a. texts that record diverse conversations
    b. conversing with one's bodymind experience
    c. collaborative inquiry in class

The dojo as a place for learning with the bodymind

9/26 Conditions of inquiry: forms of respect (*li/rei*)
Inquiry into the bodymind. Sitting (*seiza*). Meditating. Walking.
    Experiencing *ki* flow.
Stance (*kamae; hanmi*). Changing *hanmi*. Stepping and pivoting.
    Falling.
READINGS: "The dojo and its culture" (*Aikido Club Handbook*, 6–11)
Lowry, *Sword and Brush*, chap. 1, "*Do*"; chap. 11, "*Ki*"; chap. 35, "*Rei*"

9/28 Centering experiences. Testing for being centered. *Katate-dori
kokyu-nage.*
READINGS: "Why Aikido?"; teachings of Morihei Ueshiba
    (*Handbook*, 3–5, 23–24)
Lowry, *Sword and Brush*, chap. 26, "*Hara*"

II. ISSUES IN INQUIRY ABOUT SOCIAL CONFLICT

10/1   1. Conflict as a Problem for Inquiry
Simmel, "The Problem of Sociology," *On Individuality and Social Forms (OISF),* 23–30
Simmel, "The Problem of Conflict" (Selected Readings [SR], A)
Coser, *The Functions of Social Conflict,* chap. 1
Boulding, *Conflict and Defense,* xv–xvii, 1–2 (SR, A)

2. Parameters of Conflict: position; relation; awareness; attitude; interaction
Simmel, *OISF,* 71–76, 80–84
Coser, *Functions,* preface, props. 1–2, 4 (7–8, 33–48, 55–60)
Boulding, *Conflict and Defense,* 2–18 (SR, A)

Aikido Practice as Collaborative Inquiry
10/3   Attacking sincerely and falling safely (*ukemi*). *Katate-dori kokyu nage.*
10/5   Types of conjoint training. *Katate kosa-dori ikkyo.*
READINGS: Lowry, *Sword and Brush,* chap. 3, "*Keiko*"; chap. 5, "*Kata*"; chap. 27, "*Uke*"

III. FORMS OF CONFLICTUAL INTERACTION

10/8   1. Conflict and Competition
Simmel, *OISF,* 77–80, 84–97; "Competition" (SR, A)
Boulding, *Conflict and Defense,* 2–18 (SR, A)

2. Modalities of Conflict
Coser, *Functions,* prop. 3 (48–55)
Gelles and Straus, "Determinants of Violence in the Family," 549–67 (SR, C)

Elements of Martial Tradition
10/10   Proper distance and timing (*ma-ai*). *Katate-kosa-dori ikkyo. Yokmen-uchi waza.*
READINGS: Simmel, "Keeping Proper Distance" (SR, A)
10/12   Types of attack and types of response. Joining (*Musubi*). *Tai no henko* (three forms).

Katate-dori kokyu-nage
READING: Saotome, "*Musubi*" (SR, A), teachings (*Handbook,* 24–25)

IV. DYNAMICS OF SOCIAL CONFLICT

10/15   Coser, props. 5 & 6 (60–72)
Boulding, *Conflict and Defense,* chap. 2 (SR, A)
Coleman, *Community Conflict,* intro., chaps. 1 & 2 (SR, B)

Dynamics of conflictual interaction

10/17 Escalating conflict. Moving off the line. *Munetsuki kokyu-nage.*

10/19 Expressing antagonism in a relationship. *Munetsuki kokyu-nage.*
READINGS: Coser, *Functions*, props. 7–8 (72–85)

V. ALTERNATIVES TO ESCALATION

10/22 Coleman, *Community Conflict* (chap. 3)
Kerr, "Chronic Anxiety and Defining a Self" (SR, C)

Alternatives to Escalation

10/24 Positive receptivity. Reframing. *Munetsuki kote-gaeshi.*

10/26 Maintaining connections. *Munetsuki kote-gaeshi.*

VI. SOURCES OF HUMAN COMBATIVENESS

10/29 Freud, "Why War?" (SR, C)
Fromm, *The Anatomy of Human Destructiveness*, chap. 8
Wrangham & Peterson, *Demonic Males: Apes and the Origins of Human Violence*, chaps. 2–6, 9

Initiating an Attack

10/31 Punching and counterpunching. Fight/flight responses. *Shomen-uchi waza.*

11/2 Unified powers of attack and response. *Morote-dore waza.*
READINGS: Coser, *Functions*, props. 9, 14 (87–95, 128–33)

VII. THE VALUE OF COMBAT

11/5 Coser, "Some Social Functions of Violence" (SR, C)
James, "The Moral Equivalent of War" (SR, C)
Heckler, *In Search of the Warrior Spirit*, 70, 115–19, 168–73

Training for Courage

11/7 Entering the line of attack. *Marubashi* training. *Katatedori irimi-nage.*
READINGS: Lowry, *Sword and Brush*, chap. 15, "*Shin*"; chap. 19, "*Fudo*"

11/9 Staying centered under stress. Multiple attacks (*randori*). *Irimi waza.*
READINGS: Palmer, "*Irimi*" (SR, C)

VIII. THE VALUE OF NONVIOLENCE

11/12 1. Nonviolent resistance: the way of *satyagraha*
Bondurant, *The Conquest of Violence: The Gandhian Philosophy of Conflict*, 3–41
2. Active nonresistance: the *aiki* way Ueshiba, *The Spirit of Aikido*

Training for Calm Control

11/14   *Omote* and *Ura. Shomen-uchi ikkyo, omote*
        READINGS: Leggett, *"Mushin"* (SR, A)

11/16   Leading the mind. *Shomen-uchi ikkyo, ura.*

IX. CONTEXTS OF CONFLICT

11/19   Simmel, "The Conflict in Modern Culture" (*OISF*, chap. 24)
        Watson, *The Architectonics of Meaning,* chaps. 1, 4

11/21   Reciprocity in training. *Yokomen-uchi shiho-nage, omote* and *ura.*
        READINGS: Lowry, *Sword and Brush,* chap. 21, *"Omote/Ura"*

X. CONTROLLING CONFLICT: AWARENESS OF OPTIONS

11/26   Simmel, "The Nonpartisan and the Mediator"
        Boulding, *Conflict and Defense,* chaps. 15–16
        Wrangham & Peterson, *Demonic Males,* chap. 12

        Awareness of options

11/28   Hovering awareness (*zanshin*). *Happo undo. Yokomen-uchi
          shihonage.*
        READINGS: Lowry, *Sword and Brush,* chap. 32, *"Zan"*
        Heckler, "Given to Love: Warriorship in the Twenty-first
          Century" (SR, C)

11/30   Continuous Flow. *Jiyu waza.*

XI. PUTTING IT TO THE TEST

12/5   Testing *waza*

12/7   Final papers due

SOCIAL SCIENCE 271

Organizations, Methods, and Principles of the Social Sciences

I. THE ARISTOTELIAN SYNTHESIS
    A. Subject Matters, Agents, Aims, and Methods of the Sciences
        Aristotle   *Posterior Analytics* I, 28
                     Physics II, 1–2, 3, 7, 8–9
                     Metaphysics VI, 1
                     Ethics VI, 1–8, 12
                     Metaphysics I, 1–2
                     Ethics I, 1–5, 7; X, 6–9

B. The Sciences of Man: Psychology, Ethics, Economics, Politics,
and Rhetoric

Aristotle   *De Anima* I, 1; II, 1-4; III, 3, 7
             Ethics I, 13; II, 1-2, 5-7
             Politics I, 1-3, 8-10, 12-13; III, 6-9
             Politics IV, 1-3
             Rhetoric I, 1-2 (to 1356b)

II. THE KANTIAN SYNTHESIS.

A. The Critical Organization of the Sciences

Kant   Preface to the *Critique of Pure Reason*
        Preface to the *Groundwork of the Metaphysic of Morals*
        (Grundlegung)
        Introduction to *The Metaphysic of Morals* (Ladd ed., 10-21)
        First Introduction to the Critique of Judgment, sections 1-3, 11

B. The Sciences of Human Freedom and Human Behavior: Ethics,
Jurisprudence, Empirical and Pragmatic Behavioral Science

Kant   *Grundlegung*
        Introduction to *The Metaphysical Principles of Virtue,* sections 1-5
        The Metaphysical Elements of Justice, Introduction (33-48) and
        articles 1, 5, 8, 9, 41-46, and 62
        Preface to *Anthropology in Pragmatic Perspective*
        On Perpetual Peace, selections

III. THE COMTEAN SYNTHESIS

A. The Positive Organization of the Sciences

Comte   *The Positive Philosophy,* Introduction; Book VI,
         chap. 15
         The Positive Polity I, chap. 1

B. The Sciences of Humanity: Social Statics and Social Dynamics

Comte   *The Positive Philosophy,* Book VI, chaps. 3-6

IV. THE MARXIAN SYNTHESIS

A. The Dialectical Materialist Organization of Knowledge

Marx   Preface to *A Contribution to the Critique of Political
        Economy,* selection, in Feuer, ed., *Marx and Engels: Basic
        Writings* (F), 43-44; also in Tucker ed., *The Marx-
        Engels Reader* (T), 4-5

Marx and Engels   *The German Ideology,* selections, F,
                   246-61 (T, 114, 118-39)

Marx   "Theses on Feuerbach," F, 243-45 (T, 107-9)
        "Contribution to the Critique of Hegel's *Philoso-
        phy of Right:* Introduction," F, 262-66
        (T, 11-23)

"On the Realm of Necessity and the Realm of
Freedom," T, 318–20
B. Social Science, Ideology, and Utopia
Marx and Engels   *The Communist Manifesto,* sec. 3,
F, 29–39 (T, 353–61)
Engels   *Anti-Duhring,* selections, F, 270–80 (T, 666–68)
"Socialism: Utopian and Scientific," secs. 1–2, F, 68–90
(T, 605–22)
Mao Tse-Tung   "Where Do Correct Ideas Come From?"

V. THE PARSONIAN SYNTHESIS
A. The Organization of Knowledge in the Framework of the General
Theory of Action
Parsons   *The Social System,* chaps. 1, 8, 12
B. The Sciences of Action
Parsons and Smelser   *Economy and Society,* chap. 1
Parsons   "Theory and the Polity"

THE UNIVERSITY OF CHICAGO \ DEPARTMENT OF SOCIOLOGY \
SOCIOLOGY 530 \ DONALD LEVINE \ SPRING 1992

Seminar: The Forms and Functions of Social Knowledge

Students of the social sciences confront a plethora of competing perspectives,
principles, and approaches, all of which make claims to validity and significance.
This seminar explores one constructive response to that dilemma, the response
of philosophical pluralism. Its foundations were laid at the beginning of the twentieth century in the philosophies of neo-Kantianism and pragmatism, and it was
developed with unparalleled subtlety in the work of Richard McKeon.
    The seminar will proceed in three phases. First we shall consider some of the
historical and philosophical grounds for a position of epistemic pluralism and
some different ways of construing pluralism. Then we shall consider a systematic
outline of the forms and functions of social knowledge. Finally we shall apply this
schema to problems of present-day social science.
    The amount of time spent on each topic will depend on the background and
interests of the participants. A provisional outline of session topics follows.

I. HISTORICAL AND PHILOSOPHICAL FOUNDATIONS OF
PLURALISM (SIX TO SEVEN WEEKS)
A. The Presenting Problem
Booth, "The Plurality of Modes as a Problem," *Critical
Understanding,* chap. 1

    B. Topoi of Pluralism: Things, Thoughts, Words, and Deeds
       McKeon, *Freedom and History,* chap. 1
    C. Pluralisms of Words
       Gallie, "Essentially Contested Concepts"
       Levine, *The Flight from Ambiguity,* chap. 2, Epilogue
    D. Pluralisms of Things
       James, *A Pluralistic Universe,* chaps. 1, 2, 7, 8
    E. Pluralisms of Thoughts
       Simmel, *On Individuality and Social Forms,* chaps. 1, 4
       Levine, "Simmel as a Resource for Sociological Metatheory"
       McKeon, *Freedom and History,* chaps. 2–6
       McKeon, "Philosophic Semantics and Philosophic Inquiry"
    F. Pluralisms of Actions
       G. H. Mead, "A Pragmatist Theory of Truth"
       Talcott Parsons and G. Platt, *The American University,* pp. 8–17

II. PARADIGM FOR A PLURALIST EPISTEMOLOGY IN THE SOCIAL SCIENCES (ONE WEEK)
    Levine, "The Forms and Functions of Social Knowledge"

III. APPLICATIONS IN CURRENT WORK (TWO TO THREE WEEKS)

References

ARCHIVAL COLLECTIONS

Arthur P. Scott Papers, Special Collections, Joseph Regenstein Library, University of Chicago, Chicago.
Dean of the College Records, 1925–58, Special Collections, Joseph Regenstein Library, University of Chicago, Chicago.
Joseph J. Schwab Papers, University of Chicago Special Collections, Joseph Regenstein Library, University of Chicago, Chicago.
Richard P. McKeon Papers, University Archives, Special Collections, Joseph Regenstein Library, University of Chicago, Chicago.
President's Papers, Special Collections, Joseph Regenstein Library, University of Chicago, Chicago.
University Archives, Special Collections, Joseph Regenstein Library, University of Chicago, Chicago.

OTHER SOURCES

Abbott, Andrew. 2002. "The Aims of Education Address." *University of Chicago Record* 37 (2): 4–8.
———. 2004. "Academic Intellectuals." In Camic and Joas 2004, 115–40.
Adler, Mortimer J. 1977. *Philosopher at Large: An Intellectual Autobiography*. New York: Macmillan.
Allan, George. 1999. "Rethinking College Education." *Liberal Education* 85 (3): 42.
Allardyce, Gilbert. 1982. "The Rise and Fall of the Western Civilization Course." *American Historical Review* 87 (3): 695–743.
Allen, Danielle S. 2001. "The Power of Education: The Aims of Education Address 2002." Chicago: The College of the University of Chicago.

Anderson, Lorin W., and Lauren A. Sosniak. 1994. *Bloom's Taxonomy: A Forty-year Retrospective*. 93d Yearbook of the National Society for the Study of Education, ed. Kenneth J. Rehage, part 2. Chicago: University of Chicago Press.

————. 1934. *Nicomachean Ethics*. Loeb Classical Library. Cambridge, MA: Harvard University Press.

Arnason, Johann. 2003. *Civilizations in Dispute*. Boston: Brill.

Ashmore, Harry S. 1989. *Unseasonable Truths: The Life of Robert Maynard Hutchins*. Boston: Little, Brown.

Axelrod, Joseph, B. S. Bloom, B. E. Ginsburg, W. O'Meara, and J. C. Williams Jr. 1949. *Teaching by Discussion in the College Program*. Chicago: The College of the University of Chicago.

Bell, Daniel. 1966. *The Reforming of General Education: The Columbia College Experience in Its National Setting*. New York: Columbia University Press.

————. 1976. *The Cultural Contradictions of Capitalism*. New York: Basic Books.

Blake, Lincoln C. 1966. "The Concept and Development of Science at the University of Chicago, 1890-1905." PhD diss., University of Chicago.

Bloom, Allan. 1987. *The Closing of the American Mind: How Higher Education Has Failed Democracy and Impoverished the Souls of Today's Students*. New York: Simon and Schuster.

Bloom, Benjamin S., M. Englehart, E. Furst, W. Hill, and D. Krathwohl. 1956. *Taxonomy of Educational Objectives: Handbook 1; Cognitive Domain*. New York: David McKay.

Bok, Derek. 2003. *Universities in the Marketplace: The Commercialization of Higher Education*. Princeton, NJ: Princeton University Press.

Bonner, Robert J. 1927. "Teaching Originality in College." *University of Chicago Magazine*. 19 (8): 362–63.

Booth, Wayne C. 1988. *The Vocation of a Teacher: Rhetorical Occasions, 1967–1988*. Chicago: University of Chicago Press.

Boucher, Chauncey S. 1927. "The Undergraduate at Chicago." *University of Chicago Magazine* 20:76–79.

————. 1935. *The Chicago College Plan*. Chicago: University of Chicago Press.

Boyer, John W., ed. 1997. *The Aims of Education*. Chicago: University Publications Office.

————. 1999. *Three Views of Continuity and Change*. Chicago: University of Chicago Press.

Bradbury, William. 1951. "Education and Other Aspects of Personal Growth in the College Community." Unpublished report to the Dean of the College.

Brint, Steven, ed. 2002. *The Future of the City of Intellect*. Stanford, CA: Stanford University Press.

Buchanan, Scott. 1962. *Poetry and Mathematics*. Philadelphia: J. B. Lippincott.

Buchler, Justus. 1954. "Reconstruction in the Liberal Arts." In *Columbia College on Morningside*, 48–135. New York: Columbia University Press.

Byrd, Sen. Robert. 2003. Interview, May 23. http://www.moveon.org/moveonbulletin/bulletin15.html.

Camic, Charles. 1983. *Experience and Enlightenment: Socialization for Cultural Change in Eighteenth-Century Scotland.* Chicago: University of Chicago Press.

Camic, Charles, and Hans Joas, eds. 2004. *The Dialogical Turn: New Roles for Sociology in the Postdisciplinary Age; Essays in Honor of Donald N. Levine.* New York: Rowman & Littlefield.

Chadbourne, P. A. 1869. "Colleges and College Education." *Putnam's Magazine,* n.s., 4:335–42.

Ciepley, David. 2001. "Liberalism in the Shadow of Totalitarianism: The Problem of Authority and Values since World War II." PhD diss., University of Chicago, Committee on Social Thought.

Cohen, Burton, and Joseph J. Schwab. 1965. "Practical Logic: Problems of Ethical Decision." *American Behavioral Scientist* 8 (8): 23–29.

College Announcements. 1943–44. *The University of Chicago Announcements: The College and Its Divisions.* Vol. 43, no. 10. Chicago: University of Chicago Press.

College Curriculum Committee. 1934. "The Educational Objectives of the College in the University of Chicago." Unpublished report, April.

Comte, Auguste. [1839] 1969. *Cours de la Philosophie Positive.* 5th ed. Paris: Editions Anthropos.

———. 1975. *Auguste Comte and Positivism: The Essential Writings,* ed. Gertrud Lenzer. New York: Harper Torchbooks.

Corbett, Edward P. J. 1971. *Classical Rhetoric for the Modern Student.* New York: Oxford University Press.

Cornwell, Benjamin. 2004. "Notes on Bloom et al.'s Taxonomies of Educational Objectives." Department of Sociology, University of Chicago.

Coulter, Merle C., ed. 1939. *Introductory General Course in the Biological Sciences: Syllabus.* 9th ed. Chicago: University of Chicago Bookstore.

———. 1940. *Introductory General Course in the Biological Sciences: Syllabus.* 10th ed. Chicago: University of Chicago Bookstore.

Davis, Richard H. 1985. *South Asia at Chicago: A History.* Committee on Southern Asian Studies, n.s., no. 1, ed. David L. Gitomer. Chicago: Committee on Southern Asian Studies.

Dewey, John. [1915] 1990. *The School and Society.* Rev. ed. Chicago: University of Chicago Press.

———. [1922] 1988. *Human Nature and Conduct.* New York: Holt.

———. 1937a. "President Hutchins' Proposals to Remake Higher Education." *Social Frontier* 3 (22): 103–4.

———. 1937b. "'The Higher Learning in America.'" *Social Frontier* 3 (24): 167–69.

———. 1939. "No Matter What Happens—Stay Out." *Common Sense* 8 (3): 11.

Dewey, John, and Alice Dewey. 1920. *Letters from China and Japan.* New York: E. P. Dutton.

Diderot, Denis. [1755] 1961. "Encyclopedia." In *The Encyclopedia: Selections,* ed. Stephen J. Gendzier, 92–95. New York: Harper.

Durkheim, Emile. [1897] 1951. *Suicide.* Trans. George Simpson. New York: Free Press.

———. 1956. *Education and Sociology.* Trans. Sherwood D. Fox. New York: Free Press.

———. 1977. *The Evolution of Educational Thought.* London: Routledge & Kegan Paul.

Dychtwald, Ken. 1986. *Bodymind.* Los Angeles: Jeremy Tarcher.

Edgerton, Franklin. [1942] 1957. "Dominant Ideas in the Formation of Indian Culture." In *Introduction to the Civilization of India,* 398–403. Chicago: University of Chicago Press.

Eisenstadt, S. N. 1996. 1999. *Fundamentalism, Sectarianism, and Revolution: The Jacobin Dimension of Modernity.* Cambridge: Cambridge University Press.

———. 2003. *Comparative Civilizations and Multiple Modernities.* Vol. 2. Boston: Brill.

Elias, Norbert. [1936] 2000. *The Civilizing Process: Sociogenetic and Psychogenetic Investigations.* Trans. E. Jephcott. Malden, MA: Blackwell.

Eliot, Charles William. [1885] 1898. "Inaugural Address as President of Harvard College." *Educational Reform: Essays and Addresses.* New York: Century.

Emerson, Ralph Waldo. [1841] 1940. "Self-Reliance." In *The Complete Essays and Other Writings of Ralph Waldo Emerson,* ed. Brooks Atkinson, 145–52. New York: Modern Library.

Ferguson, Adam. [1767] 1966. *An Essay on the History of Civil Society.* Ed. Duncan Forbes. Edinburgh: Edinburgh University Press.

Finn, David. 2000. *How to Look at Everything.* New York: Harry N. Abrams.

Fisher, C. J., and Bella Ross-Kelly. 1996. *Aspects and Images of Kuku Yalanji Life at Mossman Gorge.* Mossman, Australia: Bamanga Bubu Ngadimunku.

Foucault, Michel. 1979. *Discipline and Punish: The Birth of the Prison.* Trans. Alan Sheridan. New York: Vintage Books.

Frank, Andre Gunder. 1991. "Plea for World System History." *Journal of World History* 2:1–28.

Frodin, Reuben. [1950] 1992. "Very Simple, but Thoroughgoing." In Ward [1950] 1992, 25–99.

Fromm, Erich. 1969. *Escape from Freedom.* New York: Avon Books.

Gallie, W. B. 1964. "Essentially Contested Concepts." In *Philosophy and the Historical Understanding,* 157–91. London: Hatteau and Windus.

Goldfarb, Jeffrey C. 1991. *The Cynical Society: The Culture of Politics and the Politics of Culture in American Life.* Chicago: University of Chicago Press.

———. 2004. "The Liberal Arts as a Dialogic Project." In *The Dialogical Turn,* 65–79. Oxford: Rowman & Littlefield.

Goodspeed, Thomas Wakefield. 1916. *A History of the University of Chicago: The First Quarter-Century.* Chicago: University of Chicago Press.

Gore, Albert. 1994. Speech, June 9. http://clinton3.nara.gov/WH/ EOP/OVP/ speeches/harvard.html.

Gorski, Philip. 1993. "The Protestant Ethic Revisited: Disciplinary Revolution in Holland and Prussia." *American Journal of Sociology* 99 (2): 265–316.

Hanna, Thomas. 1990–91. "Clinical Somatic Education: A New Discipline in the Field of Health Care." *Somatics: Journal of the Bodily Arts and Sciences* 8:1, http://www.somatics.com/hannart.htm.

Harper, William Rainey. 1905. *The Trend in Higher Education.* Chicago: University of Chicago Press.

Henderson, Algo, and Dorothy Hall. 1946. *Antioch College: Its Design for Liberal Education.* New York: Harper & Brothers.

Hendricks, Luther V. 1946. *James Harvey Robinson: Teacher of History.* Morningside Heights, NY: King's Crown Press.

Hirsch, E. D. 1987. *Cultural Literacy: What Every American Needs to Know.* Boston: Houghton Mifflin.

Horrigan, Michael W. 2004. "Employment Projections to 2012: Concepts and Context." *Monthly Labor Review* 127 (2): 3–22.

Huff, Toby E., ed. 1981. *On the Roads to Modernity: Conscience, Science, and Civilizations: Selected Writings by Benjamin Nelson.* Totowa, NJ: Rowman & Littlefield.

Humboldt, Wilhelm von. [1791] 1993. *The Limits of State Action.* Ed. J. W. Burrow. Indianapolis: Liberty Fund.

Hutchins, Robert M. 1930. "Inaugural Address: 19 November 1929." *University Record* 16:8–14.

———. 1931. "The Chicago Plan." *Educational Record* 12:24–29.

———. 1932. "The Characteristics of the University: Convocation Address, December 20, 1931." *University of Chicago Record* 18:77–81.

———. [1934] 1936. "The Higher Learning II." In Hutchins 1936.

———. 1936. *No Friendly Voice.* Chicago: University of Chicago Press.

———. 1937. "Grammar, Rhetoric, and Mr. Dewey." *Social Frontier* 3 (23): 137–39.

———. 1943. *Education for Freedom.* Baton Rouge: Louisiana State University Press.

———. 1953. *The University of Utopia.* Chicago: University of Chicago Press.

———. 1969. *The Learning Society.* New York: New American Library.

Hyde, William DeWitt. 1904. "The College." *Educational Review* 28:476.

Ichheiser, Gustav. 1949. *Misunderstanding in Human Relations: A Study in False Social Perception.* Chicago: University of Chicago Press.

Isocrates. 2000. *Antidosis.* Trans. George Norlin. In *Isocrates,* vol. 2, ed. George Norlin. Cambridge, MA: Harvard University Press.

Jacob, Pierre, and Marc Jeannerod. 2003. *Ways of Seeing: The Scope and Limits of Visual Cognition.* New York: Oxford University Press.

Jaeger, Werner. 1939. *Paideia: The Ideals of Greek Culture.* Vol. 1. Trans. Gilbert Highet, from 2d German ed. Oxford: Basil Blackwell.

Jaspers, Karl. [1949] 1953. *The Origin and Goal of History*. Trans. Michael Bullock. London: Routledge.

Jencks, Christopher, and David Riesman. 1968. *The Academic Revolution*. Garden City, NY: Doubleday.

———. 1977. *The Academic Revolution*. Chicago: University of Chicago Press.

Johnson, Mark. 1987. *The Body in the Mind: The Bodily Basis of Meaning, Imagination, and Reason*. Chicago: University of Chicago Press.

Jones, Frank P. 1976. *Body Awareness in Action*. New York: Schocken Books.

———. 1997. *Freedom to Change: The Development and Science of the Alexander Technique*. London: Mouritz.

Kass, Amy Apfel. 1973. "The Liberal Arts Movement: From Ideas to Practice." *The College* 25 (October): 1–26.

Keniston, Hayward, Ferdinand Schevill, and Arthur Pearson Scott. 1935. *Introductory General Courts in the Humanities; Syllabus*. Chicago: University of Chicago.

Kerr, Clark. 2001. *The Uses of the University*. Cambridge, MA: Harvard University Press.

Kimball, Bruce A. 1986. *Orators and Philosophers: A History of the Idea of Liberal Education*. New York: Teachers College Press.

Kissel, Adam. Forthcoming. "Interdisciplinary Deliberation and Architectonic Rhetoric." PhD diss., University of Chicago.

Klein, Jacob. 1965. *History and the Liberal Arts*. Annapolis, MD: St. John's College Press.

Kuo, Ping Wen. 1914. *The Chinese System of Public Education*. New York: Teachers College Press.

Laing, Gordon J. 1927. "The Standards of Graduate Work." In *Problems in Education: Western Reserve University Centennial Conference*. Cleveland: Western Reserve University Press.

Laton, Anita D., E. Bailey, J. Schwab, and G. Diederich. 1939. *Suggestions for Teaching Selected Material from the Field of Genetics*. New York: Teachers College Press.

Lechner, Frank. 1985. "Modernity and Its Discontents." In Alexander 1985, 157–76.

Levi, Edward H. 1948. *An Introduction to Legal Reasoning*. Chicago: University of Chicago Press.

———. 1967. "The Role of a Liberal Arts College within a University." In Booth 1967, 203–12.

———. 1969. *Point of View: Talks on Education*. Chicago: University of Chicago Press.

Levine, Donald N. 1971. "Facing Our Calling: Sociology and the Agon of Liberal Education." Paper presented at the annual meeting of the American Sociological Association, Denver, Colorado, August 30.

———. 1978. "Psychoanalysis and Sociology," *Ethos* 6 (3): 175–85.

———. 1981. "Sociology's Quest for the Classics: The Case of Simmel," in *The*

Future of the Sociological Classics, ed. Buford Rhea, 60–80. London: Allen & Unwin.

————. 1984. "The Liberal Arts and the Martial Arts." *Liberal Education* 70 (3): 235–51.

————. 1985a. "Challenging Certain Myths about the 'Hutchins' College." *University of Chicago Magazine,* Winter, 36–39, 51.

————. 1985b. *The Flight from Ambiguity.* Chicago: University of Chicago Press.

————. 1986. "The Forms and Functions of Social Knowledge." In *Metatheory in Social Science: Pluralisms and Subjectivities,* 271–83. Chicago: University of Chicago Press.

————. 1991a. "Comment on Walter Watson, 'McKeon: The Unity of His Thought.'" Paper presented at the Conference on Pluralism and Objectivity in Contemporary Culture: Departures from the Philosophy of Richard McKeon, University of Chicago, March 13–14.

————. 1991b. "Martial Arts as a Resource for Liberal Education: The Case of Aikido," in *The Body: Social Process and Cultural Theory,* ed. M. Featherstone, M. Hepworth, and B. S. Turner, 209–24. London: Sage.

————. 1991c. "Simmel as Educator: On Individuality and Modern Culture," *Theory, Culture and Society* 8:99–117.

————. 1992. Preface to paperback edition of *The Idea and Practice of General Education.* Chicago: University of Chicago Press.

————. 1995. *Visions of the Sociological Tradition.* Chicago: University of Chicago Press.

————. 1997. "Social Theory as a Vocation." *Perspectives: The ASA Theory Section Newsletter* 19 (2): 1–8.

————. 2000. "The Idea of the University, Take One: On the Genius of This Place." http://iotu.uchicago.edu/levine.html#star.

————. 2003. "Note on the Concept of an Axial Turning in Human History." In *Rethinking Civilizational Analysis,* ed. Said Arjomand, 67–70. London: Sage.

————. 2006. "Merton's Ambivalence towards Autonomous Theory—and Ours," *Canadian Journal of Sociology* 31 (2): 235–43. This article is based on a paper presented at the 37th World Congress of the International Institute of Sociology, Stockholm, Sweden, July 7, 2005.

Lind, Michael. 2006. "In Defense of Mandarinism." *Prospect 120.* March.

Linden, Paul. 1988–89. "Being in Movement: Intention as a Somatic Meditation." *Somatics* 7 (1): 54–59.

Lowell, A. Lawrence. 1934. *At War with Academic Traditions in America.* Cambridge, MA: Harvard University Press.

Lubbock, Sir John. 1896. *The Choice of Books.* Philadelphia: Henry Altemus.

MacLeish, Archibald. 1920. Professional Schools of Liberal Education. *Yale Review,* n.s., 10:362–72.

Maienschein, Jane. 1988. "Whitman at Chicago: Establishing a Chicago Style of

Biology?" In *The American Development of Biology*, ed. Ronald Rainger, Keith R. Benson, and Jane Maienschein, 151–83. Philadelphia: Philadelphia University Press.

Martin, Jay. 2002. *The Education of John Dewey*. New York: Columbia University Press.

Martindale, Don. 1981. *The Nature and Types of Sociological Theory*. 2d ed. New York: Harper & Row.

Mathieu, W. A. 1997. *Harmonic Experience: Tonal Harmony from its Natural Origins to its Modern Expression*. Rochester, VT: Inner Traditions.

Mayfield, John C. 1938. *Syllabus for Biological Science A*. Chicago: University of Chicago Bookstore.

McGrath, Earl J., ed. 1948. *Science in General Education*. Dubuque, IA: William C. Brown.

McKeon, Richard. 1937. "Education and the Disciplines." *International Journal of Ethics* 47:370–81.

———. 1949. "The Nature and Teaching of the Humanities." *Journal of General Education* 3:290–303.

———. [1953] 1990. "Spiritual Autobiography." In Richard McKeon, *Freedom and History and Other Essays: An Introduction to the Thought of Richard McKeon*, ed. Zahava K. McKeon, 3–36. Chicago: University of Chicago Press.

———. [1963] 1994. *On Knowing—the Natural Sciences*. Ed. David B. Owen and Zahava K. McKeon. Chicago: University of Chicago Press.

———. 1964a. "The Liberating Arts and the Humanizing Arts in Education." In *Humanistic Education and Western Civilization: Essays for Robert M. Hutchins*, ed. Arthur A. Cohen, 159–81. New York: Holt, Rinehart, and Winston.

———. 1964b. "The Future of the Liberal Arts." In *Current Issues in Higher Education*, ed. G. Kerry Smith, 36–44. Washington, DC: Association for Higher Education, National Education Association of the U.S.

———. 1964c. "The Flight from Certainty and the Quest for Precision." *Review of Metaphysics* 18:234–53. Reprinted in *Selected Writings of Richard McKeon*, ed. Zahava K. McKeon and Williams G. Swenson. Chicago: University of Chicago Press, 1998.

———. 1967. "The Battle of the Books." In Booth 1967, 173–202.

———. 1969. "Character and the Arts and Disciplines." In *Approaches to Education for Character: Strategies for Change in Higher Education*, ed. Clarence H. Faust and Jessica Feingold, 51–71. New York: Columbia University Press.

———. 1972. "Where We Are and Where We Are Going." *University of Chicago Record* 6:69–71.

———. 1979. "Honors Students and Honors Programs of Studies." Paper read before the National Collegiate Honors Council, University of Arkansas, October 20. In the author's possession.

———. 1987. *Rhetoric: Essays in Invention and Discovery*, ed. M. Backman. Woodbridge, CT: Ox Bow Press.

———. 1990. *Freedom and History and Other Essays: An Introduction to the Thought of Richard McKeon*, ed. Zahava K. McKeon. Chicago: University of Chicago Press.

McNeill, William H. 1958. *History Handbook of Western Civilization*. Chicago: University of Chicago Press.

———. 1963. *The Rise of the West: A History of the Human Community*. Chicago: University of Chicago Press.

———. 1991. *Hutchins' University: A Memoir of the University of Chicago, 1929–1950*. Chicago: University of Chicago Press.

Mead, George H. 1929. "National-Mindedness and International-Mindedness." *International Journal of Ethics* 39:385–407.

———. 1934. *Mind, Self and Society*. Ed. Charles W. Morris. Chicago: University of Chicago Press.

Meiklejohn, Alexander. 1922. "The Unity of the Curriculum." *New Republic* 32 (Oct. 25), pt. 2, pp. 2–3.

Merton, Robert K. [1942] 1996a. "The Ethos of Science." In Merton 1996b, 267–76.

———. 1996b. *On Social Structure and Science*. Ed. Piotr Sztompka. Chicago: University of Chicago Press.

Mitscherlich, Alexander. 1965. *Auf dem Weg zur vaterlosen Gesellschaft: Ideen zur Sozialpsychologie*. Munich: R. Piper.

Moon, Richard. 2000. The Power of Extraordinary Listening. http://www .aiki-extensions.org.

Moraitis, George. 1981. "The Psychoanalytic Study of the Editing Process and Its Applications to the Interpretation of an Historical Document." *Annual of Psychoanalysis* 9:237–63.

Morrison, Philip. 1982. *Powers of Ten: About the Relative Size of Things in the Universe*. New York: Scientific American Library.

Murphy, William Michael, and D. J. R. Bruckner, eds. 1976. *The Idea of the University of Chicago: Selections from the Papers of the First Eight Chief Executives of the University of Chicago from 1891 to 1975*. Chicago: University of Chicago Press.

Nash, Paul, Andreas M. Kazamias, and Henry J. Perkinson. 1965. *The Educated Man: Studies in the History of Educational Thought*. New York: John Wiley & Sons.

Nelson, Michael, and Associates. 2000. *Alive at the Core: Exemplary Approaches to General Education in the Humanities*. San Francisco: Jossey-Bass.

Newman, H. H., ed. 1926. *The Nature of the World and of Man*. Chicago: University of Chicago Press.

———. 1948. "History of the Department of Zoology in the University of Chicago." *Bios* 19:215–39.

Nussbaum, Martha C. 1987. Review of *The Closing of the American Mind*, by Allan Bloom. *New York Review of Books* 37 (17), http://www.nybooks.com/articles/4618.

————. 1997. *Cultivating Humanity: A Classical Defense of Reform in Liberal Education*. Cambridge, MA: Harvard University Press.

Oakeshott, Michael. 1962. *Rationalism in Politics and Other Essays*. New York: Basic Books.

Ogburn, William F. 1922. *Social Change: With Respect to Culture and Original Nature*. New York: B. W. Huebsch.

Orlinsky, David E. 1992. "Not Very Simple, but Overflowing: A Historical Perspective on General Education at the University of Chicago." In *General Education in the Social Sciences: Centennial Reflections on the College of the University of Chicago*, ed. John J. MacAloon, 25–76. Chicago: University of Chicago Press.

Palmer, Wendy. 2000. *The Intuitive Body: Aikido as a Clairsentient Practice*. Rev. ed. Berkeley and Los Angeles: North Atlantic Books.

————. 2002. *The Practice of Freedom: Aikido Principles as a Spiritual Guide*. Berkeley and Los Angeles: Rodmell Press.

Parsons, Talcott. 1942. "Some Sociological Aspects of the Fascist Movements." In *Essays in Sociological Theory*, 2d ed., 124–41. Glencoe, IL: Free Press.

————. 1961. Introduction to *The Study of Society*, by Herbert Spencer. Ann Arbor: University of Michigan Press.

————. 1964. "Evolutionary Universals in Society." *American Sociological Review* 29:339–57.

————. 1977. *The Evolution of Societies*. Ed. Jackson Toby. Englewood Cliffs, NJ: Prentice-Hall.

Parsons, Talcott, and A. L. Kroeber. 1958. "The Concepts of Culture and of Social System." *American Sociological Review* (October): 582. Repr. in *Ideas of Culture: Sources and Uses*, ed. Frederick Gamst and Edward Norbeck. New York: Holt, Rinehart & Winston, 1976.

Pirsig, Robert M. 1974. *Zen and the Art of Motorcycle Maintenance: An Inquiry into Values*. New York: Morrow.

Plochmann, George Kimball. 1990. *Richard McKeon: A Study*. Chicago: University of Chicago Press.

————. 1998. Review of *Selected Writings of Richard McKeon*, by Zahava K. McKeon and William G. Swenson, eds. *Hypotheses: Neo-Aristotelian Analysis* 25 (Spring): 4–15.

PR. *See* University of Chicago 1892–1930.

Putnam, Robert D. 2000. *Bowling Alone: The Collapse and Revival of American Community*. New York: Simon & Schuster.

Radin, Paul. 1927. *Primitive Man as Philosopher*. New York: D. Appleton.

Redfield, Margaret Park, ed. 1962. *Human Nature and the Study of Society*. Vol. 1 of *The Papers of Robert Redfield*. Chicago: University of Chicago Press.

Redfield, Robert. 1941. *The Folk Culture of Yucatan*. Chicago: University of Chicago Press.

————. [1947] 1963. "The Study of Culture in General Education." In *The*

Papers of Robert Redfield, vol. 2, *The Social Uses of Social Science,* ed. Margaret Park Redfield, 107–17. Chicago: University of Chicago Press.

———. 1953. *The Primitive World and Its Transformations.* Chicago: University of Chicago Press.

———. 1956. *Peasant Society and Culture: An Anthropological Approach to Civilization.* Chicago: University of Chicago Press.

———. 1957. "Thinking about a Civilization." In Singer 1957, 3–15.

———. 1963. "The Educational Experience." In *The Papers of Robert Redfield,* vol. 2, *The Social Uses of Social Science,* ed. Margaret Park Redfield. Chicago: University of Chicago Press. Originally published in 1955.

Reid, William A. 1999. "The Voice of 'the Practical': Schwab as Correspondent." *Journal of Curriculum Studies* 31 (4): 385–97.

Review Committee for History. 1948. "Report of the Review Committee for History to the Faculty of the College." March. Unpublished report. In personal files of Donald Levine.

Riesman, David, and Associates. 1950. *The Lonely Crowd: A Study of the Changing American Character.* New Haven, CT: Yale University Press.

Rusk, Robert R. 1965. *The Doctrines of the Great Educators.* New York: St. Martin's Press.

Sack, Saul. 1962. "Liberal Education: What Was It? What Is It?" *History of Education Quarterly* 2 (4): 210–24.

Sapir, Edward. [1924] 1949. "Culture, Genuine and Spurious." In *Selected Writings of Edward Sapir in Language, Culture, and Personality,* ed. D. G. Mandelbaum, 308–31. Berkeley and Los Angeles: University of California Press.

Scholz, Richard F. 1922. "Fitness for Freedom." *Reed College Bulletin* 2 (1): 1–9.

Schwab, Joseph J. 1935. "A Further Study of the Effect of Temperature on Crossing-Over." *American Naturalist* 69:187–92.

———. 1940. "A Study of the Effects of a Random Group of Genes on the Shape of Spermatheca in Drosophia melanogaster." *Genetics* 25:157–77.

———. 1941a. "Deriving the Objectives and Content of the College Curriculum: The Natural Sciences." In *New Frontiers in Collegiate Instruction, Proceedings of the Institute for Administrative Officers of Higher Institutions,* vol. 13, ed. John Dale Russell, 35–52. Chicago: University of Chicago Press.

———. 1941b. "The Role of Biology in General Education: Biology and the Problem of Values." *Bios* 12:87–97.

———. 1942. "The Fight for Education." *Atlantic Monthly* 169:727–31.

———. [1950] 1992. "The Natural Sciences: The Three-Year Program." In *The Idea and Practice of General Education: An Account of the College of the University of Chicago,* 149–86. Chicago: University of Chicago Press.

———. 1950. "Criteria for the Evaluation of Achievement Tests: From the Point of View of the Subject-Matter Specialist." In *Proceedings of the Educational Testing Service Invitational Conference on Testing Problems, 1950,* 82–94. Princeton, NJ: Educational Testing Service.

————. [1954] 1978. "Eros and Education: A Discussion of One Aspect of Discussion." In Westbury and Wilkof 1978, 105–32.

————. [1956] 1978. "Science and Civil Discourse: The Uses of Diversity." In Westbury and Wilkof 1978, 133–48.

————. [1958] 1978. "Enquiry and the Reading Process." In Westbury and Wilkof 1978, 149–63.

————. [1960] 1965. *Philosophical Aspects of Biology: The Decision Points of Biological Inquiry.* Chicago: Syllabus Division of the University of Chicago Press.

————. [1960] 1978. "What Do Scientists Do?" In Westbury and Wilkof 1978, 184–228.

————. 1961. "Some Reflections on Science Education." *BSCS Newsletter* 9 (September): 8–9.

————. [1961] 1978. "Education and the Structure of the Disciplines." In Westbury and Wilkof 1978, 229–72.

————. 1963. *Biology Teachers' Handbook.* New York: John Wiley and Sons.

————. 1964a. "The Religiously Oriented School in the United States: A Memorandum on Policy." *Conservative Judaism* 18 (3): 1–14.

————. 1964b. "Structure of the Disciplines: Meanings and Significances." In *The Structure of Knowledge and the Curriculum,* ed. G. W. Ford and L. Pugno, 1–30. Chicago: Rand McNally.

————. 1964c. "The Structure of the Natural Sciences." In *The Structure of Knowledge and the Curriculum,* ed. G. W. Ford and L. Pugno, 31–49. Chicago: Rand McNally.

————. 1969. *College Curriculum and Student Protest.* Chicago: University of Chicago Press.

————. [1970] 1978. "The Practical: A Language for Curriculum." In Westbury and Wilkof 1978, 287–321.

————. 1975. "Learning Community." *Center Magazine,* May/June, 30–44.

————. 1976. "Education and the State: Learning Community." In *The Great Ideas Today, 1976,* 234–71. Chicago: Encyclopaedia Britannica.

————. 1983. "The Practical 4: Something for Curriculum Professors to Do." *Curriculum Inquiry* 13 (3): 239–66.

Sennett, Richard. 1977. *The Fall of the Public Man: The Forces Eroding Public Life and Burdening the Modern Psyche with Roles It Cannot Perform.* New York: Knopf.

Severson, Stanley. 1972. "The Defeat of General Education at Chicago: A Case Study of Collegiate Conflict." M.A. thesis, University of Chicago.

Shils, Edward. 1981. *Tradition.* Chicago: University of Chicago Press.

————, ed. 1991. *Remembering the University of Chicago: Teachers, Scientists, and Scholars.* Chicago: University of Chicago Press.

Shorey, Paul. 1909. "The Spirit of the University of Chicago." *University of Chicago Magazine* 1:229–45.

Shulman, Lee S. 1991. "Joseph Jackson Schwab." In Shils 1991, 452–68.

Shusterman, Richard. 1994. "Dewey on Experience: Foundation or Reconstruction?" *Philosophical Forum* 26 (2): 127–48.

———. 1997. *Practicing Philosophy: Pragmatism and the Philosophical Life.* New York: Routledge.

———. 2000a. *Performing Live.* Ithaca, NY: Cornell University Press.

———. 2000b. *Pragmatist Aesthetics: Living Beauty, Rethinking Art.* 2d ed. New York: Rowman & Littlefield.

Simmel, Georg. [1890] 1989. "Über sociale Differenzierung." In *Georg Simmel Gesamtausgabe 2*, 109–295. Frankfurt am Main: Suhrkamp.

———. [1896] 1997. "Infelices Possidentes!" In *Simmel on Culture*, ed. David Frisby and Mike Featherstone, 259–62. London: Sage.

———. [1907] 1978. *The Philosophy of Money.* 2d ed. Trans. Tom Bottomore and David Frisby. Boston: Routledge. Originally published as *Philosophie des Geldes.*

———. 1968. *The Conflict in Modern Culture and Other Essays.* Trans. Peter Etzkorn. New York: Teachers College Press.

———. 1971. *On Individuality and Social Forms.* Ed. D. Levine. Chicago: University of Chicago Press.

Singer, Milton, ed. 1957. *Introducing India in Liberal Education: Proceedings of a Conference Held at the University of Chicago, May 17, 18, 1957.* Chicago: University of Chicago Press.

———. 1976. "Robert Redfield's Development of a Social Anthropology of Civilizations." In *American Anthropology: The Early Years*, ed. John V. Murra, 187–260. St. Paul: West.

Smith, Adam. [1759] 1976. *The Theory of Moral Sentiments.* Oxford: Oxford University Press.

———. [1776] 1976. *An Inquiry into the Nature and Causes of the Wealth of Nations.* Chicago: University of Chicago Press.

Smith, Jonathan Z. 1983. "Why the College Major? Questioning the Great Unexplained Aspect of Undergraduate Education." *Change* 15 (5): 12–15.

———. 1993. "To Double Business Bound." In *Strengthening the College Major*, ed. C. G. Schneider and W. S. Green, 13–23. New Directions for Higher Education 84. San Francisco: Jossey-Bass.

Spencer, Herbert. 1861. "What Knowledge Is of Most Worth?" Ch. 1 in *Education, Intellectual, Moral and Physical.* New York: D. Appleton.

———. [1874] 1961. *The Study of Sociology.* Ann Arbor: University of Michigan.

Stilgoe, John R. 1998. *Outside Lies Magic: Regaining History and Awareness in Everyday Places.* New York: Walker.

Storr, Richard J. 1966. *Harper's University: The Beginnings; The History of the University of Chicago.* Chicago: University of Chicago Press.

Swift, Hewson. 1991. "Sewall Wright." In Shils 1991, 568–86.

Tappan, Henry P. 1851. *University Education.* New York: G. P. Putnam's Sons.

Taylor, Joshua C. 1981. *Learning to Look.* 2d ed. Chicago: University of Chicago Press.

Thomas, Russell. [1950] 1990. "The Humanities." In *The Idea and Practice of General Education: An Account of the College of The University of Chicago.*, 103–22. Chicago: University of Chicago Press.

———. 1962. *The Search for a Common Learning: General Education, 1800–1960.* New York: McGraw-Hill.

Thomas, W. I. 1966. *On Social Organization and Social Personality: Selected Papers.* Ed. Morris Janowitz. Chicago: University of Chicago Press.

Tocqueville, Alexis de. [1840] 1988. *Democracy in America.* New York: Harper-Collins.

True, A. C. 1915. "The Relation of the College Curriculum to Human Life and Work." *School and Society* 1 (June 19): 865–69.

Tyler, Ralph W. 1984. "Personal Reflections on 'The Practical 4.'" *Curriculum Inquiry* 14:97–102.

University of Chicago. 1891. *Official Bulletin.* No. 2, April.

———. 1892–93. *Annual Register.*

———. 1892–1930. *The President's Report.* Chicago: University of Chicago Press. Cited parenthetically in text as PR, with publication years of specific edition.

———. 2001. *Courses and Programs of Study: The College; The University of Chicago, 2001–2002.* Chicago: University of Chicago.

University of Chicago College Center for Curricular Thought. 1984a. *Project 1984: Design Issues; Reports of the Task Forces.* Chicago: College Center for Curricular Thought, University of Chicago.

———. 1984b. *Report of the Starved Rock Conference.* Chicago: College Center for Curricular Thought, University of Chicago.

Veysey, Laurence. 1965. *The Emergence of the American University.* Chicago: University of Chicago Press.

Walter, E. V., ed. 1985. *Civilizations East and West: A Memorial Volume for Benjamin Nelson.* Atlantic Highlands, NJ: Humanities Press.

Ward, F. Champion. 1949. Preface to *The People Shall Judge*, by Staff, Social Sciences I, eds. Chicago: University of Chicago Press.

———, ed. [1950] 1992. *The Idea and Practice of General Education: An Account of the College of the University of Chicago.* Chicago: University of Chicago Press.

———. 1962. "Principles and Particulars in Liberal Education." In *Humanistic Education and Western Civilization: Essays for Robert M. Hutchins*, ed. Arthur A. Cohen, 120–37. New York: Holt, Rinehart and Winston.

———. 1992. "Requiem for the Hutchins College." In *General Education in the Social Sciences: Centennial Reflections on the College of the University of Chicago*, ed. John J. MacAloon, 77–100. Chicago: University of Chicago Press.

Watson, Walter. 1985. *The Architectonics of Meaning: Foundations of the New Pluralism.* Chicago: University of Chicago Press.

———. 2000. "McKeon: The Unity of His Thought." In *Pluralism in Theory and Practice: Richard McKeon and American Philosophy*, ed. E. Garver and

R. Buchanan, 10–28. Library of American Philosophy. Nashville: Vanderbilt University Press.

Weber, Max. 1978. *Economy and Society*. Ed. Guenther Roth and Claus Wittiich. Berkeley and Los Angeles: University of California Press.

Weinstein, Fred, and Gerald M. Platt. 1969. *The Wish to Be Free: Society, Psyche, and Value Change*. Berkeley and Los Angeles: University of California Press.

———. 1973. *Psychoanalytic Sociology: An Essay on the Interpretation of Historical Data and the Phenomena of Collective Behavior*. Baltimore, MD: Johns Hopkins University Press.

Westbrook, Robert B. 1991. *John Dewey and American Democracy*. Ithaca, NY: Cornell University Press.

Westbury, Ian, and Neil J. Wilkof, eds. 1978. *Science, Curriculum, and Liberal Education: Selected Essays*. Chicago: University of Chicago Press.

Whitehead, Alfred North. 1933. *Adventures of Ideas*. New York: Macmillan.

Wilcox, Clifford. 2004. *Robert Redfield and the Development of American Anthropology*. Lanham, MD: Lexington Books.

Wilkins, Ernest. 1927. *The Changing College*. Chicago: University of Chicago Press.

———. 1932. *The College and Society: Proposals for Changes in the American Plan of Higher Education*. New York: Century.

Wilkinson, David. 1981. "Global Civilization." In *The Boundaries of Civilizations in Space and Time*, ed. Matthew Melko and Leighton R. Scott, 338–40. Lanham, MD: University Press of America.

Wilkof, Neil J. 1973. "History and the Grand Design: The Impact of the History of Western Civilization Course on the Curriculum of the University of Chicago." A.M. thesis, University of Chicago.

Williams, Joe. 1999. "Thinking about What We Don't Know." *College Faculty Newsletter* [University of Chicago] 1 (2): 8–10.

Williams, Raymond. 1983. *Keywords: A Vocabulary of Culture and Society*. Rev. ed. New York: Oxford University Press.

Wilson, Woodrow. 1925. "Should an Antecedent Liberal Education Be Required of Students in Law, Medicine and Theology?" In *College and State: Educational, Literary and Political Papers 1875–1913*, vol. 1. New York: Harper & Brothers.

Wirth, Louis. 1934. "Nature, Scope, and Essential Elements in General Education." In *General Education: Its Nature, Scope and Essential Elements*, ed. William S. Gray, 25–38. Chicago: University of Chicago Press.

Wittrock, Björn. 2000. "Modernity: One, None, or Many? European Origins and Modernity as a Global Condition." *Daedalus* 129 (1): 31–60.

Wriston, Henry M. 1934. "Nature, Scope, and Essential Elements in General Education." In *General Education: Its Nature, Scope, and Essential Elements*, *Proceedings of the Institute for Administrative Officers of Higher Institutions*, vol. 6. Chicago: University of Chicago Press.

Index